The
HIGHLANDERS
of Central China
A History 1895-1937

The
HIGHLANDERS
of Central China

A History 1895~1937

Jerome Ch'en

An East Gate Book

Routledge
Taylor & Francis Group

LONDON AND NEW YORK

An East Gate Book

First published 1992 by M.E. Sharpe

Reissued 2018 by Routledge
2 Park Square, Milton Park, Abingdon, Oxon OX14 4RN
711 Third Avenue, New York, NY 10017, USA

Routledge is an imprint of the Taylor & Francis Group, an informa business

A Library of Congress record exists under LC control number: 90009156

ISBN 13: 978-1-138-89537-9 (hbk)
ISBN 13: 978-1-138-89513-3 (pbk)
ISBN 13: 978-1-315-48961-2 (ebk)

At the Chengdu end of my life, for C.C. and Yu
At this end of my life, for Laura and Barbara

CONTENTS

TABLES

Note: Tables are gathered at the end of each chapter.

FIGURES

ACKNOWLEDGMENTS

THIS PROJECT has been funded with a generous grant from the Social Sciences and Humanities Research Council of Canada and several minor research grants from my own university, York University in Toronto. While on two field trips in China, the Social Sciences Academy in Beijing, the Social Sciences Academy in Shanghai, and the provincial Social Sciences Academies of Sichuan and Hunan kindly extended their friendship and hospitality to me. I am most grateful.

In my research, I have received the courtesy and untiring assistance of the staffs of several libraries—in North America, the East Asian libraries of the University of Toronto and the University of Michigan at Ann Arbor; in Japan, the Toyo Bunko, the East Asian Studies Centre Library of Todai, and the library at the Jimbun Kagaku Kenkyujo of Kyodai; in China, the Peking National Library, the Municipal Library of Shanghai, the Provincial Library of Sichuan, the Municipal Library of Chongqing, and the Library of the Hunan Social Sciences Academy. I remain deeply in their debt.

Everywhere I went on my field trips in Central China, I was unselfishly helped by the local historians who were then engaged in revising their gazetteers, and by journalists, teachers, and party cadres. I was privileged to share their peerless local knowledge in many sessions of discussion. The villagers and townsmen regarded me as an oddity and stopped me with their questions in the street or in the marketplace. I learned a great deal from them.

I asked for and obtained the guidance of an economist friend, Professor John Buttrick, to eliminate the howlers in my manuscript. In my own field, professors David Buck, Edward Friedman, Diana Lary, and Mark Selden read the draft with minute care and gave me their most insightful comments. In return I offer them my sincerest thanks.

Last, but not least, I must thank Ms. Anita O'Brien for her excellent and painstaking editing of the manuscript.

WEIGHTS, MEASURES, AND MONIES

IN A PERIOD of profound confusion (1895–1937), little in China was standardized. Weights and measures were snafu; the monetary system was skimble-skamble. Even the sentence structure and pronunciation of the language were far from consistent. The marvel was that all of them somehow worked. In spite of local and trade variations, the weights, measures, and monies, like Chinese words, were understood by their users, if only vaguely.

All the units listed below were certainly in use, but they varied from place to place or from trade to trade. All attempts to make them uniform ended in failure. The *mu*, for example, was first decreed to equal 6.144 *are* (*gongmu*) by the Beijing government and then to equal 6.667 *are* by the Nanjing government. No one seems to have paid much attention to the decrees; the old *mu* continued to reign. At some places it was smaller than 2 *are* and at other places larger than 32 *are*. In the highlands, peasants hardly used the *mu* at all; they used weight units, a basket or a picul of rice, to measure areas of land.[1] Zhang Xiaomei's book on Sichuan indicates that even such a simple unit as the *jin* (catty) led an extremely complicated life.[2] At each central market in Sichuan, it received dozens of definitions among the trades and then several more dozens of definitions from one market to the next.

Commonly Used Weights and Measures

li	0.5760 km; 1.1520 *shili*; 0.3579 miles
mu	0.06 hectares; 0.9216 *shimu*; 6.144 (later 6.667) *are*; 0.15 acres
jin	1 catty; 0.5279 kg; 1.0557 *shijin*; 1.1637 lbs
dan	1 picul; 100 catties

Sichuan Salt

zhai	900 piculs; 90,000 catties
bao	200 catties; 80 Sima catties

piao	1 picul
yin	100 piculs

A new *jin* for Sichuan salt was enacted and introduced at the end of 1933 by the Ministry of Finance. It was considerably lighter than the old: 100 old catties equaled 127 new ones. This was obviously a way to increase the rate of the gabelle, but it only succeeded in provoking widespread resentment and protest. Early in 1934 it was abandoned.[3]

Tong Oil

Containers

Sichuan:	Fuling *tong* (barrel)	200 catties
	Wanxian *lou* (basket)	200 catties
	Yunyang *lou*	200 catties
Hubei:	Xiangyang *lou*	200 catties
Hunan:	*long* (basket)	100, 75, or 50 catties
	tong wood	105 catties
	iron	330 catties
	guan (jar)	30 catties

The basket was made of wicker covered with oiled paper to make it water-tight.[4]

Catty and Picul of Oil

Fengdu	1 catty = 18 taels; 1 picul = 112.5 catties
Fuling	1 catty = 18 taels; 1 picul = 112.5 catties
Wanxian	1 catty = 17.4 taels; 1 picul = 109 catties
Yunyang	1 catty = 18 taels; 1 picul = 121.5 catties
Zhongxian	1 catty = 18 taels; 1 picul = 112.5 catties

Ton for Export of Oil

1 ton = 1,680 Customs catties; 1,016.047 kg; 2,032.094 catties; 2,040 lbs

Money

Officials, money exchangers, silversmiths, and other people who had to deal with different monies frequently used no fewer than 170 kinds of scales to weigh the taels and smaller units of the monetary metals, chiefly silver and copper. The Treasury tael (*kupingliang*) contained 373.1256 grams of fine silver. Before its abolition, there were as many as sixty-five different kinds of the Treasury tael in use. The Customs tael (*guanpingliang*), weighing 376.8 grams of fine silver, was proudly uniform. There were more than one hundred kinds of taels.

In the highlands, people used the *zhiqian* (what E. Kann called the hole-cash), sycee (shoe-shaped silver ingots), silver and copper coins of different denominations, and paper monies of various face values. The first two had been gradually disappearing since the end of the nineteenth century, but they continued to be used in the mountains. Their place was being taken by some twenty-six kinds of legitimate silver coins, fifteen kinds of copper coins, and paper currencies issued by national and provincial banks, local banks and money shops, military authorities, and shops.

Perhaps the best indicator of the purchasing power of the Customs tael was its Sterling exchange rate. As indicated by Woodhead, it showed a gradual decline before World War I, a sharp rise during the war, and a rapid decrease thereafter:[5]

1895 3s 3d 1915 2s 7d
1900 3s 1d 1920 6s 9d
1905 3s 0d 1925 3s 3 1/4d to 3s 1/4d
1910 2s 8d 1930 2s 3/4d to 1s 4 3/4d
1935 1s 8 3/8d to 1 2 3/8d

The changes in the external value of the Customs tael naturally affected the value of all silver coins, be they of the 1-yuan denomination or smaller. The latter also decreased.

The internal purchasing power of silver coins was normally expressed in their exchange rates with copper coins. The par was fixed by the imperial government in 1903 at 50-hole cash or 100 copper coins of the denomination of 10 wen to a silver coin of 1 yuan. The market rate of exchange fluctuated in Shanghai as follows (in 10-wen copper coins):[6]

1912 132   1925 240
1915 136   1930 265
1920 141.5 1935 300

The rate of depreciation of the copper coins accelerated in the 1920s and 1930s. In Sichuan, the depreciation was much sharper:[7]

1910 1,000 wen   1930 14,500–16,000 wen
1918 2,000   1935 28,400
1926 5,000–6,000

On the other hand, the silver yuan was treated by the Sichuan government with scanty respect. In 1915 when the silver yuan was adopted as the governmental unit of account and exchange in place of the Treasury tael, 1.60 yuan was fixed as the official rate of exchange for the tael. The county of Fuling, for instance, had traditionally paid 5,317.16 taels per annum as its land tax proper (*diding*). In 1915 this was converted to 8,507.456 yuan. By 1933 the rate of conversion was raised to 16.64 yuan for 1 tael. Fuling was by no means alone; other Sichuan highland counties used these rates of conversion in 1933:[8]

Fengdu   15.38 yuan   Wushan   11.96 yuan
Fengjie   8.61   Wuxi   13.10
Nanchuan   19.22   Xiushan   5.30
Pengshui   4.35   Youyang   4.79
Qianjiang   7.45   Yunyang   19.45
Shizhu   18.41   Zhongxian   14,72

In Hubei and Hunan the situation was similar.

I have collected some price indices for Chongqing and for eastern Sichuan counties. Unfortunately, as time series, they cover too short a period to allow one to see any long-term trends. Since local conditions were drastically different from those of a central market like Chongqing or Wuhan, the price and cost of living indices there could hardly be applied to the mountain counties. One set of figures is given in table 1.

To sum up, this confused monetary system worked because, out of necessity, people gravitated toward 1-yuan silver coins and 10-wen and 20-wen copper coins, in spite of their different fineness and weight. Other, better currencies, such as the tael and the *zhiqian*, were driven out of circulation; still other, inconvenient and untrustworthy ones, such as many types of irredeemable paper notes and ruthlessly debased copper coins, were rejected. The external values of the silver and copper coins were on the decline, except during World War I.

Table 1

Fluctuations in the Price of Rice

	1912	1931	1932	Jan. 1933	April 1933	July 1933	Oct. 1933	Jan. 1934	April 1934	July 1934	Oct. 1934
Cili	104	—	—	100	104	104	65	91	87	152	169
Dayong	—	160	160	100	104	120	—	—	—	—	—
Fengdu	—	—	—	100	—	—	—	113	166	128	163
Fengjie	—	—	—	100	—	—	—	109	145	145	127
Shimen	—	160	160	100	—	80	—	—	—	—	—
Xiushan	57	—	177	100	111	—	—	96	108	90	108
Yunyang	54	—	143	100	—	—	119	165	—	—	151
Zhaohua	50	63	90	100	53	100	—	—	—	—	—
Zhongxian	—	—	156	100	72	120	120	178	167	178	133
Zigui	—	188	125	100	100	100	—	50	80	—	—

Source: Nongqing baogao 3/12, 254–70.

Their internal purchasing power was also in decline, but that of copper dropped more sharply than that of silver, and that of subsidiary silver coins fell more sharply than that of the 1-yuan denomination.

The year 1935 was the year of currency reform. In essence, the fiat money issued by the central banks of the Nanjing government replaced all the existing currencies at fixed rates of exchange. From November 1935, the new 1-yuan notes became the only legal tender while the exchange rate of the Customs tael was pegged at 1s 2 1/2d. In Sichuan, the provincial bank was allowed to issue subsidiary coins. Suddenly there was a serious shortage of both legal tender and token money, as people hoarded all the metallic currencies. The tense monetary situation did not ease until the eve of war in 1937.

The
HIGHLANDERS
of Central China
A History 1895-1937

1
INTRODUCTION

BETWEEN the end of the first Sino-Japanese War and the beginning of the second (1895–1937), the Central China highlands went through rapid changes, set in motion by the enormous and swift commercialization of several of the area's agricultural products and consequently by its enhanced economic and strategic importance to the contending cliques of armed forces on both sides of the north-south divide. Central China became the civil war belt between north and south; its heightened expectations were ravaged by the wars, and poverty was bred in the midst of plenty. Against this background, the Red armies under He Long in the 1920s and under Zhang Guotao and Xu Xiangqian in the 1930s invaded and created rural soviets, arousing the highlanders to revolt.

In addition to telling the story of an area and a period in which agricultural commercialization failed to lead to anticipated social changes, thus frustrating the people's hopes and breeding dissatisfaction, this study tries to test the theories of rural social change and revolution. The area under study comprises seventeen counties in western Hubei, twenty in eastern Sichuan, and thirteen in western Hunan. It lies to the east of the Jialing and the Wu (or Qian) rivers in Sichuan; to the west of where the Han and the Dan meet, the Yangzi reaches Zigui, and the Qing flows just past Changyang in Hubei; and to the northwest of the upper reaches of the Yuan and the Li, extending eastward to Lixian, almost to where the Li empties into the Dongting lakes. The rivers, of course, have contributed to shaping the topographical features and social life in this area; the other powerful factor is the mountains.

Interposed between the Qinling range in the north and the Yunnan-Guizhou plateau in the southwest, between the Hubei-Hunan plains in the east and the Sichuan basin in the west, the great ranges of Dabashan (including Wudang and Guanmian mountains), Wushan (including Jingshan and Fangdoushan), and Wulingshan form a system of mountains in the eastern section of the middle (or upper) reaches of the Yangzi. Some of the mountains soar above 3,000 meters, such as the well-known Shennongjia northeast of the Wushan Gorges, to look down at the folds of 1,000–2,000 meters or lower in all directions.

Climate

Shaded by the Qinling range, the whole area enjoys a mild climate, especially in the basins and on the valley floors. In western Hubei, the average temperature in January is 3.3° C and in July 18.4° C, with the annual average at 7.8° C. Moving south to the southwest basin along the Qing, the climate is even more comfortable—warmer in the winter and cooler in the summer.[1] Throughout eastern Sichuan from north to south, both the winter and summer are warmer (respectively 6–8° and 26–30° C) while in western Hunan they are 4–5° and 26.6–28.8° C.[2] The entire area is blessed with adequate rainfall, generally over 1,000 mm annually, although less occurs in northern Hubei and Sichuan but considerably more (1,250–1,500 mm) falls south of the Yangzi. Much of it is concentrated in spring and autumn, but without the hazards of a long rainy season in the autumn to ruin the rice harvests as it does in the Sichuan and Hubei plains.[3] The climate assures a long and beneficial growing season for food crops and citrus fruit. It passes with flying colors all the critical tests—3°, 10°, 15°, and 20° from winter to autumn—desired by rice and fruit growers. The only drawback is a lack of sunshine in the Qing valley when there are excessive clouds and rain in the growing season, as the temperature rises from 10° to 20°.[4] However, drought is seldom known in these mountains.

Soil

The yellow earth of western Hubei is rich in organic nutrients, suitable for growing maize, sweet potatoes, legume, rape-seeds, winter wheat, and paddy rice. The clayey and acidic soil found on the slopes is only good enough for maize and sweet potatoes. Higher up, poorer soil and colder temperatures make a home for trees, chiefly pines and firs.[5] The red earth of Sichuan is generally acidic, at some places even excessively so. It is suitable for growing a variety of food and cash crops.[6] In northwestern Hunan one finds similar types of soil, similar crops, and similar trees and bushes.[7] On the grounds of climate and crop patterns, this whole area forms an entity. In addition, social and political factors bind it into a historical unit in the period under investigation.

Demography

The seventeen counties of western Hubei spread over an area of 58,035 sq. km, in other words, 26 percent of the total area of Hubei; the twenty counties of eastern Sichuan, 111,346 sq. km, or 25.5 percent of Sichuan; the thirteen counties of northwestern Hunan, 34,448 sq. km, or 16 percent of Hunan. In the mid-1930s, about 12,878,311 people lived in this area of 203,829 sq. km: 3,180,353 in western Hubei (about 12 percent of Hubei's total population), 6,829,914 in eastern Sichuan (about 14 percent of Sichuan's total population), and 2,868,584 in northwestern Hunan (about 10 percent of Hunan's total population).

How had the demography of this area changed? The Qing valley was unique (see table 1.1); elsewhere the situation was different (table 1.2).

If the demographic records are more or less reliable, the Qing valley stands out as the only exception whose population showed remarkable stability. This may have been due to the scarcity of cultivable land for food crops. According to the mu (acreage) surtax register, the average of the seven counties there was a miserly 2.6 percent cultivable land, with Jianshi having the highest percentage at only 17.49 percent cultivable land.[8] The inconvenience of overland transport between counties before the construction of modern highways may have been another factor. Even the Red Army under He Long found the place unsuitable for creating a soviet. Its inhospitableness ensured the safety of the primeval forests and many of their valuable plants from invading hordes of men. In the other regions of this highland, however, the first wave of immigration may have been brought about by the spread of "American food crops" in the seventeenth and eighteenth centuries.

It is difficult to prove that the aftermath of the Taiping Rebellion (1850–64) caused any considerable influx of migrants, even along the navigable Yangzi. In 1816, Fengdu (Sichuan) recorded a population of 106,025, and in 1868, 82,155. Wanxian (also Sichuan) had a population of 137,878 in 1816, but by 1858, only 101,696. Other short-term factors that may have affected the demography of this area were the great Yangzi floods of 1931, the devastating drought in the Sichuan basin in 1935–36, and the continual civil wars, especially the wars against the Communists in northeastern Sichuan in 1932–35 and in northwestern Hunan in 1929–35. Nonetheless, the long-term trend of population for this area continued to increase at a rate faster than that of the three provinces as a whole (table 1.3). This faster rate of increase, I believe, should be partly attributed to a lack of epidemics in the mountain areas and, more importantly, to the commercialization of highland agriculture, which made a larger population sustainable.

The population density of all the mountain regions under consideration was well below that of the respective provinces in spite of the increases. Taking the highland as a whole, the average density was 63.2 persons per sq. km, compared with 146.61 in Hubei, 133.81 in Sichuan, and 143.21 in Hunan in 1928.[9]

The Rim

The whole area may be called a "periphery" or "rim," although I do not follow here the Skinnerian scheme of dividing China into eight macro regions.[10] Skinner's theoretical framework and considerations are of reference value nonetheless. If the area fits somewhere in his macro regions, it may be in the middle Yangzi region, where it towers over the lowlands and the greater as well as lesser cities on them. Skinner's partitioning of China does not, of course, exclude any other, and the area under study here is by no means the only one that serves the research objectives I have outlined. In fact, the southern Jiangxi-western Fujian area looks remarkably similar to it.

Skinner stresses two major human geographic factors in defining a region—homogeneity and interrelatedness. Homogeneity may be hard to discover; common features, both natural and human geographic, are not. I have discussed the system of mountain ranges and the relatively low population density of this highland; I have mentioned briefly the similar vegetation and crops, and similar infrequency of natural hazards. In addition, portions of the rim relied in a similar way on trade and credit supply from the nearby core areas, used similar traditional means of transport, shared a scarcity of villages, and exhibited backwardness in handicrafts. As to interrelatedness, in addition to administrative and economic linkages, the systems of armed forces (warlords' men, Red armies, militia, and bandits) as this area was de facto the dividing line and bone of contention between the northern and southern

leagues of militarists, education, communications, and cultures (both the great and little traditions). It was the infrequent and inconvenient interrelatedness between the valleys and basins that tied them more to the nearest core areas than to themselves. Like all the other linkages, the ebb and flow of the influence between the great tradition of the plains and the little traditions of the mountains have always been mutual. The crude ideas and patterns on the highlands were taken to the plains, to become refined and established there, and finally to return to the highlands. I shall discuss the details of all this in chapter 8.

As one travels from core to rim (I did it several times from Chengdu to the north side of Qinling, from Nanchang to Jinggangshan, from Changsha to Fenghuang and the Guizhou border, from Chengdu to Gulin, and from Changsha to Dayong, Sangzhi, Mayang, Huaihua, through Guizhou to Chongqing and Chengdu), one's impression is that the size and density of cities, towns, and villages decrease as one goes farther away from the center. This is what Skinner describes as the urban-rural continuum.[11] The Chinese tradition makes it more complex by ranking the counties: Fuling, a first-class county, surrounded by third- and fourth- ones such as Nanchuan and Xiushan; Wanxian, another first-class county, surrounded by Kaixian (second class), Yunyang (third class), and Wushan (fourth class).[12]

To go further toward the rural end of the continuum, the southern tip of southeastern Sichuan provides an extreme case. The three counties there—Pengshui, Xiushan, and Youyang—were all of the fourth class.

In 1940 Pengshui city had 1,042 households, 40 inns, 21 taverns, 12 teahouses, and itself a hundred-day (year-round) market dealing in salt, food, cloth, and tong oil. Its Yushanzhen market town, also a hundred-day market, rivaled the city cum market by having a population of 566 households, 20 inns and taverns, and 5 teahouses. It too dealt in salt, cloth, and tong oil.[13] The county seat of Qianjiang to its east was even smaller, having only 500 households but no city wall.[14] Gongtan, shaped like a ribbon, was a market town par excellence. Situated at the junction of the Tangyan and the Wu, it boasted 1,300 households and over 30 wholesalers handling salt, tong oil, foodstuffs, and a variety of mountain goods.[15] Youyang had a smaller population, mostly officials, scholars, and militia officers, than either Gongtan or Longtan, another market town; it was a sleepy place, similar to Xiushan.[16] Both these cities depended on Liye across the border in Hunan for the supply of arms and ammunition[17] and on Longtan for other, less destructive imports. Longtan was by far the largest market town in this corner of Sichuan, close to 2,000 households and 68 inns and taverns. Its tong oil wholesalers numbered 30. It also dealt in cotton, yarn, cloth, salt, herbal medicine, and alcoholic drinks.[18] Crouching among hills and mountains, these central market towns were nodes rather than hinterlands—to and from them goods, information, defense forces, public revenues, and subsidies were sent.

Transport

Traditionally the distance between Hanyang in Hubei and Chengdu in Sichuan, 3,480 li (or 1,740 km) took a mounted courier nine days, at an average speed of 400 li a day.[19] However, from Donghu westward to the Hubei-Sichuan border there were neither courier stations nor courier roads. The deliverer would be slowed down to 240 li a day or had to abandon his mount. This was the normal speed from Yidu, at the junction of the Yangzi and the Qing, west to, say, Hefeng (590 li in two or three days) or from Badong southwest to Enshi (390 li in two days).[20]

A porter or a drover (of horse or donkey) proceeded at a much slower speed. In northeastern or southeastern Sichuan, carrying 100 catties, a porter could walk 76 li a day, for a pay of 1.50 yuan in the 1930s, while a drover, loading twice as much on his beast, could do 70 li a day for 1.80 yuan. Either of these compared unfavorably with a boat laden with 25 piculs or 2,500 catties and sailed down at 120 li a day for 0.50 yuan in the northeast or at 60 li a day for 0.80 yuan in the southeast.[21] Take Chengkou to Wanyuan (330 li), for instance. It would require a porter five days on a road that was described as "over one foot wide."[22] To reach the market and steamers in Fuling either by the Sichuan-Hunan motorway or the Yuan, one came to Xiushan first. Cargo had to be borne by a porter to Longtan (94 li in two days) and then to Gongtan (400 li in six days) before it could be loaded on a boat down the Wu to the final destination.[23] The roads were good, and both Longtan and Gongtan were pleasant places to stay, but there and elsewhere one ran the risk of being robbed.[24]

The novelist Shen Congwen once in the 1920s traveled on foot from Chadong (Hunan) through Songtao (Guizhou) and Xiushan to Longtan. It took seven days.[25] In his home region in western Hunan, nearly all the border cities, towns, and garrison fortresses were linked up with narrow, winding, hazardous roads, only occasionally suitable for horse and sedan-chair. The traveler would be happy to cover thirty li a day, and that was Shen's speed. He had to endure this snail's pace until he reached Enshi in the Qing valley, Gongtan in the Wu valley, or Yuanling in the Yuan valley.

To go by motorway in this mountain area was frightening and uneconomical from the user's point of view. By 1937 Hubei had 2,000 km of motorways in use, western Hubei, 737 km; Sichuan had 7,500, eastern Sichuan 1,631; and Hunan, had 2,000, western Hunan, 200. Most of these roads were built in the mid-1930s for military operations against the Communists. Since the Communist threat was more ominous in northern and southern Sichuan (the Second and First Front armies, respectively) than in northwestern Hunan (the Second and Sixth army corps), more motorways were cut in Hubei and Sichuan than in Hunan.[27]

Road building was a painful experience for the people, to say the least. The construction of the Qijiang-Chadong section of the Sichuan-Hunan highway was typical. It was budgeted for 5.5 million yuan at 7,879.7 yuan per kilometer, which included 0.20 yuan for food per worker per day. The authorities planned to hire 265,390 workers for a month. Thus, the food budget alone, 15.9 million yuan, would have exceeded the budget by 300 percent! The Highway Board of Sichuan had no option but to conscript workers who had to bring their own food and tools.[27] Their foremen were mostly local ruffians, secret society bosses, or army officers whose handling of the workers was ruthless to the extreme—no medical care, no proper accommodation, and no compensation for death (over two thousand died) or injury.[28] Desertion and riots were naturally rife.

Few of the roads in the region were surfaced. When it rained, they were slippery; when it was fine, they were bumpy.[29] Not until 1935 when the Highway Board of Sichuan was reorganized were some three hundred new buses bought to replace the twenty dilapidated ones.[30] Still, for a distance of ninety km a ticket cost five yuan while an open sedan-chair (*huagan*), carried by two men, cost only about three. There was only one bus every three days from Santai to Mianyang, but there were many sedan-chairs for the passenger's convenience, comfort, and safety, although they were slower.[31]

To transport goods by truck in Hubei, the average cost per 100 kg per kilometer was 0.23 yuan; in Sichuan, 0.17 yuan; and in Hunan, 0.16 yuan. By cart, the average cost was 0.03 yuan; by porter 0.04 yuan; by donkey, 0.026 yuan; and by boat, 0.023 yuan.[32] There did not seem much to choose among these alternatives. With luck, the motor road was faster, only three days from Chongqing to either Guiyang or Changsha at a speed of 330–400 km a day, whereas the courier could at best ride 300 km a day or a sedan-chair cover about 50 km a day.[33]

Wherever steamer traffic was possible, it tended to replace traditional types of boats in passenger as well as cargo services. In the area under study this meant the section of the Yangzi from Fuling to Sandouping (just west of Yichang, Hubei), a distance of 469 km, and on the Jialing from Chongqing to Hechuan, 98 km. Elsewhere the ingenuity and adventurism of the old-fashioned boatmen prevailed. To give a few examples: the 275 km between Fuling and Gongtan was essential for rice and mountain goods moving downstream to reach Fuling and salt moving upstream to Gongtan and beyond. The journey up required a month, that is, less than 10 km a day; the trip down took only six to ten days depending on the water level. Here a boat could carry as much as 30 tons, and the 224 boats were organized into 24 *bang* (guilds representing boatmen of different localities).[34] The freight charge for a barrel of tong oil (280 catties) was 1.50 yuan or 0.003 yuan per 100 kg per km, less than one-tenth of the cost of hiring a porter.[35] The You is a smaller river. From Longtan down to Yuanling (Hunan), a distance of 287 km, took three or four days. On the Chen, from Fuling down to Chenxi (Hunan) needed four days.[36] There were hundreds of boats, carrying from a couple to 20 tons of cargo. These too were organized into *bang*. On them the import of salt and textiles and export of mountain goods depended.[37] It was safer for passengers to use wood or bamboo rafts downstream on these treacherous rivers, which at the same time also sent timber to places like Yuanling and Chenxi.[38]

What questions can one raise about these highlands, and about the people who lived there between 1895 and 1937? In his important work on the Chinese peasant economy, Ramon Myers, for the convenience of discussion, divides the major theoretical approaches to recent Chinese agrarian problems into the distribution theory (chiefly Marxian, with greater emphasis on institutional factors than on technological ones) and the eclectic theory (reversing the emphases).[39] More recently, Phillip Huang's *Peasant Economy and Social Change in North China* takes a giant step forward. His integrated analysis differentiates the three faces of the prerevolutionary peasantry—those of the subsistence, entrepreneurial, and exploited producer, each of which has carefully been studied by the substantivists in the tradition of A. V. Chayanov, by the formalists in that of T. Schultz, and by the Marxists. The main questions Huang tries to answer are: Why did the highly sophisticated Chinese peasant economy fail to break through the precapitalist constraints to become modern (the question of underdevelopment)? How did the village disintegrate to give rise to harsher exploitation by the state and the elite as well as to revolution?[40] Both of these works are enormously inspiring and stimulating, although in scope and focus they are different from the present study. In the first place, their factual base is the North China plains, whereas mine is the Central China highland. Their periodization is much longer, whereas here it covers only forty years. As Huang's study addresses the question of agricultural commercialization and the rise of managerial farms, it is more instructive to this work which also deals with the process of commercialization and its failure to effect a breakthrough due to vastly different circumstances and reasons.

Sources

Both Myers and Huang have been helped to a great measure by the South Manchurian Railway's survey material on the rural socioeconomic conditions of North China. It is the consistency of the survey material that has convinced them and others of its reliability. This luxury is beyond any study of highland economy, society, and particularly individual decision making. The Japanese fieldworkers were prevented from venturing very far away from railway lines and county seats by the dangers to their personal safety;[41] by the same token, their Chinese counterparts seldom went up to the highlands.

Later Qing and Republican materials on this area abound, however. Provincial, prefectural, and county gazetteers were compiled from the 1860s to the 1930s, to mention only what is relevant to this study, especially the northern Sichuan gazetteers compiled under the auspices of General Tian Songyao of the Twenty-ninth Army, who controlled that garrison region (*fangqu*). One must not overlook the fact that the three provincial governments inaugurated a large number of periodicals; the Sichuan government alone accounted for some thirty-five titles. There are also daily newspapers such as the Changsha *Dagongbao*, *Wuhan ribao*, and Chongqing *Xinshubao*. Monographs on taxes, local products such as tong oil and bristles, and ethnographic material collected before the advent of communism are available. At a less formal level, travelogues (books and articles), novels, and stories by local writers like Shen Congwen, Zhou Wen, Sha Ding are helpful in attaining a deeper, more realistic understanding of the cultural traits of this highland area. One may legitimately inquire about the availability of county government archives. And in 1983 and 1989, when I was traveling in the mountains, all the counties were busy bringing local histories up to the present day. The local historians who were engaged in this enterprise must have had old and new archives to assist them, but no one was prepared to tell me where they were kept or whether they were available to visiting researchers like myself. Only in Gulin was I given a copy of the old county gazetteer, and that is easily obtainable at any respectable East Asian library in the West. Let us hope that future historians will have better luck.

These sources of information are naturally of uneven quality. By collating them with great care, however, it is not impossible to make them consistent, intelligible, and as reliable as possible. In most cases, opportunities for collation do exist.

After verification, what can be described as the special characteristics of this highland? First, there is an absence or paucity of villages as observed by G. W. Skinner and others.[42] Villages anywhere perform roughly similar functions, some being more attentive to religious activities (as in Mexico) and others to economic welfare (such as poor relief in England). Chinese villages normally shoulder the duties of defense, tax collection, public works, adjudication of disputes, and ceremonial arrangements.[43] Where they are absent and only homesteads or hamlets exist, there is insufficient supply of food and water to sustain a large group of people.[44] When peasants live in smaller and more widely scattered communities they make do with fewer and simpler ceremonies, they may take their disputes directly to formal adjudication instead of informal village arbitration, and the government may design a new way to collect taxes, but they still need safety and goods they cannot produce themselves. For defense in the highlands, the inhabitants, with or without government help, built fortresses at strategic places against invaders. In time some of the fortresses grew to become sizable settlements indistinguishable from natural villages or market towns, although they still bore the name of "fortress" (*zhai* or *bao*), such as Longjiazhai in northwestern Hunan and the twenty-nine *zhai* in Nanjiang, northeastern Sichuan. Along water routes markets were to be found, for the exchange of mountain products in return for what traders brought from the plains.

The landscape of the mountains was thus dotted with county seats, market towns, government and private fortresses, usually nestling on valley floors and drawing nourishment from the irrigated crop land around them, and farmsteads and hamlets on the mountain slopes with enough resources for the people to eke out a living and to give aid to each other. Highlands can seldom be closed economically, however the larger environment changes, for their dependence on trade with the plains below is always high. Even when a mountain community is self-sufficient in food, it can hardly be so in salt, metals, and clothing. As A. T. Bambo says,

> Truly open peasants do not live in village communities at all but rather are most often found living in scattered settlements of homesteaders in underpopulated frontier areas. These pioneer farmers engage almost exclusively in the production of cash crops for the national and world markets and are dependent in turn on these markets for many of their most basic subsistence needs, just as, lacking organic local defensive institutions, they are dependent on the police institutions of the state to provide their personal security. Such peasants are unable to respond to deterioration in their political and economic environment by

increasing the degree of closure of their settlements. They cannot close
the gate in times of unrest because there is no gate.[45]

In the highlands, though, Bambo's picture is overdrawn.

In the highlands the peasants did, as they still do, engage in food
production and rely on local defense arrangements—militia, fortresses,
and regional armies—against bandits and other forms of armed invasion. They could withstand a short siege or blockade. For that matter,
because of scarce means for survival, invaders could hardly mount a
protracted war of aggression. Larger communities—cities, towns, and
fortresses—could be "shut" for short periods when necessary.[46]

A second characteristic of the highlands was the important role of
the lineage. The existence of the village depends on village loyalties
and kinship ties; the individual does not count.[47] The individual asserts
himself only in the absence or dissolution of the village. As long as it
exists, kinship ties, real or fictive, inherent or derivative, form the basis
of village solidarity, and their main principles guide all activities of the
villagers, from the lineage mode of production to recreation. In the
long run, the strength of these ties is based on the economic and
political resources of a lineage, as Watson points out. He goes on to
say that in the mountains the lineage is generally weak.[48] While the
scattered homesteads had to fend for themselves, on the valley floors,
by contrast, large lineages and their halls were not unknown. There
were examples in Guiyang, Dayong, and Sangzhi in southern and
northwestern Hunan and in Hechuan, northern Sichuan.[49] Their chief
function seemed to be to defend their members and others in time of
invasion. Social welfare, such as free ferry services and famine relief
and education, due to lack of funds had to rely on government allocation.[50]

The port city of Wanxian is an interesting case. In the city itself
there was an array of welfare arrangements to give aid to the underprivileged, aged, and orphaned, with funds coming from both the government and the wealthy. For famine relief there were county and
village granaries (changpingcang and shecang), but no privately financed charity granaries (yicang). The granaries did not come into
existence until 1820. In the 1860s, the five colleges in the city received donations of 11,020 taels of silver and 17,500 mu of land, while
the twelve charity schools did no better than 3,600 taels of silver.[51]
Starved of money, peasant education there and elsewhere depended on

elite handouts until the government stepped in in the final years of the Qing,[52] a state of affairs detrimental to educational development in the highland counties. The shift from private to public funding in the early years of the Republic did little to uplift their cultural backwardness, probably because of elite poverty and diversion of government money to meet military needs. Right to the end of the period, Wanxian, in spite of its rise to be a major port city and greatly enlarged tax revenue, had only 308 primary schools that taught only 16,852 pupils, 1 pupil in every 2,600 people, compared with 1 in every 1,165 in Baxian (Chongqing) and 1 in every 6,230 in another port city, Fuling.[53] Although private tutorial classes (sishu) were ordered to close down in 1933, Wanxian still had 868 of them in the second half of the 1930s. The tutors collected fees.[54] Wanxian was by no means typical as it was relatively better off; the poorer counties fared worse.

The third characteristic was trade. Because of its low degree of self-sufficiency, the highland economy has to have two components: for subsistence and for exchange. The ratio of the two depends on local resources and accessibility to a market, the latter of which could come to the doorstep (itinerant traders) or could lie as far away as countries overseas. Therefore, it is hard to say whether highlanders had a fear of markets.[55] It is the itinerant traders and branches of wholesalers at market towns who gather mountain goods for shipping to larger markets on the plains. The inconvenient transport between highland settlements not only renders it impossible to develop trade relations across the mountains, but also thwarts the growth of local handicrafts on a scale larger than subsistence needs. In other words, this is a world of "petty producers and petty traders."[56] It is difficult to find even a "family workshop" that hires a couple of journeymen and a couple of apprentices.[57] If there is an oil press or a paper mill, it is likely to be situated in a market town.

The highlanders exchanged staple goods (food that could be spared), timber, wood oil, bristles, opium, herbs, and so forth, for processed consumer goods (cloth, salt, sugar, haberdasheries, etc.). These may well have been the two most developed types of markets. The difference was that the former was likely to be oligopolistic between a few landowners who possessed the staples and merchants who wanted them, whereas the latter was between small retailers and small buyers, thus far more competitive.[58] These markets could exist side by side with barter, loans of goods, gifts, and mutual assistance.[59]

The tong oil trade system may be used as an example to show the marketing structure:

peasant grower → landowner or rich peasant → itinerant buyer
                oil press   who carries oil
                                             to Chadong
→ oil merchant at a standard market who ships oil to Taoyuan
   (at Chadong, Huayuan County)
→ wholesaler → *guozaipu* (large wholesaler) → foreign firm
(intermediate market)   (central market)
at Taoyuan   at Changde and Hankou

The transport of oil was organized by brokers and guilds (*bang*), licensed by the government and responsible for paying taxes. In the upper reaches of the rivers, on the You, for instance, small boats that carried only a few piculs sailed to a standard market whence by larger boats or small steamers, holding a few thousand barrels, it was sent to the central market. As the distance between the grower and the nearest standard market might be well over what could be comfortably covered in a day's return journey on foot, by riding a donkey, or by boat, the grower was left out of the market world. There were many on the mountains to whom the market was a far-away place of trade but not yet a state of mind.[60] If there was any exchange of views and information between these isolated highlanders and the outside world, it was through an itinerant merchant, intruder, or occasional "returnee."

This traditional marketing system, *mutatis mutandis*, proved capable of handling a greatly expanded volume of trade from the highlands. Take tong oil again as an example: no reference to its export is to be found in the *Shangwu guanbao* published by the Ministry of Agriculture, Industry, and Commerce from 1907 to 1911, nor in the *Nongshang gongbao* by the Ministry of Agriculture and Commerce in 1915. It was insignificant, too small. Li Changlong recorded an export of Hunan tong oil in 1869 worth a miserly amount of 62 Mexican dollars; this was to rise to 3 million HG taels in 1930.[61] Likewise its export from Wanxian in 1917 was only 31,180 piculs or 314,606 HG taels, but in 1930, 312,555 piculs or 4,688,326 HG taels.[62] Other exports from the highlands made similar impressive advances. But the old trading system remained almost intact.

Fourth, agricultural commercialization on the highlands is of crucial importance to this study. Here as elsewhere in China, it failed to free agriculture from the grips of what Geertz calls the agricultural involution. There are two explanatory models of this failure. The first is the demographical model. When population increases, it touches off a chain reaction of price increases and increases in the agricultural profit rate while the real incomes level falls and the terms of trade turn against agricultural goods. This involutionary process cannot be arrested by a mere diversification of crops.[63] The second is the commercialization model in which price increases can mean a fall in the fixed income of landowners' rent. This may lead land to be allocated to new uses and cause peasants to migrate to the city or become wage laborers. Hence urban industry and commerce flourish.[64] Structurally there would be the change from family-bound production toward productive enterprise that draws the surplus labor and raw materials from and sends manufactures to the countryside; there would be the movement from neighborhood communities toward a national class society; and there would be the growth from a variety of parochial cultures toward a national one.[65] From the individual's point of view, there would be change of lifestyle from the traditional to a more complex, technologically more advanced, and frequently changing one.[66]

R. Brenner thinks that both models miss the point by ignoring rural class relations and feudal control. In any discussion on the long-term changes in income, the working of legal and social institutions and class relations, such as landownership and decisions on rent, must be brought into play. With powers of ownership and rent decisions, the landlord could control various aspects of the peasant's life. Take the stagnation of eastern European agriculture in the eighteenth century, for instance. It was not simply a matter of lack of available technological improvement. As long as the landowner had attractive feudal rent, no market incentive would induce him to adopt innovations.[67] Brenner argues further against the commercialization model. "Serfdom was a relationship of power which could be reversed, as it were, only on its own terms, through a change in the balance of class forces." As long as the peasantry had no freedom of decision and action, corvée would remain corvée. He concludes: "it is the structure of class relations, of class power which will determine the manner and degree to which particular demographic and commercial changes will affect long-term trends in the distribution of income and economic growth—and not *vice versa*."[68]

In the North China situation, Huang describes how an increase in rural population led to an increase in cotton production and small-scale cotton textile industry as well as sweet potato growth, which actually retarded the growth of what he calls managerial farming. None of these could solve the question of capital formation, which was critical for agriculture to break away from the involutionary situation. The other critical question was power of control, which remained in the hands of large, leasing landowners and outsiders, the civil and military establishments.[69]

In the case of the highlands, there was also a failure to break away from involution and usher in modernization through the process of commercialization. The old settlers had developed a trade in timber and charcoal, herbs and furs, mushrooms and fungi, tong oil and tea oil, bristles and later opium in exchange for daily essentials. They felled trees and opened up virgin land to make room for dry crops— winter wheat and buckwheat, maize and tubers, beans and peas. During the Miao uprisings and sectarian rebellions, notably the one at the turn of the nineteenth century, they built fortresses and manned them with local and garrison troops to begin a military tradition. With the collapse of the central authority in 1911–12, the military seized greater power and larger stretches of land at the expense of the older landowners. The new owners were mostly military officers, civil officials, and militia commanders, supported by local ruffians and armed forces.

In this structural change and confusion, a rural anomie, the perpetual rights of the lease, gradually ceased to operate. A series of decisions sent down by the Supreme Court in 1914–15 permitted owners to abolish or revoke perpetual leases on grounds of rent payment in arrears, public law and order, and changed economic conditions.[70] Forest land that had not belonged to anyone was taken over by individual claimants in the usual pioneer manner by scratching marks on trees. This was later recognized by the Mountain Land Clearance Bureau (Qingshanju) established in Beijing in 1917, which issued title deeds to and collected taxes from the claimants.[71] The same new owners also privatized public land, temple estates, and clan association estates. Legalized by the Supreme Court's decisions of 1913, 1914, and 1917, this practice put an end to the tradition that clan members had the priority in purchasing clan estates.[72] To add insult to injury, the new owners treated their tenants with much less customary courtesy. Worse still, they and their bailiffs, with fire-arms behind them, collected taxes according to their whim.[73]

These changes in the class structure and redistribution of power led to two observable trends that were characteristic of these highlands. First, Huang points out what he calls the atomization of the village, which entailed the emigration of poor peasants from their native villages in the 1930s, a fact much discussed by contemporary Chinese scholars.[74] Similar emigration was to be found in Hubei, Sichuan, and Hunan, involving mostly tenants working on a farm smaller than ten mu of land.[75] It was generally attributed to famine, which was frequent in North China, Shaanxi, and the lake district of Hunan. It was also attributed to indebtedness, especially among those whose families were large and productive power small, and to heavy taxation, particularly in Sichuan. Factors facilitating emigration were nearness to a sparsely populated area, such as Manchuria to Shandong, or to a high employment opportunity region, as the Canton delta to overseas. In the Republican period, soldiering and road building could lure peasants away from their homes. Nowhere, however, was high rent or declining ancillary businesses a contributory factor to their departure. In the highlands throughout this period, peasant emigration was never a problem of any significance. The trend was a reverse flow of people up the mountains, interrupted probably by such civil wars as the war in aid of Hubei in 1920–21, the invasion of Guizhou troops in southeastern Sichuan in 1923–24, Xiong Kewu's Sichuan troops fighting their way through western Hunan in 1924–25, and above all the anti-Communist campaigns in northern Sichuan in 1932–35.

Second, in western Hunan owner-cultivators and partial owners occupied a higher percentage in the rural population than the provincial average. The situation was the same in northern and eastern Sichuan. But western Hubei presented a different picture—a higher percentage of owner-cultivators and lower percentages of both partial owners and tenants. From 1912 to 1937 there were no prominent changes in western Hubei, but a slight increase in partial owners and a slight decrease in owner-cultivators there and in eastern Sichuan.[76] The worsening relations between landowners and tenants did not so increase the tenants' misery as to drive them to give up their farms. The other side of the coin was that the entire peasantry, thanks to the enhanced income from cash crops, found their financial situation either comfortable or tolerable, but made miserable by taxes.

A fifth characteristic of the highlands was immiserization. The highland peasant's growing schedule was roughly as follows: When fields were irrigated, paddy rice was grown from spring to autumn; when drained, wheat or rape seeds were raised from autumn to spring. Maize grew from spring to autumn, sweet potatoes from June to October or November, potatoes from spring to summer and from autumn to winter (two crops a year), and opium from autumn to spring. Other products included tea for cooking oil, timber, tong oil (harvest and oil pressing in October), medicinal herbs, and winter hunting. Here I will concentrate on a few cash crops of considerable value to the peasant—tong oil, opium, and bristles.

In the Li valley of western Hunan in the 1930s, tong oil brought in an estimated 1,473,000 yuan a year. This gave each grower household an extra income of 3.4 yuan (or 0.68 yuan per person), which had not been available before 1895. My estimates based on available figures of the gross revenue from selling tong oil from 1912 to 1937 (inclusive) are 6.3 million yuan for western Hubei, 90 million yuan for eastern Sichuan, and 9 million yuan for western Hunan. The average per annum was 3.9 million yuan.

Being an illegal drug, opium output and revenue are variously and often unreliably estimated. Let me begin from what I regard as a trustworthy piece of reporting in the *Dongfang zazhi*.[77] With due emendation, the cost of producing opium in the 1930s can be broken down as follows:

From breaking the earth to harvesting, 134 days
Wages, 10.21 yuan
Food, 14.18 yuan
Fertilizers, 32.50 yuan
Rent for 2 mu, 3.00 yuan
Tax on 2 mu, 0.45
Wear and tear of tools and interest, 0.55 yuan
Total cost, 60.89 yuan

Revenue gained is listed below:

200 taels of opium (say, at 450 yuan a picul or 1,000 taels), 90 yuan
Stalks, 1.50 yuan
Poppy seeds, 3.20 yuan
Leaves, 0.50 yuan
Total revenue, 95.20 yuan

The net profit from the two mu would be 34.21 yuan, or 17.10 yuan
of profit per mu. If the same mu were planted in wheat in the same
season, the net profit would be 5–6 yuan.[78] If the price of opium is
assumed at 350 yuan a picul, the net profit per mu would fall to only
7.15, hardly worth the grower's while to run the risk and endure the
hard work of growing poppies.

Opium prices did fluctuate wildly under the influence of supply and
demand and government intervention. Take Fengdu in 1936, for example. In the summer, a picul fetched 500 yuan. This rose to 600–700 in
August and September, leaped to 1,500 in October, dropped back to
1,000 in November, and climbed up again to 1,300 in December.[79]
These highly attractive prices of course included an outrageous amount
of taxes. In Fuling in 1932, each picul of opium bore 434.80 yuan of
taxes, of which 300 yuan went to the garrison region government and
the rest to the county government.[80]

A. C. McAllum estimated that in 1908 Sichuan produced 175,000
piculs of the drug.[81] Assuming that in the 1930s the total output had
increased to some 200,000 piculs, each of which bore 434.80 yuan of
taxes, the total tax yield would have been in the neighborhood of
86,960,000 yuan a year—the garrison region governments' share about
60,000,000 and county governments' 26,960,000.

Sichuan may have had 500,000 soldiers in the 1930s, each of whom
may have received 120 yuan or less per annum from the garrison
governments. This sounds reasonable. The rest shared by the 166
county governments of the province would have been an average of
162,410 yuan each. This also sounds reasonable.

If, as assumed above, the price of a picul of opium on leaving the
farm was 450 yuan, this meant 11–13 yuan of net profit from a mu of
land devoted to poppy cultivation, or 110–130 yuan per picul of
opium. From 200,000 piculs, the rural population of Sichuan was better off by 36,000,000 yuan. To use the Sichuan government's estimate
of the rural population of 34,225,854 in the early 1930s, this also
meant that each person was benefited by just over one yuan a year. The
share of eastern Sichuan was 7,000,000 yuan annually.

Sichuan again was the bristle producer par excellence, taking a
share of 15 percent of the national total output. In 1932 its bristle was
worth 4,503,250 yuan.[82] In 1936, a picul of black bristles was worth
100 yuan on the highlands. On reaching Chongqing for processing and
export, it fetched 324 yuan.[83] This rise in price was chiefly due to taxes

collected by the garrison and county governments, only secondarily due to the cost of transport and processing and middlemen's profit. For instance, from Chengdu to Chongqing, some 100 yuan was levied on a picul, and on leaving Chongqing the export duty was 77.29 yuan a picul.[84] If this was an indication of the state of affairs, at least 79 percent of the price rise was due to taxes, and only 21 percent to the middlemen and processors. To put it another way, only one-third of the total revenue from the bristles was retained in the countryside while two-thirds went to the cities (see chapters 5 and 6). About a quarter of the provincial total was produced in the highland, for a value of 341,250 yuan, or about 0.25 yuan per rural household (0.05 yuan per person).

We know very little of the bristle production in western Hubei and northwestern Hunan. Local historians in Dayong, for instance, say that it was of little importance. Three or four dealers regularly bought bristles from butchers and made some money. The amount purchased was small, however.[85] But Sichuan alone was likely to have contributed more than 40,000,000 yuan in the twenty years from 1916 to 1936 to the coffers of the various governments of the province. In addition, the inhabitants of the highlands paid other taxes—the land tax, surtaxes, and advances on it; a multitude of inland excise taxes, both traditional and newly introduced; the salt gabelle and its surtaxes. This burden they shared with their brethren on the plains. They also shared the use of the irredeemable currencies issued by the governments and garrison region commanders.

What was taken away by the commanders and governments was spent largely on what may be called "the scramble for garrison regions"—the civil wars, too many to be enumerated, between themselves and against Communist guerrillas. The total tax burden of these three commodities alone amounted to more than 11,000,000 yuan a year in eastern Sichuan, a share of 1.60 yuan or 2 yuan per person of the rural population.

The highland peasants knew that they had toiled mainly for the benefit of the commanders and governments for internecine fighting, only marginally for their own interests. They may not have known, however, that the surplus exacted from them could have been invested in improving production and transport. Here as elsewhere, capital had to come from landowners, bureaucrats, and townsmen. But no such capital was supplied there and then. Whatever investment that was carried out came from peasants themselves in the traditional, small-scale, and costly ways. Conspicuously absent was large-scale invest-ment in processing these three products in the highlands to create employment, cut middlemen's profit, and economize on transport costs. Small producers remained small producers; their agriculture stagnated; and spectacular commercialization failed to promote mod-ernization and high rates of returns in this half-century.

I now come to more theoretical issues, even if they are beyond my ability to solve. I shall return to them in chapter 8 where I offer a detailed description of the cultural characteristics of the highlanders. Here as there I candidly admit that because of lack of factual material some of the issues cannot be answered convincingly. Nonetheless, there is a considerable amount of material on the highlanders' tradi-tions and behavioral patterns which depict their martial and romantic characteristics.

When the highlanders became aware of their surpluses being appro-priated directly by the state (local governments and garrison com-manders) or indirectly through the new landowning class, the result was their discontent—"the spiritual problems behind the economic mechanism."[86] From discontent, they were to take action in protest, rebellion, or even revolution. Although anger alone would not lead to revolution, as Scott cautions us, the feeling was there and real. What he calls the righteous anger (or the standards of justice or moral values) indicates that the peasants had a problem—who was responsible for their plight? Scott assumes that peasants hover closely above the star-vation level. A bad crop due to natural or manmade reasons or both might threaten their survival. Out of this situation a notion of economic justice, the subsistence ethic, emerges to show the normative roots of peasant politics.[87]

It is because of this concern with survival that they eschew risk-taking to increase profit either by themselves or by others. By the same token they resent the claims to their surplus by landowners and by the state. They were and still are, therefore, cautious, conservative, "safety first, profit-making second." In this sense, small producers behave not very differently from their counterparts in the transition from medieval to early modern Europe, whose mentality was articulated by the church in terms of just price, unjust usury, reasonable rent, and profit; nor very differently from the small investors who buy blue chips instead of more speculative stocks in the city. In the case of producing tong oil, opium, or bristles, the highlanders originally exchanged them for daily necessities, not for profit. When the demand for these goods greatly expanded, they responded by increasing the production of these goods for the international market, whose workings and fluctuations were entirely beyond their ken. They did not expect that the governments would step in to grab so much of the proceeds from the trade. In spite of the benefit brought about by the commercialization, the landowners, mostly absentees, showed scant concern with peasants' welfare, let alone with the modernization of processing, transport, and marketing. They appropriated wooded land and privatized timber and tong trees. Although they violated the traditional norm of reciprocity, they did not go so far as to endanger peasants' right to survival. It was the state, represented by the militarists with their taxation and civil wars, that disrupted the peasants' productive pursuits and personal safety.[88]

Scott is by no means the only moral economist; historians like B. Moore, J. Blum, E. Le Roy Ladurie, and R. H. Tawney, and anthropologists like E. Wolf and E. Banfield share this conviction. On the general level, moral economy, which is based on cultural and psychological observations, is weak precisely in the empirical study of peasants' culture and psychology or at least in the study of culture as an expression of psychology. J. Davis, for example, shows his suspicion of the validity of Banfield's moral economic study in an article, "Morals and Backwardness."[89] Then there is the frontal attack launched by S. Popkin. Aware of this weakness, Scott follows up with his recent study of the day-to-day resistance of the peasants, *Weapons of the Weak*. There are, of course, other criticisms such as those from area specialists in the *Journal of Asian Studies* of August 1983. Here I shall concentrate on J. Polachek's essay in that issue on southwestern Jiangxi, whose hill peasants bore a strong resemblance to the highlanders under study here.

To test Scott's theory, Polachek points out that traditional rural society in Jiangxi provided a number of competing institutional arrangements to help the peasants tide over crises: the clan villages, the temple fair organization, and the blood-oath Brotherhood. The first had at their disposal some corporate estates that could be leased to the needy of the clan and some surplus grain and cash that could be loaned at low rates of interest. They were by far the most important institution, for they were the most resourceful. The temple fair organization often

took steps to maintain law and order and to defend the village community. These two types were to be found on the valley floor. The Brotherhood, however, spread chiefly among the hill settlements. Poor as they
were, its members assisted each other on an egalitarian principle and
by whatever means they possessed when times were hard.[90]

What Polachek does not mention is that in the last decades of the
Qing and the early years of the Republic, most of the village granaries
had become empty, corporate estates privatized, and the temple fair
organization and Brotherhood quite ineffective in giving aid. The welfare arrangements between the valley floor villages and hill settlements, though theoretically neat, were in fact intermingled, not only in
Sichuan and Hunan, but also in Jiangxi and Fujian.[91] For instance,
although the government and privately sponsored granaries were found
only in the walled city and some major market towns, the Brotherhood
chapters and members were everywhere. The risk-sharing arrangements in Jiangxi could hardly have survived intact the civil wars of the
1910s and 1920s and the Communist wars of the 1930s. The picture
seems to validate rather than invalidate Scott's general observation that
the peasants' subsistence ethic had been violated before the arrival of
the Communists. To prove this, scholars should search for the
peasants' own expression of their anxiety and anger, a step neither the
moral economists nor their critics have taken (see chapter 7).

C. Keyes suggests that just as Scott's theory fits the poor peasants
well, Popkin's applies better to the slightly better off, the peasants who
have a hope of improving their standards of living.[92] In his recent
study, Huang supports and elaborates on this suggestion.[93] Popkin begins by asking a series of searching questions that the moral economists have overlooked. How is the subsistence level determined? How
are the competing claims for village resources weighed? What is the
difference between need and poverty? If there is the moral obligation
to help poor peasants, how is a village community stratified? Because
of these previously unasked and unanswered questions, individual decisions and village functions have to be considered anew. However
poor, a peasant must have a little surplus for investment, in the short
run for maintaining the crop cycle, and in the long run for the life
cycle. The well-off naturally also invest, not merely for the benefit of
the poor, but chiefly for preserving the dyadic relations between themselves and their clients, thus for preserving their power. As to investing
for collective welfare if the villagers are poor, their demand for it

would be large and contribution to it small. They would contribute only when the collective welfare could benefit them more and cost them less. Otherwise, they would refrain from doing so, to become free riders.[94] All this points to the peasant's rationality in decision making.

> Individuals evaluate the possible outcomes associated with their choices in accordance with their preferences and values. In doing this, they discount the evaluation of each outcome in accordance with their subjective estimate of the likelihood of the outcome. Finally, they make the choice which they believe will maximize their expected utility.[95]

That is to say, first there are individual preferences that are subjective; then there is the individual estimate of the likelihood of success of a choice; finally, there is the amount of utility one expects to reap when the decision succeeds.[96] The preferences are not necessarily for money; nor is the utility entirely selfish.

Without any obstruction from the patron, whose chief concern is to preserve his power, a peasant would be willing to pursue commercial agriculture for his and his neighbors' benefit. Indeed, commercialization of agriculture is beneficial to him. And it is he who chooses to pursue it; he is not forced to do so. By the same token, he is not afraid to adopt innovations; rather, he is afraid of incompetent leadership that may make a mess of it. The relations between patron and client are not as harmonious as the moral economists would have one believe; they are in fact full of conflict, and the village is stricken with clashes between different groups of people, particularly between patrons and clients. The procedure in the village often favors the rich and powerful who lead in order to gain at the expense of the led.[97] It is the conflict between the social classes, not the "subsistence ethic" or "righteous anger," that prompts the peasants to protest and rebel.

In the case of Vietnam (studied by both Scott and Popkin), Popkin says that there was no trace of peasants longing for a return to the good old days. Their revolution was against the ancient regime as well as colonialism. If, as moral economists insist, their individual subsistence was threatened, why, asks Popkin, was the pattern of collective response so different from individual sentiments? Why did the middle peasants, better off than the tenants and landless laborers, respond more violently than their less fortunate brethren? Quoting from Mancur Olson's study of collective action, Popkin believes that "unless there is coercion or some other special device to make individuals act in their common interest, rational, self-interested individuals [i.e., peasants] will not act to achieve their common or group interest."[98] Powerless peasants needed a leader or leadership to convince them that his (or its) way would be effective and beneficial.[99]

What these two schools are trying to explain is the process starting from the peasants' perception of suffering to their revolutionary action. To one school, it is from perception of suffering to moral indignation and finally to action; to another, it is from perception to inaction, to an outside influence or coercion, to the acceptance of the influence or coercion, and finally to action. The moral economists need impetuosity and courage whereas the political economists want calculation, planning, and organization, as argued out in the last chapters of Scott's and Popkin's books. The former emphasize the existence of combustible material; the latter, the arsonist's hand. Nonetheless, both are based on an understanding of the peasant's mind—irrational or rational. Concluding his *Moral Economy*, Scott writes: "It is especially at the level of culture that a defeated or intimidated peasantry may nurture its stubborn moral dissent from an elite-created social order."[100] But his book contains little direct evidence to show the peasants' moral dissent. Popkin's has even less.

Rural culture created by the peasants is a product of history which has to be studied in the context of its urban counterpart if it is to be understood.[101] As to its contents, Le Roy Ladurie lists religion and folklore while Scott enumerates myths, jokes, songs, linguistic usages, and religions to meet peasants' survival and spiritual needs so that they can explain and control their environment.[102] In essence, this is also what Geertz means in his several studies of culture in general and peasants' culture in particular.[103]

To contrast rural culture with its urban equivalent is a research device, to underline their differences, but it must not be carried to the misconstruction that the twain never meet or that whatever influence there exists between them, it flows only from one to the other. However secluded, a folk society is seldom completely cut off from the outside world.[104] On the other hand, however modern, an urban society has never totally obliterated its rural vestiges. For instance, to say that peasant logic is "the logic in use" or "situational logic" does not mean that the townsman's is entirely general or universal.[105] Likewise, to assert that the peasant has developed a shame culture is not to assert at the same time that the townsman is immune to the feeling of shame.

By shame I mean that one is exposed in the view of others in a painfully diminished sense.[106] It is synonymous with a feeling of inferiority, shyness, or modesty.[107] It arises out of a tension between the ego and the ego ideal (including collective ideal). When the goal set by the ego ideal is unattained, one feels the anxiety of abandonment and social ostracism. Guilt, on the other hand, arises out of a tension between the ego and the superego (say, conscience). A transgression of the boundary set by the superego leads to another type of anxiety, the anxiety of mutilation. These two types of anxiety often overlap and fuse, one turning into another.[108] In a society where the realm of privacy is either extremely limited or nonexistent, guilt tends to be swamped by shame, and social sanction tends to depend on the watchful eyes of others who are always nearby. In a society where the private world is more spacious, one tends to become one's own arbitrator, and social sanction relies mainly on oneself.[109]

Peasants are said to be passive, and their passivity is usually attributed to a feeling of inferiority in the presence of townsmen, masters, and outside authorities. They are a people of diminished pride and self-respect.[110] If they dare to break free from the constraint of passivity by taking their grievances to the authorities, they may not obtain redress to justify what it might cost them for their recklessness. This explanation may be more acceptable than the so-called psychology of undernourishment, which is no more than conjecture.[111]

With few resources at their disposal and a long history of exploitation by others, peasants have to socialize their children to conform rather than to innovate. To act against village traditions or standards accepted by one's kin and neighbors may cause gossip and criticism, if nothing worse. To set one's goals low, to strive for what everyone else has been doing, is to be free from unnecessary anxiety and sanction by shame. Therefore the peasants of Languedoc were nearly all Catholics; southern Italians eschew education and new technology; and Aztecs have been making the same handicraft objects and dancing the same steps as far back as they can remember.[112] The new is never as good as the old. In other words, the peasants are conservative.

Peasants distrust not only outsiders, but also each other.[113] Montaillou was a world of spies and betrayals, and among the Aztecs Lewis found malice, hidden and indirect hostility, envy, and harsh and unrelenting gossip.[114] This leaves the immediate family the only dependable people. Without them "the individual stands unprotected and isolated, a prey to every form of aggression, exploitation, and humiliation."[115] Their distrust may be an expression of their resentment of the repressive social order in which they live, a weapon their feeble arms can still hurl.[116] From G. Foster's point of view, it is an attitude shaped by "the image of the limited good."

"The image of the limited good," as far as I know, is the only systematic explanation of peasants' attitude and behavior, whatever Foster's critics care to say to the contrary. Under the assumptions of insignificant improvement in the technology of production and essentially a closed society, "all of the desired things of life [including health and love] exist in finite quantity and are always in short supply."[117] It is a "one man's meat another man's poison" situation. In such a situation, (1) one's best strategy is to maximize security by preserving one's relative position in the existing order of things—one poses no threat to anyone else; (2) one must not stick out like a nail only to get hit; (3) one must do one's best to conform with the rest of the community, by doing no better and no worse, by being neither admirable (or enviable) nor contemptible, even to the extent of denying one's admirability; (4) one has to use gossip, slander, back-biting, character assassination, witchcraft, even physical aggression to keep everyone in line, in one's relative position.[118]

Foster's assumption of a closed society has been the major point of criticism. Once opened, the "limited good" may become "expandable good" by the introduction of outside technology and capital, ideas and attitudes, and even outsiders themselves. This of course happens normally.[119] But one must not exaggerate its importance; otherwise the contrast between town and country would disappear and with it our problem. The influx of all the things mentioned above has been going on for many decades, if not centuries, among Chinese, Polish, and southern Italian peasants. Their friends and relatives who emigrated overseas have come and gone and have sent back to their native villages letters and other reading materials, modern gadgets and technology. In some cases their own "image of the limited good" is taken to and held fast in the metropolis whither they have emigrated, and the others who remain in their native villages of course continue to subscribe to it.

In their daily life, distrustful and suspicious peasants tend to conceal truth. They regard frank and direct persons as either naive or exceedingly crafty. "You must always hide something or [sic] from someone;

everyone lies about everything: money, food, friendship, love, God."
Even an expression of affection is but a fulfillment of reciprocal obligations—in other words, prim and proper and ritualized. Friends and
relatives must be guarded against and kept at arm's length.[120]

In the final analysis, however, one has to trust one's family for
security, not necessarily for love. Family, not the individual, is the
center of a peasant's life. The patriarch is to be obeyed; his character is
the character of his wife and children; his duty is to discipline them by
corporal punishment whenever it is needed;[121] Love-making between
husband and wife should be infrequent so as to save energy for the
back-breaking labor during the day; masturbation is harmful; bodily
contact between parents and children over the age of five should cease.
Since the whole family normally sleeps on the same bed or in any case
in the same room, neither intercourse nor masturbation is convenient.[122] As to socialization, peasant children's formal education is
never a matter of importance. A boy is first trained to be dependent
and reserved for the convenience of the patriarch's rule and the boy's
social acceptability, and then to be independent and assertive in preparation for succeeding to the patriarchal mantle.[123]

Is there any fun in a peasant's life? Eating and drinking seem to be
what pleasure means to him. Then there are games and jokes, rituals
and songs to make the daily drudgery tolerable. This is the grim picture
learned from the studies of plains peasants. Can it be applied to the
Chinese highland?

On my visits to Hunan and Sichuan mountain regions in and before
1989, I found some but not many differences between the lifestyles of
the highlanders and plainsmen. The sameness was not surprising after
forty years of political socialization and educational popularization
since the 1949 revolution. I have the feeling that the highland characteristics recorded in the gazetteers and other documents have purposely
been eradicated so that all peasants, indeed, all Chinese, are supposed
to conform to the image of the socialist citizen. There is, of course,
another consideration: in the presence of local party leaders and a
visitor from afar, the highland peasants I met behaved with greater
circumspection. For instance, they all told me that they had left the age
of superstition behind. In a sense this appeared to be true, as I discovered that none of the old temples were still in use except for a few
priests who carried on worship, and made a living through them; nor
did I discover any form of worship at peasants' homes. In the cities

and suburbs, however, places of worship were often jam-packed with pilgrims and tourists. What lies beneath the atheistic appearance was difficult for me to fathom.

However, all the relevant local gazetteers compiled before 1949 say that the highlanders were given to believe in gods and spirits, often different from those worshiped by townsmen. They also say that these highlanders were extremely frugal, straightforward, physically strong (both sexes), arrogant, and quarrelsome. The compilers, urban scholars themselves, took a disapproving view of these strange, unruly attitudes and behavior, particularly the highlanders' sexual libertinism and their litigiousness. People of this breed were prone to protest and revolt. Their history in the nineteenth and twentieth centuries is indeed frequently punctuated by insurrections.

Another source of information on the highlanders' cultural traits is their own folktales and folksongs collected both before and after 1949. I rely almost entirely on those published before 1949, for the gatherers, individual scholars, who censored them only on moral grounds, discarded what was regarded as obscene. The gatherers did not differentiate between obscenity for monetary gain and that purely for expression of sexual humor and pleasure. After 1949, indeed even during the soviet period of the 1930s, the moralistic censorship was reinforced with political censorship; the gatherers' attitude became haughtier, and their fidelity to the original version less meticulous. Most of the tales and songs are of the heroic deeds of highlanders, their uprisings, and their sexual love. Their love songs differ from plainsmen's, not only in clinical candor but also in the absence of tearful and unrequited lamentations (see chapter 8).

The highlanders grew very distinct stripes from plainsmen for several reasons. First, an ethnic conflict existed between the dominant Han majority and the minorities—the Miao, Tujia, and others who inhabited parts of the mountain land in northwestern Hunan, southeastern Sichuan, and western Hubei. The animosity has not really died out. Second, there was an insider-outsider conflict between natives and immigrants and between old and new immigrants. The immigrants were nearly all Han and mostly ne'er-do-wells. Third, highlanders lacked opportunities to learn the great tradition of the Han, due to a high rate of illiteracy, a dearth of newspapers, magazines, and other reading material, and very few schools to acculturate the highlanders who may have been reluctant to accept the instruction. Fourth, the

isolated life of homesteaders made it imperative that they defend themselves and cope with a pattern of daily life independently. "Hanification" was not a program of education they needed.

How did they resist, protest, and fight for their interest against the
Han and all types of intruders? I admire Scott's description and analysis of the daily resistance of the Malay peasants, but his model unfortunately cannot be applied to Central China's highlanders. Since the
majority of the latter lived in small, isolated groups and were said to be
straightforward to the extent of being blunt, they might not habitually
indulge in gossip and back-biting. Instead, they resorted more to direct
confrontation—a shouting match, a fist fight, or litigation—to give an
impression that they were quick tempered. It is reasonable to assume
that they felt inferior to the plainsmen and townsmen. To conceal their
defects and shortcomings, they might use rage or righteous indignation
for self-protection.[124]

Defense, protest, and revolt need an ideology for justification, for
fighting the battle of value conflict and for what Gramsci calls
"counter-hegemony."[125] On this issue, Scott makes a telling point,
warning against an overly passive view of the subordinate classes
(such as the highlanders) whose own experiences may on occasion
have helped them see through the platitudes and falsehood of the elite
and its ideology. Even if they accepted the great tradition of the Han,
they did so only through a process of cogitation and contestation.
Moreover, when a new class takes power, its ideology is far from
entirely revolutionary or entirely in sympathy with the oppressed. It
has to incorporate elements of the tradition for its governance.[126]
Scott's point confirms the one made earlier that the ideologies of the
rulers and the ruled, like the cultures of the rural and the urban, are
mutually influencing, forming a continuum from the cities to the
mountains. They shape and reshape each other in order to accommodate each other. Paternalism on a small producer's farm and that in an
early bourgeois enterprise are obvious examples; the variegated patterns of Christianization of Europe are another. Unlike water, ideological influence can often defy the law of gravity to flow up and down.

The rebellious ideology of the peasants usually takes the form of a
religion, an ethos and world view, to make sense of existence and
guide action.[127] M. Freedman wisely advises us to see Chinese religions as different versions of each other. "Every religious phenomenon
to be found among the common people in China was susceptible of

transformation into the beliefs and rites among the cultivated elite. Heterodoxy might be a transformed version of orthodoxy and vice versa."[128] In the case of the highlanders, the stress is on the mutual influence in religious and social philosophies of the elite and the small producers, dating back before Confucius and forward to after Mao.

Ancestor worship was common between the elite and the rustic. But one's ancestor was another's ghost; the former was ascribed rights and duties by his worshiper while the latter was not; the former was revered while the latter was dreaded; the former was benevolent while the latter was malevolent.[129] If ancestor worship grew out of the socioeconomic practices of the small producer, the belief must have spread to the rural elite and then the urban elite. The indoctrination of Confucianism through the study of texts and scriptures and ritualistic observations was of course the counterflow. That there is a difference between refinement and crudity, between an emphasis on doctrine and on utility, is beyond doubt, but it is never clear-cut.[130] More important, perhaps, was what was rejected—the elite disregarded the worship of Nuoshen and Sanwang in western Hunan whereas the mountain peasants refused the incomprehensible and abstruse.

The distance that separates the central metropolis and the remotest country is, however, never unconquerable. For one thing, outside upheavals, a Seven-Year War, a French Revolution, or a Taiping Rebellion, could hardly fail to stimulate villagers and homesteaders to take appropriate action. For another, people came and went, passing on information and ideas during their visits. These were not just soldiers and migrants, but also itinerant tradesmen, "returned" scholars, porters, even cultural "mestizos" born to and brought up by a mixed parentage, thus equally at home in both, say, native and immigrant heritages, fluent in both dialects, to perform the functions of "cultural mongers."[131] There are many examples to illustrate this interaction. The verselet, *zhuzhici*, of eastern Sichuan was adopted and adapted by the poet Liu Yuxi (772–842) to become an established form of poetry. Several enthralling tales of the minorities who lived in Hubei and Hunan were incorporated in the Han tradition as its own—creating the universe by Pangu, shooting down the nine suns by Houyi, knocking down the pillars of skies by Gonggong, and so forth. On the other hand, the minority peoples have absorbed some Han stories into their own heritage, such as the widely known one on Mengjiang who wailed and the Great Wall (or simply the great wall in western Hunan) collapsed.

They worshiped the three kings (Sanwang), who were supposed to be immensely strong and fought against the Han, like Gonggong had done before them. Also like Gonggong, they were tragic heroes followed by others—Wu Bayue of the 1795 rebellion, Li Yuanfa of the 1849 rebellion, Zhang Xiumei of the 1855 rebellion, and so on. It was this defiant tradition and these hero models that encouraged the highlanders to become the "Divine Army" (Shenbing), to support the Red Armies of He Long and Xu Xiangqian, and to join Long Yunfei's antirent war in 1937.

The *wu* witches were many and widely believed to have supernatural powers. These young and middle-aged women appeared to be possessed by gods once in every season when they could do spiritual healing, exorcism, and particularly create a time-bomb type of poison known as *gu*.[132] If a plainsman, the husband of a Miao wife, decided to abandon her, the "time bomb" would "explode" for the weak to get even with the heartlessly strong—a direct form of revenge less subtle than gossip but believed to be more deadly and effective.

Of course, not all highlanders were fierce fighters; nor were most of them tame and subservient. These peasants had ambitions and backbones with a tradition to stiffen them. After each defeat, they quieted down and waited for the next opportunity.[133] Shen Congwen, the celebrated novelist from western Hunan, observed that their militancy and heroism seemed to have dissipated after 1916. Yet he immediately contradicted himself by saying that in 1917 there were still "vengeful duels among them."[134] Probably after a period of calm, the mountains would roar again, not so much against landowners as against the state of the Han people.

T. Skocpol maintains that a revolutionary theory must explain both the emergence of a revolutionary situation within the old regime and the intermeshing of the various actions of the diversely situated groups that shape the revolutionary process and give rise to the new regime. It is mainly structural and yet does not discount subjective factors completely. She lists four interpretations of the emergence and process of revolution. Marxist theory explains the structural contradictions of a society and the development of the consciousness of the ruling and revolutionary classes. Aggregate-psychological theories explain people's psychological motivations for engaging in political violence. System/value consensus theories focus on the violent responses of ideological movements to severe disequilibrium in a social system.

And political conflict theories stress the growing anger of the revolutionaries whose organizations have access to some resources, which leads to collective violent action fighting for goals contradictory to those insisted upon by the government. Of these theories, only the Marxists, and to a lesser degree the system-value dissynchronization theorists, attach greater importance to situation and structural contradictions that cause the growth of grievances to win Skocpol's sympathy and support.[135]

In an agrarian society, the correlation between inequality of land distribution and instability of political situation is often very high, especially in the process of agricultural commercialization.[136] The experiences of Mexico and Latin America in general have particularly attracted scholarly attention.[137] From another point of view, political instability occurs frequently when a long-term prosperity is followed by an economic downturn and the hardships of the downturn cannot be mitigated by the benefit of industry or commerce.[138] Under such circumstances, peasant protests have to be suppressed by naked force to turn a dangerous situation into a revolution. Who, then, is the main force of the struggle? The middle or the poor peasant or the farm laborer? With all the experiences to back him up, Mao unswervingly insisted that the poor peasants and laborers were.[139] Mao's insistence may also have been based on his conception of misery and dispossession—the most wretched was potentially the most revolutionary.

> It is true the poor peasants are not afraid of losing anything. Many of them really have "neither a tile over their heads nor a speck of land under their feet." What, indeed, is there to keep them from joining the [peasant] associations? This great mass of poor peasants, or altogether 70 percent of the rural population, are the backbone of the peasant associations, the vanguard in the overthrow of the feudal forces and the heroes who have performed the great revolutionary task which for long years was left undone. Without the poor peasant class (the "riff-raff," as the gentry call them), it would have been impossible to bring about the present [1927] revolutionary situation in the countryside, or to overthrow the local tyrants and evil gentry and complete the democratic revolution.[140]

Lenin, of course, also expounded this view.[141]

E. Wolf, on the other hand, disagrees. Poor and landless peasants "depend on a landlord for the greatest part of their livelihood or the totality of it, have no tactical power; they are completely within the power domain of their employer, without sufficient resources of their own to serve them as resources in the power struggle."[142] This position has the support of D. Feeny, who concludes his study of Vietnamese peasants with the thought that only those peasants who have some surplus resources and are organized are prepared to take a gamble on rebellion.[143]

The disagreement seems to spring from the activism or passivism of the wretched. One theory maintains that the more one owns, the less revolutionary one is likely to be. The spectrum ranges from the most revolutionary—the most wretched—to the most conservative—the wealthiest. The other has it that, leaving the most passive—the poorest—aside for the time being, the spectrum begins from the middle peasants—the most rebellious—and ends in the richest—the most conservative. In the revolutionary process, the poorest can be activated to participate.

Is Mao's thesis solidly supported by his own experiences and surveys, or does it only appear so? Throughout the two land revolutions, 1927–34 and 1947–49, his view on the poor peasants being the main force and the middle peasants being the indispensable allies seems to have remained unchanged. From 1928 onward, however, he was less enthusiastic about the spontaneous revolutionary fervor of these two groups. By implication, the activism had to be aroused and protected by the Chinese Communist Party (CCP) and the Red Army. The poor peasants "could be deceived by the intermediate classes [rich peasants and small landlords] to become inactive" while the middle peasants, like small landlords, could be ambivalent toward the revolution.[144] Mao knew that in the spring of 1930 the active elements in the district soviet government of Xingguo, Jiangxi, were ten riff-raff who were not peasants at all: three rich and middle peasants, one impoverished landlord, one woman, and three educated persons, but not a single poor peasant. He knew also that in Ruijin and Shangyou, Jiangxi, in November 1930, the CCP branches absorbed mostly landlords and rich peasants.[145] The revolutionary process needed two waves and two kinds of activism. First, when associations were being organized, the promised economic benefits attracted the poor peasants to join.[146] This first wave belonged to the poor and to those more aroused by promised gains. Protests against high rent, interest, and taxes thus took place, to be followed by guerrilla operations, land redistribution, and the formation of temporary and permanent soviet regimes.[147] It was in the redistribution of land and establishment of a regime that the second wave of activism arose, usually from the middle and rich peasants. It was stimulated by power, and again by economic gain. Even if the better-off people did not seize all the fruits of revolution, their literacy and management skills would lead them to positions of considerable local importance. Of course, the process of revolution did not end in land redistribution and government formation; it went on if the CCP and Red Army wanted sincerely to benefit the poor peasants and to consolidate their support. Further redistribution of land and its investigation would be necessary. The highland experiences in eastern Sichuan and western Hunan conformed to this central soviet pattern.

Was this a democratic revolution against feudalism and for rice and freedom?[148] Skocpol fears that the fragility of the revolutionary elite and the anarchist tendencies in a context of popular turmoil and counterrevolutionary threats, the need to defend the revolutionary regime, entailed a need for dictatorship rather than democracy.[149] Even if the elite was strong enough to curb anarchic tendencies and the context conducive to freedom and individual rights, a revolution based predominantly in the countryside offered little hope for democracy. In the Chinese case, the leadership consisted almost entirely of educated people, the majority of whom were from a rural background. Their ideal of democracy was a government dedicated to the welfare of the people; they strove for justice, incorruptibility, and a reasonable standard of living for the underprivileged. These paternalistic ends, in their best sense, were what they and their supporters had internalized in their youthful socialization and reaffirmed by their adult learning and experiences. To achieve these cherished ends, both democracy and dictatorship were available means for them to choose. Neither had any intrinsic value in it; neither was absolutely necessary. This was the attitude that guided the agrarian policies of the Krestintern for the Balkans in the 1920s; those who adopted this attitude were what Hobsbawm calls "political father or mother figures"; the state they made would be a patron state.[150] The fight for democracy had to wait for another day.

Table 1.1

Demographic Changes in the Qing Valley

	1880s–90s	1910s	Percent + or −
Enshi	269,984	267,546	−0.9
Jianshi	182,121	204,606	+12.0
Laifeng	180,391	93,615	−13.6
Lichuan	173,766	217,295	−25.0
Xianfeng	101,761	172,275	+69.0
Xuanen	181,182	99,789	−44.9
Total	1,017,205	1,055,126	

Sources: Fu and *xian* gazetteers; *Hubei tongzhi* (1921, chap. 43); *Xinzhonghua* 1934, 25/7: 83–84.

Table 1.2

Demographic Changes in Central China

East Sichuan along the Yangzi

	1880s–90s	1910s	Percent + or −
Fuling	541,898	612,522	+13.0
Wanxian	101,696	811,465	+697.0
Yunyang	102,637	456,279	+344.5

East Sichuan South of the Yangzi

Nanchuan	149,562	181,722	+21.5
Xiushan	384,379	456,279	+18.7

Northwest Hunan

	1746	1815	1890	1921
Cili	78,000	155,000	315,200	690,970

Sources: Local gazetteers; *Zhongguo shiyezhi* 1935/3:21–40.

Table 1.3

Population Changes (1873 = 100)

	1893	1913	1933
Hubei	105	116	145
Sichuan	118	135	157
Hunan	118	129	144

Source: Tongji tiyao (1935).

Table 1.4

Sichuan Bristles

Year	Piculs	Value (yuan)	Government revenue (yuan)	Middlemen's revenue (yuan)	Growers' revenue (yuan)
1912–16 (avg.)	8,156				
1917–21 (avg.)	8,712				
1928–32 (avg.)		3,006,708			
1932		4,503,250			
1936	13,650	4,422,600	2,420,009	637,591	1,365,000

Sources: Decennial Report; Zhonghua nongxuehuibao, nos. 7–8 (1936): 154; *Sichuan yuebao* 9/3, 26–32.

2
FOOD

NESTLED in a river valley, a highland city depends on the arable land adjacent to it and the roads and waterways connecting it to the world beyond the hills and mountains, beyond the reach of one's eyes. Though sitting on valley floors, there are chiefly two types of highland cities: those immediately surrounded by relatively flat land (e.g., fig. 2.1), hence largely dependent on rice for subsistence; and those surrounded by hilly land (e.g., fig. 2.2), hence largely fed by such dry crops as maize and sweet potatoes. What the cultivated land, mountains, and rivers can provide for them together with their own skills and sweat would determine the size of the city's population and the denizens' standards of living. There are no available records, meaningful or reliable, of the land progressively brought under cultivation in the forty years since the commercialization movement began, in spite of fairly reasonable records of the demographic changes on the highlands. It is known that trees were felled and sold in great quantities, an indication that population increases made land reclamation imperative, but it seemed to be a situation of first-come first-served, a free-for-all. A fierce struggle for survival must have been waged until the warlords' rule became more stabilized, toward the end of the 1920s.[1]

At first the reclaimed land was a gold mine to the tiller. Then it settled into a routine of heavy fertilizing and back-breaking work, until it was abandoned because the rate of return fell too low to justify its continued use. In the meantime, it was possible that soil erosion might turn the slope into a barren waste.[2]

The land reclaimed could have been owned by public institutions or by individuals and used for growing trees and bushes and for burying the dead. When reclaimed, it grew sweet potatoes, maize, and legumes, if there were sufficient labor and capital.[3] Terracing was the way to stabilize the value of the reclaimed land, and thus ownership and lease of it became worthwhile.[4]

Of the three subregions under consideration, eastern Sichuan attracted

Figure 2.1. **Lixian County Seat and Environs. (The city is surrounded immediately by paddy fields.)**

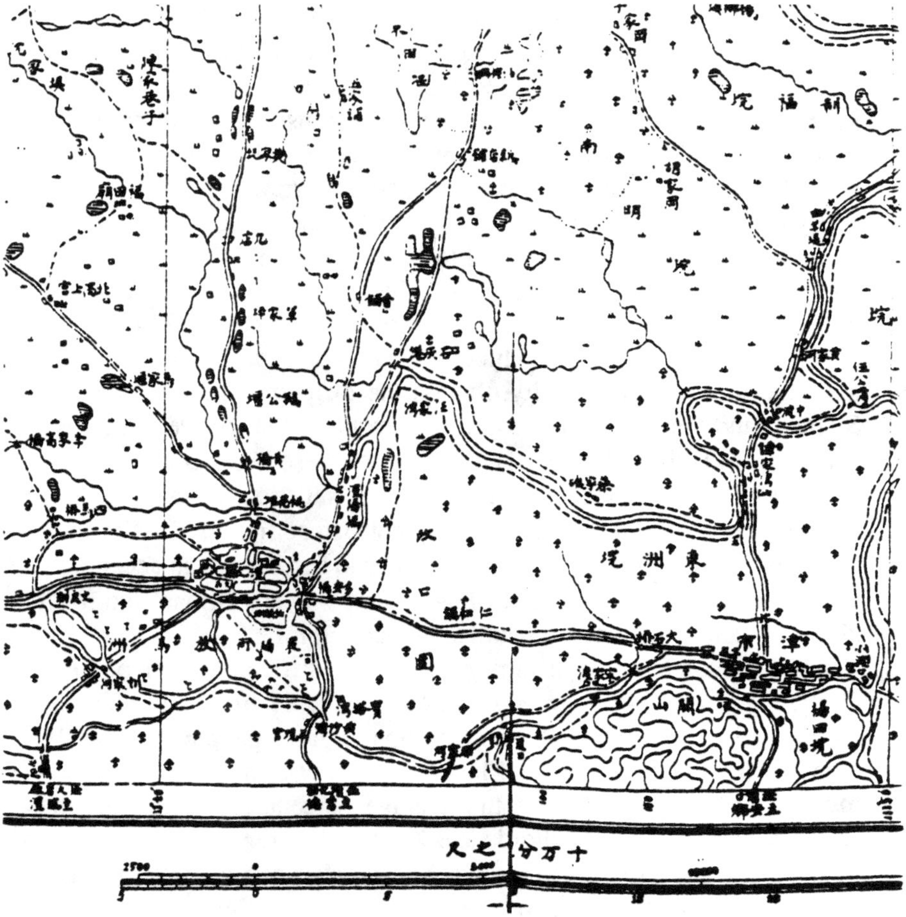

the largest number of new settlers, an increase of 74 percent from the 1880s to the early 1930s; western Hunan, the second largest number, an increase of 57 percent from 1816 to the early 1930s; and western Hubei, the least, an increase of merely 7 percent from the 1880s to the 1930s. In all cases, however, the increase on the highlands was much faster than in the respective provinces as a whole: Sichuan increased 11 percent from 1850 to 1937; Hunan, 40 percent from 1820 to 1940; and Hubei declined 21 percent (see tables 2.1 and 2.2). To explain this phenomenon, it is necessary to examine the capacity of the highlands to grow food and cash crops, to facilitate export and import, and to keep whatever additional income for their own use—a question of how much the highlanders earned, spent, and saved. This chapter is concerned with estimating the amount of food they grew.

By the early 1930s the arable land actually under rake and hoe in the three subregions may be assumed to have reached its limit (table 2.3). At that time, eastern Sichuan, with the highest percentage of cultivated area, appeared to be the most productive in food crops, followed by western Hunan and western Hubei. In terms of paddy fields, this was also the order of productivity, though the difference between eastern Sichuan and western Hunan was smaller while that between the two and western Hubei widened. The fertility of these lands is indeterminable, however, because of insurmountable statistical problems. By a stroke of luck, we do have generally consistent figures for the food crops of western Hubei. But when it comes to sorting out an acceptable impression of those in eastern Sichuan and western Hunan, the local historians and data I have consulted are not helpful.[5]

Let me indicate how insurmountable the difficulties can be. The *Dongfang zazhi*, 24/16 (p. 34) carries a valuable time series on the increase and decrease in the four groups of farm people—landlords, owner-cultivators, tenants, and laborers—in northern Sichuan, covering the period 1912–26. But the average percentages of two of the categories are 22.5 for landlords and 27.2 for laborers! I have not seen another time series of its kind and the available one makes no sense. Chinese statistics of this period are generally unreliable; those concerning the highlands are even more so. One often has to rely on one's common sense and on descriptive literature. I discuss the statistical material further in appendix A.

The highlander began to prepare for the spring-summer season early in March, hence the saying: "To plan for the whole year in the spring,

Figure 2.2. **Fenghuang County Seat and Environs. (The city is surrounded im-mediately by hilly land.)**

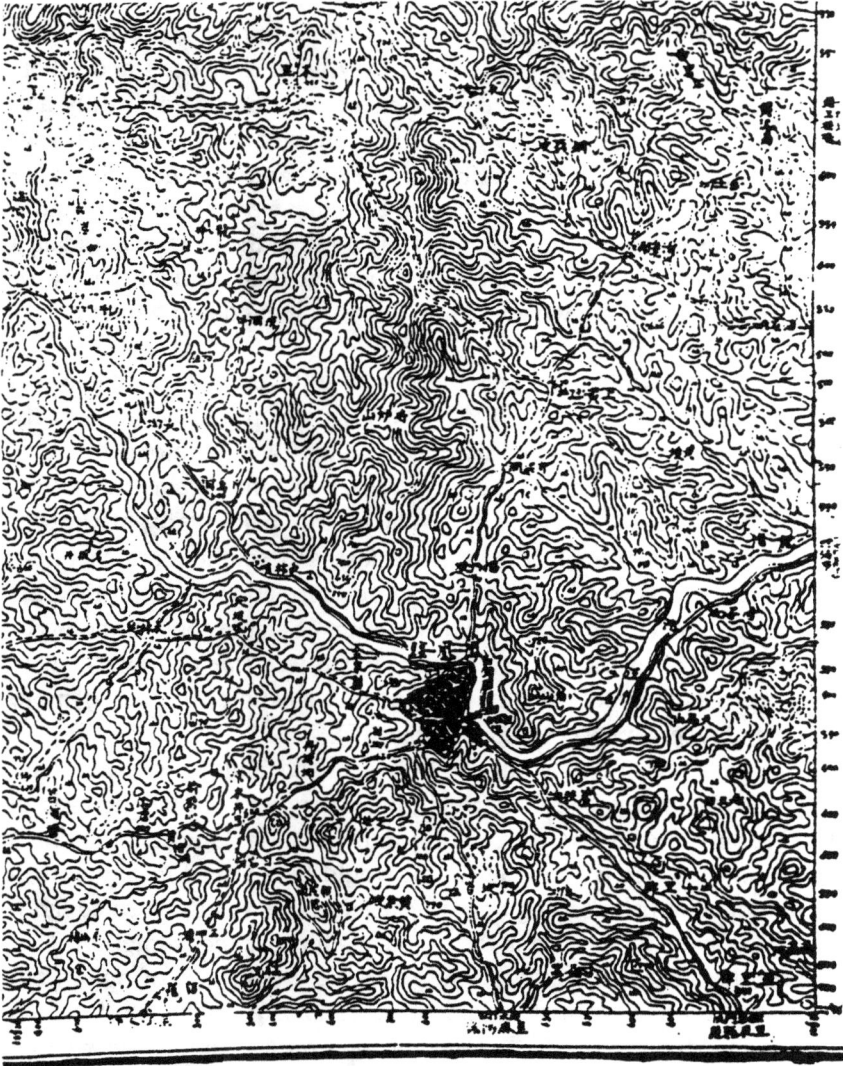

to plan for the whole day in the morning." Seeds of rice, soya, and maize must be ready, and fields must be drained for sowing. At about the same time Irish potatoes had to be put in the earth. Peasants grew only one crop of rice and maize, but two seasons of the potatoes: spring-summer and autumn-winter. As soon as the laborious work of rice transplanting and weeding was done, the highlander had to get sweet potatoes ready. A staple food, they were as needed and labor-consuming as rice, but they required much less fertilizers. In July and August, rice and maize were harvested, followed almost immediately by the planting of wheat, barley, rapeseeds, and legumes (see table 2.4). The fields left fallow through the winter were submerged under water, as an insurance against a possible drought the next year and as a respite from the strain on the tillers and on their limited supply of fertilizers. During the winter fallow, farmers hunted and gathered and carried goods to the market.[6]

Under the assumption that there was little trade in staple foods between the counties of the highlands, what was produced was locally consumed, perhaps a larger share of rice and wheat among the residents in the county seat and a larger share of other grains in the villages and hamlets. This assumption holds true particularly in western Hubei and west Hunan; less so in eastern and southeastern Sichuan. That is to say, there existed a very close correlation between the pattern of production and that of consumption of staple food in the highland area. Except for western Hunan, much less rice and wheat were consumed compared with the province as a whole, but much more grain and tubers were consumed (table 2.5).

The shortage of arable land and transport difficulties for heavy and bulky food either upstream or uphill put a firm limit on the increase in food supply, hence also the increase in population. One can imagine a situation in which a highland tenant would be allowed to pay rent in opium or cash from selling opium instead of rice to his absentee landlord, thus keeping the rice in the highlands for local consumption. This seldom happened, and after 1930 when the prohibition of opium became more effective it was seldom profitable. Another situation did occur: the increase in the demand for tong oil and opium drew many people up to the highlands who hewed the trees, reclaimed the land, and created new settlements. The resulting prosperity began to show signs of decline in the late 1920s; from 1930 onward the decline accelerated.

I do not believe that this turn in the fortunes of the highlands could be attributed to any significant degree to the extreme vagaries of nature. I have mentioned that the great Yangzi floods of 1931 that affected Hubei and Hunan (as well as Jiangsu, Anhui, and Jiangxi) did little damage to the highlands, although I am quite prepared to ascribe the decrease in Hubei's population to the successive inundations from 1931 to 1935.[7] Also, the devastating droughts in Sichuan in the 1930s, especially the one in 1936–37, had some impact on some highland counties, but the brunt was born by the basin, not the rim. This, together with the civil war between the Nationalists and Communists in southern Shaanxi and northern Sichuan and in the border region among the three provinces, contributed to the decline of the affected areas; however, a decline in the rest of the highlands has to be explained by other reasons.

In the radical 1930s, Chinese scholars blamed what they called "the general rural bankruptcy" (nongcun pochan) on imperialism and feudalism. Imperialism meant chiefly the import of cheap and preferred manufactures to the detriment of rural handicrafts, and international market fluctuations that could benefit Chinese peasants if the profit was not taken away by the state or landlords but could also damage them, as happened after the autumn of 1929. Unfortunately, the highlands had developed no handicrafts of any importance, and, shielded by the silver standard, the Great Depression did not hurt China until after 1932. If China had ever been a feudal country, feudalism, according to the scholars of the 1930s, manifested itself through the concentration of landownership, higher rates of exploitation (i.e., principally high rates of rent and secondarily those of taxes and interest), and local militarization for the defense of this state of affairs. If this was in fact the situation, land values and rents should have risen in the 1920s and 1930s; they did not, as I shall soon discuss.

There were at least three indicators pointing to the gradual decline of the rural highlands—a decline in population, a decline in land value, and a decline in the rates of rent. These indicators occurred against the background of a gradual decrease in the production and export of tong oil and opium. In the following chapter I shall explain that the boom and bust in tong oil and opium production and sales had a great deal to do with the prosperity and depression of the highland communities as a whole.

How much staple food did a highlander need to keep body and soul together, and therefore how much land must an individual have to work on in order to feed oneself? Leaving aside the various nutrients an adult must have for a relatively healthy life, I shall concentrate only on the basic 2,800–3,000 calories a day. The staples produced in the highlands—rice, wheat, maize, legumes, and millet—generated roughly the same amount of calories (1,920–2,200 a catty). If one assumes that a peasant paid rent in rice and consumed only the other grains and tubers (sweet potatoes at 544.7 calories a catty, for example), he or she would need either 1.5 catties of polished grain or 5 catties of sweet potatoes a day. In other words, the individual had to have at least 1.82 mu for growing grains (other than rice) and another 1.82 mu for growing tubers to meet the demand for a mixed diet. A family of five would therefore require the minimum of 18.2 mu of dry land for their survival. With a little help from his wife or adolescent son, the master of the house was quite capable of working the 18 mu of land. If a family had less than this, it suggested one or a combination of several of the following possibilities: the family had cash crops that they sold to pay the rent on all the land they leased; they earned sideline incomes from butchery, construction work, or porterage; they could reduce the number of mouths in the family to be fed; they would migrate.

Ownership

Against the background of population increase, more explosively in eastern Sichuan than in western Hubei and Hunan, and the rise of a new landowning class to destabilize the traditional rural elite, the public land[8] was gradually bought or forcibly taken over by private owners. They were in most cases local strongmen in command of armed forces or in civil office. In Sichuan, public land used to take a share between one-third and one-half of the utilized land. Later, much of it became privatized.[9] Similar developments occurred in Hubei and Hunan.[10] By 1932 less than 2 percent of the cultivated areas in Hubei and less than 5.5 percent in Hunan remained under public ownership.[11] In the latter case, the garrison field system in the Miao area accounted for the relatively high percentage of public land. Ironically, the system itself was the cause of much tension and conflict.

Simultaneous with this change in ownership was the gradual disappearance of the system of lease in perpetuity commonly in use in the highlands. Such leases were originally granted as an encouragement to reclaimers of land. They bore unusually low rates of rent and could be passed on to the leaseholders' children and grandchildren.[12] As time went on, these leaseholders and their descendants were brought in line with other types of tenants. They were required to pay rent deposits, to convert sharecrops into a fixed rate of monetary rent, and even to advance rent payments before the autumn harvest. Their financial obligations grew heavier as perpetuity ceased to be perpetual.[13] By the 1920s this system had largely faded into history, leaving only scattered traces on the highlands.[14]

Leases themselves existed only in one copy in the hands of the owner; the tenant, the supposed leaseholder, held nothing.[15] One could argue that since the tenant was likely to be illiterate, he did not need a copy. On the other hand, the landowner could carelessly or purposely damage, destroy, or lose the only copy. In such a case, a new lease had to be drawn up, usually in a way more favorable to the owner than the old one.

When an owner had land to lease, he either passed the word around or posted a notice at a market place, to draw the attention of any would-be tenant. The procedure, of course, was for the would-be tenant to "look see" (*kantian*) and to ask questions about the productivity of the land under consideration. Having been introduced to the owner by "middlemen" (*zhongren*) and agreed to the terms, the tenant would sign a document as follows:

> I, the lessee, B, in the presence of X, Y, and Z, agree to lease from Mr. A the land situated at Liangluxiang, including the house, its doors and windows in good order, the pigpen, cowshed, well, stone-mill, and threshing ground, at 120 yuan of the national currency in circulation, without any further charge of interest, on this day [May 11, 1940]. Hereafter, I shall be responsible for sharing 50 percent of the annual crop of unhusked rice of the aforesaid land with Mr. A and for sending the rice to the threshing ground in front of Mr. A's house. I shall have the rice measured in Mr. A's presence. Apart from grazing my animals on the wooded part of the land, I have no right to fell the trees and bamboos. When the house needs repairs, Mr. A will supply the required material and I shall provide the labor. When I decide to terminate the lease, the aforesaid money will be returned to me by Mr. A.
>
> This lease is signed to guard against human hearts being not as good as they used to be.
>
> Witnesses X, Y, Z signed   Lessor A signed; Lessee B signed
> Written by W
>
> The 29th year of the Chinese Republic, the 5th month, the 11th day [May 11, 1940].[16]

Another example is a simplified form of lease used in Luxi, western Hunan:

> I, the lessee, B, have leased from Mr. A x mu of land, located at Y, from this day (a precise date). It is agreed that Mr. A and I shall divide equally the yield of the aforesaid land every autumn when the harvest is in. If I do not work the aforesaid land, Mr. A has every right to work it himself or lease it to another person.
> Witnesses signed, leasor signed, lessee signed.[17]

The statistics on the percentage changes of the three categories of peasants in the three provinces from 1912 to 1937 (table 2.6) do not show a clear trend of increase in tenants accompanied by a trend of decrease in owner-cultivators and part-owners.

Although there are no time series to denote one way or the other similar changes on the highlands, there is no reason to assume a polarization of the rural society in this regard. The data from the 1930s make it clear that there was a higher share of owner cultivators among the highland peasant population. Furthermore, the poor counties on the highlands, such as Bazhong, Tongjiang, and Xiushan in Sichuan and Baojing, Fenghuang, and Luxi in Hunan, had startlingly high percentages of owner-cultivators in the late 1930s. Their poverty was shown by their population in decline, and by their tiny shares of cultivated land whose productivity also was tiny.

Rent

With the productivity of all grades of land on the highland being inferior to that on the plains, and the variety of dry crops being grown there, it was expected that a smaller percentage of fixed rent in rice and correspondingly a larger percentage of fixed rent in cash and sharecrop were paid. Agricultural commercialization brought more cash to the highlands to facilitate the commutation to money rent (table 2.7). The rates of rent were generally lower than those on the plains, but there were exceptions due to specific local conditions.

The customs of rent payment differed from district to district and region to region. In western Hunan, for instance, some took the rent to the landowners; others waited for the bailiffs to collect it. Some had fixed periods of tenure, as in Baojing; others left them flexible. Some had only verbal agreements; others wrote them down.[18] In Sichuan the lease specified all the details—the feast on the day of closing the deal; the grain (usually wheat and maize) for the spring-summer payment; the labor service and gifts at the end of the year.[19] On the whole, the length of the tenure was left vague. This gave the tenant an incentive to make long-term plans and invest in the land in the hope that if he could keep up with the rent payments, the owner would have no good reason to terminate the tenure contrary to the usual practice. This vagueness also offered the owner more room to maneuver—to renegotiate a lease, to change the rent, and so forth. A deposit was imposed on nearly all tenants on the highlands. It was higher in Sichuan than in Hubei and Hunan,[20] in each case amounting to a year's rent.[21] In 82 percent of the cases, the tenants had to borrow either all or part of the money for the deposit.[22] In his important study of the Sichuan economy, Zhang Xiaomei observes that the rents for dry land, hill land, and poorer grades of land were proportionately higher than for better-quality land by about 10 percent.[23] This is borne out in table 2.8. The reasons are not difficult to see. The rent in absolute terms (piculs of grain or yuan of money) and the value of such poor land being already low, either the tenants who came along to rent such land were poor enough for landowners to exploit ruthlessly or it might be more profitable but certainly less troublesome for the owner to sell the land instead of charging a lower rent.

There is no evidence to prove that there had been increases in the rent deposits in Sichuan, as Lu Pingdeng asserts.[24] Nor is there evidence to say that the rates of rent on the highlands had been rising throughout the 1920s and 1930s.[25] In fact, the falling rates in Hubei spoke exactly to the contrary (see table 2.8).

Value of Land

It is hard to imagine that the value of land rises when rent is falling. In the highland area, the general trend of both land values and rents, from what little is known, rose steadily, especially after the collapse of Yuan Shikai's monarchical attempt, but by the end of the 1920s a reverse trend, which was particularly noticeable in the value of dry land, set in (table 2.9).

In the case of Sichuan, the value of land began to rise spectacularly after 1916 and then began to fall after 1929. Lu Pingdeng attributes the rise to four factors: the purchase of land by new warlords and their political supporters; the restoration of law and order in the countryside because of the establishment of a more or less effective militia system; the depreciation of a variety of currencies in circulation in Sichuan; and the economic growth in the heart of the basin between Chengdu and Chongqing. He attributes the fall in value to a host of economic and noneconomic causes, if causes they were. Of the economic ones, there was a general decrease in the productivity of land and a general fall in the purchasing power of the people. These in turn were caused by a rise in the rates of interest and consequently a shift of investment from agriculture to industry and commerce. Among the other, non-economic, causes, Lu especially includes heavy taxation, banditry, and the Communist invasion in 1932.[26] Some of his causes are difficult to prove, such as, the decline in the productivity of Sichuan land. Since his book was published in 1936, he obviously did not consider the widespread drought in that year. Equally difficult to prove is the general fall in the purchasing power of the people, which in 1929 could not yet be blamed on the Great Depression. However, Lu's observation of the rise and fall and some of the other causes mentioned above may be hard to deny. Perhaps these phenomena should be analyzed from a different perspective. Rent in Sichuan and in the other two provinces under consideration was paid largely in cash, if one includes the rent deposit, and in rice. The tenant's ability to pay money rent evidently depended on the receipts from sales of his cash crops (e.g., opium, tong oil, medicinal herbs). Since the lion's share of the owner's rent receipt in rice was to be sold, rice, from his point of view, was a cash crop whose quantity of production and price determined its profitability and to a large extent the profitability of his investment in land. Evidently, the value of land depended on the returns of land in terms of rice and major cash crops; its cycle must correlate with the cycles of rice, opium, and tong oil.

It is true that in the 1930s, Sichuan's rice output showed a slight decrease, but this was more than compensated for by an increase in the price of rice (table 2.10). The output and value of opium rose continuously from 1895 to 1912, and after the years of Yuan Shikai's suppression it picked up where it had left off and grew again until 1932. The tightening up of the opium prohibition in Sichuan and elsewhere brought the boom to a temporary end before the outbreak of the Japanese war in 1937. The tong oil upswing had maintained itself from the end of the nineteenth century to 1928–29. Then it slumped, picked up again in 1935–37, only to decline irreparably in 1938. The rise and fall in rent and land value corresponded unsurprisingly to those of rice, opium, and tong oil.

Summary

Because of the inconsistency of highland statistics, a benchmark must be etched to start with. This work is made easier because of the highlands' self-sufficiency in staple foods; both imports and exports of such products were negligible. Except for the import of salt and sugar and the exchange of Guizhou rice for salt (down and then up the Wu) in southeastern Sichuan, food trade was insignificant across the highland area. Under the traditional transport conditions, it was physically cumbersome and economically unfeasible to import bulky and heavy foodstuffs uphill, even if the highlanders had the money to buy it. Assuming each hardy and hard-working highlander needed 2,800–3,000 calories a day (the equivalent of 1.82 mu of land for growing grain and another 1.82 for growing tubers) for his or her survival, a family of five therefore had to have 18.2 mu of dry land for their basic living. Based on this, it can be said that the reliability of the estimates of average landholdings per household of 2 mu for Zigui, 5 mu for Zhushan, and even 11 mu for Enshi in western Hubei, 9 mu for Fengjie and Wanxian in eastern Sichuan, or 6–7 mu for Chenxi and Mayang in western Hunan is questionable.[27] Before sinking to that depth of misery, the highlander must have either left or perished.

If in the 18.2 mu there were a few paddy fields, the family could pay rent in rice and enjoy a few meals of it on festive days. If not, he would have to have land for cash crops and earn enough money to pay rent. In either case, the family lived on a mixed diet of some rice and much maize, sweet potatoes, and legumes. Thanks to the low prices of hill land, at least at the beginning of the mass migration in the closing years of the nineteenth and the opening decades of the twentieth century, the new settlers could afford to buy land and to become owner-cultivators. Later on, in spite of the land grab by warlords and bureaucrats and the population explosion on the highland, a large percentage of the peasants remained as owner-cultivators. If an increase in the tenancy rate denoted the impoverishment of peasants, such an increase was nowhere noticeable on the highland. Instead, one notices in some poverty-stricken counties a decrease in population in the late 1930s.

Table 2.1

Demographic Changes in Hubei, Sichuan, and Hunan

Year	Hubei population	Changes (%)
1850	33,738,000	—
1895	34,427,000	20
1908–11	27,646,651	-20
1928–29	26,696,253	-3
1934	26,553,434	-0.5

Western Hubei

	1880s	1910	1934	Changes(%)
Badong	—	206,284	200,000	-3
Baokang	—	—	110,000	—
Enshi*	269,980	267,546	272,777	1
Fangxian	—	299,420	263,510	-12
Hefeng	—	66,016	67,080	1
Jianshi*	182,121	204,606	206,397	13
Laifeng*	108,391	93,615	116,794	8
Lichuan*	173,766	217,195	141,813	-18
Wufeng	—	—	90,000	—
Xiangeng*	101,761	172,275	140,000	38
Xuanen*	181,182	99,789	120,527	-33
Yunxi	—	229,181	219,912	-4
Yunxian	—	411,328	409,785	-0.3
Zhushan	—	266,237	263,294	-1
Zhuxi	—	191,004	203,431	7
Zigui	—	189,461	226,989	20
*Six counties' total	937,201	1,055,026	998,308	+13

Year	Sichuan population	Changes (%)
1850	44,164,000	—
1908–10	44,140,462	-0.5
1928	47,992,282	8.7
1936–37	48,861,434	1.8

Eastern Sichuan

	1816	1880s–90s	1935–36	Changes (%)
Bazhong	—	—	644,247	—
Chengkou	—	—	77,805	—
Fengdu*	106,025	88,435	525,323	395
Fengjie*	118,654	180,310	365,541	208
Fuling	166,007	—	1,041,688	527
Guangyuan	92,288	—	164,842	79
Nanjiang	84,688	—	218,270	158
Pengshui	82,797	—	210,162	164

Qianjiang*	70,590	94,308	115,461	64
Shizhu	93,569	—	189,445	102
Tongjiang	86,287	—	223,092	159
Wanxian	137,828	—	811,465	489
Wanyuan	—	—	152,266	—
Wushan*	84,563	196,853	150,492	78
Wuxi	—	—	150,063	—
Xiushan*	93,404	284,379	314,112	236
Youyang	121,381	—	362,620	199
Yunyang	102,637	—	509,317	396
Zhaohua	—	—	106,814	—
Zhongxian	—	—	505,889	—
Five counties' total		844,285	1,470,929	74

Year	Hunan population	Changes (%)
1820	18,929,000	—
1840	19,891,000	5
1860	20,940,000	5
1880	21,002,000	0.2
1898	21,174,000	0.8
1919	28,443,279	34
1940	27,186,730	−4

Western Hunan

	1816	1921	1934	Changes (%)
Baojing	96,840	126,866	133,939	38
Chenxi	192,932	140,682	150,352	−22
Cili	139,560	690,970	341,626	148
Dayong	128,370	186,730	136,811	6
Fenghuang	74,739 (1822)	126,483	133,676	79
Lixian	300,310	898,980	694,700	131
Longshan	143,630	533,585	210,061	46
Luxi	93,560	106,673	104,834	12
Mayang	163,630	184,286	114,900	−30
Sangzhi	99,306	114,071	297,000	199
Shimen	176,465	192,523	323,045	83
Yongshun	302,690	165,517	227,640	−25
Total	1,822,656	3,593,849	2,868,584	57

Sources: Hubei: Ping-ti Ho (1959, 283); Li Wenzhi (1957, 1:17); *Tongji yuebao* 1/1; government report in *Wuhan ribao*, March 2, 1934.

Western Hubei: Respective local gazetteers; *Hubei tongzhi*, ch. 43; *Sichuan jingji yuekan* 4/2, 60; cf. *Zhongguo jingji pinglun*, August 31, 1936, 4–5.

Sichuan: Ping-ti Ho (1959, 283); *Jingji nianjian* 3/C2–5; *Tongji yuebao* 1/1; Zhang Xiaomei (1938, B6–12).

East Sichuan: *Sichuan tongzhi*, ch. 65; respective local gazetteers; Zhang Xiaomei (1938, B1–22)

Hunan: *Hunan sheng zhi* 2; *Zhongguo shiyezhi*, 30–40[a] for 1934 figures; respective county gazetteers.

Table 2.2

The Highland Region: Area and Population

	Area (sq. *shili*)	Population 1935–36	Population density
Western Hubel			
Badong	11,680	201,308	17
Baokang	9,120	110,000	12
Enshi	17,867	271,216	15
Fangxian	29,627	261,323	8.8
Hefeng	14,133	66,675	4.7
Jianshi	11,280	198,640	17
Laifeng	8,933	117,622	13
Lichuan	11,893	141,813	12
Wufeng	8,853	85,918	9.7
Xianfeng	9,920	167,114	17
Xingshan	8,053	113,180	14
Xuanen	8,347	120,698	14
Yunxi	18,453	219,912	12
Yunxian	23,867	412,076	17
Zhushan	10,667	265,100	25
Zhuxi	10,533	207,508	20
Zigui	7,307	220,250	30
Total	*220,533*	*3,180,353*	*15.2 avg.*
Hubei total	*707,776*	*26,553,434*	*37.5 avg.*
Eastern Sichuan			
Bazhong	18,948	644,247	34
Chengkou	17,229	77,805	4.5
Fengdu	22,082	525,323	24
Fengjie	17,830	356,541	20
Fuling	23,888	1,041,688	44
Guangyuan	24,604	164,842	6.7
Nanjiang	18,742	218,270	12
Pengshui	36,522	210,162	5.8
Qianjiang	22,932	115,461	5
Shizhu	29,727	189,445	6
Tongjiang	19,921	223,092	11
Wanxian	14,668	811,465	55
Wanyuan	16,469	152,266	9
Wushan	10,585	150,492	14
Wuxi	12,626	150,063	12
Xiushan	25,812	314,112	12
Youyang	52,203	362,620	7
Yunyang	13,477	509,317	38
Zhaohua	6,165	106,814	17
Zhongxian	18,686	505,889	27
Total	*423,116*	*6,829,914*	*18.2 avg.*
Sichuan total	*1,662,143*	*49,300,771*	*29.7 avg.*

Western Hunan

Baojing	6,681	133,939	20
Chenxi	8,416	150,352	19
Cili	20,493	341,626	16
Dayong	5,559	136,811	27
Fenghuang	8,849	133,676	17
Guzhang	4,769	—	—
Lixian	10,267	694,700	52
Longshan	10,612	210,061	20
Luxi	7,174	104,834	16
Mayang	5,980	114,900	22
Sangzhi	9,855	297,000	13
Shimen	17,125	323,045	19
Yongshun	15,122	227,640	13
Total	*130,902*	*2,868,586*	*19.8 avg.*
Hunan total	*822,364*	*28,514,044*	*34.7 avg.*

Sources:: Cheng Lichang (1938); *Hubei sheng nianjian* (1937, 13, 74–75); Zhang Xiaomei (1938, ch. 1, sec. 1; ch. 2, sec. 1); *Zhongguo shiyezhi* 1936/3:8–11, 36–41 (*jia*); *Hunan shengzhi* 1982/2:A; *Hunan nianjian* (1933, 12–16).

Table 2.3

Cultivated Areas in the 1930s

	Percentage of total county area	Paddy fields (percentage of cultivated areas)
Hubei		
Badong	4.11	13
Baokang	2.63	7
Enshi	6.78	17
Fangxian	2.34	19
Hefeng	5.28	17
Jianshi	17.49	14
Laifeng	8.36	29
Lichuan	3.36	23
Wufeng	7.23	6
Xianfeng	6.45	21
Xuanen	7.03	15
Yunxi	5.35	7
Yunxian	3.12	19
Zhushan	4.25	29
Zhuxi	4.56	18
Zigui	2.55	29
Sichuan		
Bazhong	24	32
Chengkou	5	33
Fengdu	79	33
Fengjie	25	28
Fuling	60	32
Guangyuan	15	31
Nanjiang	22	29
Pengshui	15	23
Qianjiang	15	36
Shizhu	31	38
Tongjiang	20	34
Wanxian	60	38
Wanyuan	13	39
Wushan	10	27
Wuxi	5	37
Xiushan	30	54
Youyang	39	25
Yunyang	25	30
Zhaohua	34	30
Zhongxian	50	41
Hunan		
Baojing	22	43
Chenxi	7	49
Cili	13	25
Dayong	10	41
Fenghuang	12	57

Guzhang	15	50
Lixian	20	53
Longshan	10	40
Luxi	21	55
Mayang	22	15
Sangzhi	18	33
Shimen	5	52
Yongshun	15	36

Sources: Hubei: Cheng Lichang (1938); Anon. (1977). Sichuan: Wang Chengjing (1944, 7–9); Zhang Xiaomei (1938, A14–7); *Sichuansheng jingji jikan* 2/1, 86–88 (figure for Guanfyuan is from *Sichuansheng nongqinq baogao* 1/4). Hunan: Zhongguo shiyezhi (1935, Hunan, 2–7[*yi*]); *Hunan nianjian* (1933, 12–16); *Hunan shen zhi, dilizhi* 1982/1:1.

Table 2.4

Diet of Staple Food, 1934

	Rice		Wheat		Other	
	A	B	A	B	A	B
Hubei	34	24	21	21	45	55
Sichuan	33	30	12	8	55	62
Hunan	49	66	4	11.5	47	22.5

Sources: Column A based on survey by the Central Agricultural Experiment Institute, in *Jingji yanjiu* 1/6:66–67; Column B based on my own estimates of the diet in the highland (see table 2.5).

Table 2.5

Staple Food Output, Early 1930s

Western Hubei, Sixteen Counties

	Total area (thousand mu)	%	Total output (thousand piculs)	%	Average output per mu (piculs)
Rice	708	16	2,107	24	3
Wheat	1,005	22.7	1,870	21	1
Barley	372	8.4	432	5	1.3
Maize	1,355	30.5	1,603	18	1.2
Sorghum	242.4	5.5	219.5	2.5	0.9
Sweet pot.	199.2	4.5	1992	22.7	10
Legumes	541.8	12	558	6.7	0.9

Eastern Sichuan, Eight Counties (thousand piculs)

	Fengdu		Guangyuan		Nanjiang		Qianjiang	
Rice	463	26.7%	248	35.4%	342	26.7%	300	50%
Wheat	170	9.8	62	8.8	10	0.8	45	7.6
Barley	80	4.8	42	6	7	0.5	–	–
Maize	124	7	164	23.4	4.8	0.37	65	11
Sorg./ millet	130	7.5	20	2.8	7.5	0.6	–	–
Sweet pot.	249	14.4	79	11	900	70	180	30
Legs.	509	29.4	86	12.3	11.3	0.8	4.4	0.7
Rice	1,096	22.3	550	27	446	21.7	693	33.7
Wheat	223	6.7	162	8	175	8.5	285	13.9
Barley	52	1.6	96	4.8	112	5.5	116	5.6
Maize	301	9	422	21	192	9.4	88	4.3
Sorg./ millet	77	2	18	0.9	168	8	52	2.5
Sweet pot.	760	23	373	18.6	630	30.8	575	28
Legs.	809	24	384	19	323	15.8	247	12

Rice Output per Mu, Eastern Sichuan

	Piculs
Bazhong	3
Chengkou	2.8
Fengdu	2.5
Fengjie	2.5
Fuling	2.5
Guangyuan	3.3
Nanjiang	3.2
Pengshui	2.6

Qianjiang	2.6
Shizhu	2.6
Tongjiang	2.1
Wanxian	2.25
Wanyuan	2.1
Wushan	2.88
Wuxi	3.2
Xiushan	2.2
Youyang	2.1
Zhaohua	3.2
Zhongxian	2.7

Western Hunan (thousand piculs)

	Rice	%	Wheat	%	Barley	Maize	Sorghum	Sweet potatoes	%
Baojing	231	41	12	—	22	64	—	162	29
Chenxi	460	93	18	—	1	—	—	9	—
Cili	1,520	82	66	—	17	76	4	106	6
Dayong	698	86	48	—	—	14	—	—	—
Feng-huang	230	59	89	23	12	—	0.1	—	—
Lixian	5,388	97	21	—	—	—	33	56	—
Longshan	540	44	320	26	68	—	36	—	—
Luxi	708	88	42	—	—	5	0.5	22	—
Mayang	875	59	156	14	34	1.2	0.2	8	—
Sangzhi	290	54	88	16	27	14	36	10	—
Shiman	150	33	68	15	16	—	—	200	47
Yongshun	831	58	288	—	162	—	31	45	—

	Legumes	Percent	Average per person (piculs)
Baojing	66	17	4.2
Chenxi	6	—	3.3
Cili	47	—	5.4
Dayong	53	—	6
Fenghuang	57	17	3
Lixian	32	—	7.9
Longshan	255	21	5.6
Luxi	29	—	8
Mayang	61	—	10
Sangzhi	77	14	2
Shimen	14	—	1
Yongshun	67	—	6

Staple Food Output per Mu, 1933–34, Western Hunan (piculs)

	Rice	Wheat	Barley	Maize	Sweet potatoes	Legumes
Baojing	5	2	2.6	2	4	2.2
Chenxi	2.3	1	1.1	—	5.7	1
Cili	7.2	2.6	2.6	3.6	9	4
Dayong	4.4	—	—	3.3		1
Fenghua	5	1.5	1.6	2	—	1
Lixian	5	—	—	1.6	7	1
Longshan	3.6	—	—	—	—	1.7
Luxi	3.8	—	—	0.8	6	—
Mayang	5	2	3	3	4	4
Sangzhi	2	—	1	1.8	—	1
Shimen	5	2.8	3.3	—	—	4
Yongshun	3.9	2.4	1.5	—	5	1.8

Sources: Hubei nianjian, 138, 164–69; *Sichuansheng jingji jikan* 1/1, 409; 1/3, 426; 2/1, 265, 384–85; 2/2, 374–78, 398–99; *Sichuan wenxian* 80, 16–17; 84, 16; 93, 29–31; 97, 26–28; 98, 17; 99, 26–28; 100, 13; 101, 22; 124, 17–19; 126, 15–16; 130, 30–31; 133, 26–28; *Sichuan yuebao* 4/6, 100–1; 5/4, 93–93; 6/3, 143; 7/5, 115–20; 8/2, 139–53; Wang Chengjing (1944, 9–13); Lu Pingdeng (1936, 119, 264–75); *Sichuansheng jingji jikan* 2/1, 86–7, 364, 384–83; *Zhonghang yuekan* 1935/5, 86; *Xinshubao*, November 26, 1935; Zhang Xiaomei (1938, A8); Zhang Youyi (1957, 3:50); Zheng Wanggu (1934); *Zhongguo shiyezhi*, 14–49, 162–64 [*ding*].

Table 2.6

Classification of Peasants and Farmland Distribution (percent)

Classification of Peasants, Hubei

Year	Owner cultivators	Part owners	Tenants
1912	34	28	38
1931	30	30	40
1932	28	30	42
1933	30	32	38
1934	33	28	39
1935	31	31	38
1936	33	26	41
1937	39	25	36

Classification of Peasants, West Hubei, 1934–36

Location	Owner cultivators	Part owners	Tenants
Enshi	30	30	40
Hefeng	50	11	39
Laifeng	40	20	40
Lichuan	60	20	20
Xianfeng	40	30	30
Yunxi	60	10	30
Zigui	29	28	43

Classification of Peasants, Sichuan

Year	Owner cultivators	Part owners	Tenants
1912	30	19	51
1930	22	21	57
1931	25	19	56
1932	23	19	58
1933	22	19	59
1934	20	22	58
1935	28	19	53
1936	29	20	51
1937	24	24	52

Classification of Peasants, Northeast Sichuan, 1938–39

Location	Owner cultivators	Part owners	Tenants
Bazhong	42	24	34
Chengkou	18	21	61
Guangyuan	22	22	56
Nanjiang	37	22	41
Tongjiang	46	27	27
Wanyuan	41	29.5	29.5
Zhaohua	22	39	39

Classification of Peasants, East and Southeast Sichuan, 1938–39

Location	Owner cultivators	Part owners	Tenants
Fengdu	47	25	28
Fengjie	23.4	13.7	62.9
Fuling	37	15	48
Pengshui	33	33	34
Shizhu	22	11	67
Wanxian	26.5	13.5	60
Xiushan	47	42	11
Yunyang	15.9	9.6	74.5
Zhongxian	20.6	18	50.5

Distribution of Farmland, Sichuan

Peasant category	–10 mu	10–19	20–29	30–39	40–49	50–59	60+
Owner cultivators	14	61	16	5	2	1	1
Part owners	20	46	15	4	4	2	2
Tenants	70	11	8	2	2	1	3

Classification of Peasants, Hunan

Year	Owner cultivators	Part owners	Tenants
1912	29	23	48
1930	34	32	34
1931	28	25	47
1932	26	25	49
1933	26	25	49
1934	24	30	46
1935	23	30	47
1936	22	28	50
1937	27	29	44

Classification of Peasants, West Hunan

Location	Owner cultivators	Part owners	Tenants	Laborers
Baojing	49.80	29.20	21.00	—
Chenxi	25.40	36.35	38.25	—
Cili	53.26	15.90	29.41	1.43
Dayong	27.70	31.26	39.36	1.62
Fenghuang	73.81	8.14	11.57	6.48
Lixian	32.85	18.00	32.50	16.65
Longshan	35.21	26.54	32.45	5.80
Luxi	68.17	6.92	24.91	—
Mayang	12.53	41.70	44.54	1.23
Sangzhi	33.13	27.42	33.03	6.42
Shimen	30.30	15.15	45.46	9.09
Yongshun	40.00	30.00	20.00	10.00

Distribution of Land among Peasants in the Early 1930s

	1912	1931	1932	1933
Owner cultivators				
Hubei	28	30	30	32
Sichuan	19	10	19	19
Hunan	23	25	25	25
Part owners				
Hubei	34	30	28	30
Sichuan	30	25	23	22
Hunan	29	28	26	26
Tenants				
Hubei	38	40	42	38
Sichuan	51	56	58	59
Hunan	48	47	49	49

Sources: Zhongguo zudian (1942, 6–8); Jingji nianjian 1, G16–17; Jingji yanjiu 1/7, 32; Sichuansheng jingji jikan 2/2, 267–68; Sichuansheng nongqing baokao 1/12; Zhang Xiaomei (1938, A24, M16–20); Zhongguo shiyezhi 3:43–47[yi]); Nongqing baokao, no. 8, quoted from Zhongguojingji 2/1.

Table 2.7

Frequency Distribution of Different Forms of Rent (percent)

Hubei, Sichuan, and Hunan, 1930

	Counties surveyed	Fixed rent in rice	Fixed rent in cash	Sharecrop
Hubei	28	58	20.2	21.8
Sichuan	58	57.8	26.4	15.8
Hunan	39	74.2	7.4	18.4

Sichuan, 1938

				Labor service
East	63.5	9.2	20.2	7.1
Northeast	44.1	11.1	31.7	11.1
North	63.7	22.1	9.4	4.8

East Sichuan counties, 1934

Fengdu	25	50	25
Fengjie	50	20	30
Fuling	36.6	47	16.4
Xiushan	28.2	8.5	63.3
Youyang	58	12	30
Yunyang	20	—	80
Zhongxian	44.1	53.9	2

West Hunan, 1934

Cili	55	45	—
Dayong	67	—	33

Sources: Zhujichu, 1942, 33–40, 43; *Jingji nianjian* 1:G41–44.

Table 2.8

Rates of Rent in Hubei, Sichuan, and Hunan (in different grades of fields)

1930	Fixed rent in rice (percent of crop)			Fixed rent in cash (percent of land value)			Sharecrop		
Paddy	1st	2nd	3rd	1st	2nd	3rd	1st	2nd	3rd
Hubei	36.1	35.9	39.4	17.0	17.2	15.3	58.3	46.0	40.0
Sichuan	66.7	64.9	53.5	20.3	19.7	18.9	65.0	58.2	55.2
Hunan	53.9	55.0	45.0	—	—	—	45.0	40.0	—
Dry									
Hubei	38.3	43.2	25.8	15.1	14.8	18.5	41.5	33.0	25.5
Sichuan	55.6	41.4	46.3	9.0	8.6	7.6	50.0	48.0	46.0
Hunan	—	—	—	13.0	10.0	10.0	—	—	—

Hubei Paddy Fields: Per Mu Rent in Cash (yuan)

1st grade			2nd grade			3rd grade		
1913	1923	1934	1913	1923	1934	1913	1923	1934
5.61	5.58	3.26	4.81	3.44	2.37	2.83	2.80	1.48

West Hubei: Fixed Rent in Kind, 1930s (percent of crop)

Enshi	38
Fangxian	50
Hefeng	50
Jiangshi	40
Laigeng	50
Xuanen	50
Yunxi	31
Yunxian	30

Sichuan, 1938 (per Mu)

	Fixed rent in rice (piculs)			Fixed rent in cash (yuan)			Sharecrop (percent)		
	1st grade	2nd grade	3rd grade	1st grade	2nd grade	3rd grade	1st grade	2nd grade	3rd grade
Paddy fields per mu									
East	2.94	2.09	1.56	9.43	7.42	5.69	65:35	58:42	65:35
N-east	2.63	2.08	1.62	8.83	6.62	4.51	60:40	54:46	45:55
North	3.00	2.52	2.01	9.14	7.23	5.59	60:40	53:47	43:57
Dry fields per mu									
East	1.15	0.93	0.62	4.51	3.47	2.44	61:39	53:47	42:58
N-east	1.16	0.84	0.60	4.20	2.96	2.27	68:32	50:50	36:64
North	1.34	1.05	0.81	5.08	3.80	2.74	56:44	48:52	38:62

East Sichuan, 1938: Rent per Mu

	Fixed rent in rice (piculs)			Fixed rent in cash (yuan)			Sharecrop (percent)		
	1st grade	2nd grade	3rd grade	1st grade	2nd grade	3rd grade	1st grade	2nd grade	3rd grade
Paddy fields									
Bazhong	3.54	2.79	2.31	6.52	4.32	3.24	6:4	5:5	4:6
Fengdu	3.09	2.72	2.32	10.85	9.22	7.59	7:3	6:4	5:5
Fengjie	3.38	2.86	2.22	—	—	—	6:4	6:4	4:6
Guang-yuan	—	—	—	—	8.68	4.36	—	—	—
Nanjiang	2.36	1.51	0.98	7.22	4.58	3.96	5:5	5:5	5:5
Pengshui	1.95	1.63	1.30	—	—	—	6:4	5:5	5:5
Shizhu	2.06	1.71	1.31	—	—	—	5:5	5:5	5:5
Tong-jiang	1.39	1.11	1.00	—	—	—	7:3	5:5	5:5
Wanxian	3.26	2.67	1.17	11.38	7.79	5.18	7:3	6:4	5:5
Wanyuan	3.13	2.61	2.09	10.53	8.42	6.32	7:3	6:4	5:5
Xiushan	2.83	2.45	1.98	8.14	6.51	4.88	6:4	6:4	5:5
Yunyang	2.25	1.91	1.36	8.15	6.51	4.88	7:3	6:4	5:5
Zhaohua	—	—	—	—	—	—	—	5:5	4:6
Zhong-xian	2.23	1.81	1.46	11.24	9.66	7.86	7:3	6:4	4:6
Dry fields									
Bazhong	1.79	1.48	1.08	3.90	3.12	1.78	5:5	5:5	4:6
Fengdu	1.36	1.13	0.84	7.05	6.42	3.8	7:3	6:4	5:5
Fengjie	1.30	1.02	0.79	—	—	—	6:4	5:5	4:6
Guang-yuan	0.66	0.39	0.26	—	—	—	—	—	—
Nanjiang	0.84	0.4	0.37	—	—	—	6:4	2:8	2:8
Pengshui	0.95	0.76	0.57	—	—	—	5:5	5:5	5:5
Shizhu	1.10	0.88	0.66	3.26	2.17	1.63	5:5	5:5	5:5
Tong-jiang	1.30	0.73	0.65	—	—	—	5:5	4:6	3:7

Wanxian	1.10	0.82	0.61	3.36	2.38	1.44	6:4	6:4	5:5
Wanyuan	0.90	0.72	0.54	3.32	2.49	1.65	5:5	4:6	3:7
Xiushan	1.38	1.09	0.84	3.26	2.17	1.63	5:5	5:5	5:5
Zhaohua	1.08	0.97	0.86	—	—	—	—	—	—
Zhong- xian	0.72	0.58	0.46	7.05	6.42	3.8	6:4	6:4	5:5

Sources: Sichuansheng nongqing baogao 1/12, 399; *Jingji nianjian* 7:G63–5; *Tongji yuebao*, no. 31, 9; *Hubei sheng nianjian*, 150–51; *Zhongguo jingji* 1/4–5, 11); *Sichuan zudian zhidu*, 17;

Table 2.9

Changes in Land Value

In the Three Provinces (1933 = 100)

Province	Paddy fields			Dry fields			Hill land		
	1912	1931	1932	1912	1931	1932	1912	1931	1932
Hubei	82	113	102	83	106	100	79	107	101
Sichuan	78	110	107	78	105	104	76	103	102
Hunan	89	107	109	76	110	104	67	102	110

Land Value, 1933 (yuan per mu)

	Average	Median	Mode
Hubei	28.26	22.05	15.57
Sichuan	56.59	59.82	17.74
Hunan	40.12	35.00	10.00

Land Value 1930 or 1931 (yuan per mu)

	Paddy fields			Dry fields		
	Highest	Inter-mediate	Lowest	Highest	Inter-mediate	Lowest
Hubei	150	33.8	8.0	150	12.6	0.6
Sichuan	225	64.0	7.0	120	34.2	2.0
Hunan	120	35.5	6.8	77	15.0	2.5

Changes in the Value of Dry Land (yuan per mu)

	1912	1930	1931	1932	1933	1934
Hubei:						
fields	26.34	20.14	20.58	20.55	22.28	22.39
land	9.38	13.35	12.79	12.59	12.35	11.8
Hunan:						
fields	15.8	22.74	22.3	22.95	22.84	21.54
land	9.38	13.35	12.79	12.59	12.35	11.8

West Hubei Land Value, Early 1930s (yuan per mu)

	Paddy fields	Dry fields
Badong	90	80
Lichuan	54	48
Jianshi	90	60
Xianfeng	60	10
Laifeng	8	7
Yichang	50	48

East Sichuan Land Value, Early 1930s (yuan per mu)

	Paddy fields	Dry fields
Bazhong	110	90
Pengshui	100	80
Chengkou	41.7	25
Shizhu	70	35
Fengdu	65	33
Tongjiang	30	15
Fengjie	40	30
Wanxian	50	30
Guangyuan	15	6
Xiushan	8	7
Nanjiang	40	20
Yunyang	57	40
Chengdu	140	70
Jiangjin	225	145

Sources: Nongqing baogao 1/11, 3; Zhujichu (1942, 24); *Jingji nianjian* 1:F22–26); 6:F32–3; *Tongji yuebao*, 9–10–11–12/1832); Lu Pingdeng (1936, 104–6).

Table 2.10

Sichuan Rice Output and Value

Total Output (thousand piculs)

Normal	1931	1932	1933	1934	1935	1936
158,098	160,436	183,537	153,430	146,559	153,763	129,333

Price of Rice per Peck (yuan)

	1931–32	1932–33	1933–34	1934–35	1935–36
Bazhong	—	—	—	—	11.30*
Chengkou	—	—	—	—	6.60*
Fengdu	2.07	—	2.30	2.30	—
Fengjie	1.90	—	—	3.15	—
Fuling	2.30	—	—	—	2.90
Guangyuan	—	—	—	4.90	—
Nanjiang	—	—	—	4.00	8.50*
Pengshui	2.37	—	—	—	—
Qianjiang	—	—	—	2.30	—
Shizhu	1.97	—	—	3.80	3.10
Tongjiang	—	—	—	—	5.60
Wanxian	1.83	—	—	—	3.40
Wanyuan	—	—	—	—	9.80*
Wushan	1.70	—	—	—	—
Wuxi	1.90	—	—	—	2.90
Xiushan	—	—	—	—	8.30
Youyang	2.26	—	—	5.00	8.80
Yunyang	1.70	—	—	2.00	3.10
Zhaohua	—	—	—	—	6.10*
Zhongxian	2.30	2.60	3.00	3.50	3.50

Sources: Zhang Xiaomei (1938, 01, V4–33); Lu Pingdeng (1936, 117, 254–56; *Sichuan yuebao* 2/2, 45–46; 4/6, 93–94; 5/1, 114).
*Counties affected by the anti-Communist war in northern Sichuan.

3
GOODS FOR TRADE

A NUMBER of goods were economically significant to the highlanders. The first that comes to mind is the preserved vegetable, *brassica juncea*, heavily salted and spiced with chili and cayenne (*zanthoxylum bungeanum*), delicious if eaten in morsels. It is better known as *zhacai*. Fuling was, and still is, the center of production; Changshou and Jiangbei up the Yangzi and Fengdu and Zhongxian down are also famous for it.[1] Its history as a mass-produced delicacy cannot be traced further back than the short reign of Xuantong (1909–12), but it may not be unreasonable to assume that housewives in these counties knew how to make it long before the advent of steamer transport during the same reign. It was the steamer that made it possible to send the vegetable in large quantities through the Wushan Gorges to the rest of the country.[2] In 1936–37 some 170,000 jars of it (weighing 60 catties a jar) were sold at 7 yuan each at a central market like Wuhan, or a total of 1,190,000 yuan. The industry engaged some thousand people in four hundred workshops in Fuling alone,[3] whence the export of *zhacai* amounted to 60,000 jars in 1931, 50,000 in 1932, 60,000 in 1933, 80,000 in 1934, 120,000 in 1935, and 130,000 in 1936, declining to 65,000 in 1937.[4]

Fengdu produced about half as much as did Fuling. If the total output of 170,000 jars is acceptable, the whole industry must have employed about three thousand people in the five or six *zhacai*-producing counties.[5]

The second product to be mentioned here is the fungus *auricularia auricula-judae*, which comes chiefly in black and sometimes in white (bleached) or brownish yellow. In Chinese these three varieties are called *muer* (black), *yiner* (*tremella fuciformis*, white), and *huanger* (produced in southern Sichuan, outside the highland area). They are all parasitic fungi, special to the oak (*quercus serrata*, *Q. chinensis* and *Q. dentata*), growing under an altitude of 1,700 meters in spring and summer. Three or four days after the seeds begin to sprout but before the sprouts begin to wither, they have to be picked. The black type must be dried in the sun while the white type is baked dry with oak charcoal and bleached with sulphur.[6] *Yiner* was grown in Nanjiang, Tongjiang, Wanyuan, and Zhongba. It was used as a cough medicine and a general strengthening or repairing agent. In the 1930s about 20,000 catties were produced. *Muer* was harvested in Guangyuan, Nanjiang, Tongjiang, Zhongba, and southern Shaanxi. Its crispiness added to the texture of some Sichuan dishes. About 30,000 catties were gathered. *Huanger* was raised in southern Sichuan and Huili.[7]

Tongjiang and *yiner* seem to be synonymous, but two factors caused the industry there to decline: the planting of poppy, a more profitable enterprise, and the invasion of the Fourth Front Red Army in 1932.[8] Then Wanyuan replaced Tongjiang as the *yiner* center for a period. By 1940, this luxury trade could just manage to survive in the disruption of the Sino-Japanese War and the austerity of the wartime economy.

The production of *muer* and *yiner* was a sideline business of the peasants who grew a few catties of them at a time of the year when they were busy transplanting rice. What little amount they produced was sold to itinerant traders from Hubei at about 8 yuan for a catty of *yiner*.[9] Adding the taxes (5 yuan a catty) and other expenses and a profit margin, it was sold to the consumer at between 120 yuan a catty for the highest grade and 30 yuan for the lowest.[10] At the peak of the industry, *yiner* brought 160,000 yuan to the peasants in northern Sichuan.

The third commodity is salt, well salt, but not that produced in the pocket between the Tuo and the Min. It is produced in eastern Sichuan near the Wushan Gorges and at Pengshui. Anything to do with table salt anywhere in China is an immensely complicated business. Here I am concerned only with its production (table 3.1), not its distribution, which I shall discuss in a later chapter.

Fengjie had 60–70 salters who normally began making salt when the water level of the Yangzi fell and the wells near the banks were exposed. It was strictly an occupation during the winter fallow and a household activity for a little additional money to tide them over the New Year festival. The small producers needed the money; aware of this, the itinerant buyers struck a hard bargain with them. Someone tried to put an end to this state of affairs by setting up a large-scale saltern, but the government was alarmed by it. The project might deprive the small producers of their additional income in the winter, and it might well produce so much salt that it would encroach upon other salters' markets and lead to unpleasant consequences. Therefore, the government turned the project down. At the same time, it decreed that neither the number of salters nor the number of boilers they had could be increased.[11]

Daning in Wuxi had a larger-scale salt industry than that in Fengjie. Production began each year in the winter when the salt content of the solution in the wells was the highest. Sixty salters there used firewood, and 120 used coal to dry the solution. But at a given time, 40 of them were not producing any salt for various reasons. Each of the operating ones could make in a season between 600 and 700 piculs of salt. This means that each of the 100,000 people who took part in the industry would end up with a share of 1.2 piculs.

At Yunyang, there were eighty salters; at Zhongxian a few dozen; and at Pengshui, forty-one.[12] Not only was the scale of production smaller here, the quality of salt was poorer. There was hardly any profit worth mentioning. The salt was for the makers, not for the market. That the salters here and elsewhere on the highlands could survive was chiefly due to the arrangement Sichuan authorities made with Hubei and Hunan to have Sichuan salt sold at western Hubei and Hunan (the Chu markets), in competition with the sun-baked and therefore much cheaper salt from the Huai coastal region. I shall return to this in the next chapter.

It would be untrue to say that throughout this vast area there were no mineral resources to exploit. In western Hunan, Chenxi had deposits of coal and produced small quantities for local use;[13] Cili offered a variety of mineral products, tin, realgar, sulphur, and arsenic. Needless to say, they were all small in scale and traditional in technology. They lacked capital investment and suffered at the hands of bandits and unruly soldiers.[14] Eastern Sichuan had a fairly important, though widely scattered, industry of coal and iron before World War I; however, by the 1930s, it was gasping for life.[15] The story was the same for mining in western Hubei.[16] At the peak of the mining on the highlands, there were 1,400 miners in 1917 in Badong, Hubei; 11,928 in Cili, Hunan; and 38,808 in Fenghuang. In 1914 in Fengjie, Sichuan, there were 890; and in Guangyuan, 1,372.[17] In the chaotic 1920s and 1930s, mining languished.

Then there were the medicinal herbs for which Sichuan, particularly western Sichuan, was famous. Like the mineral products, they too were embattled and went into decline early in the 1920s. A short resurrection in 1924 was interrupted by the year-long strike and boy-cott at Guangzhou (Canton) against British Hong Kong. Recovering again, they enjoyed a period of prosperity up to the Great Depression and the Japanese occupation of Manchuria, which traditionally had been the most important market for Sichuan herbs. Another deadly enemy of this industry was tax—a picul of *angelica sinensis* was worth 9.70 yuan, but taxes brought the price up to 22 yuan.[18]

The most important species and their annual production value were as follows: *Codonopsis tangshen*, at Wuxi, c. 300,000 yuan; *coptis chinensis*, at Shizhu, 33,000 yuan; China roots, at Bazhong, 5,560 yuan; *eucommia ulmoides*, at Bazhong, Guangyuan, 70,000 yuan; *liriope spicata*, at Fuling and Wanxian, 15,000 yuan. Another important product was *rhus semialata* (gall nuts), essential in making Chinese black ink, of which Sichuan's contribution, in the east and along the Wu in the south, was 26.15 percent of China's total production.[19]

The best bristles are grown near the hunch on the back of the beast; they are long and resilient. The most suitable condition for their growth is the cool climate of the highlands.[20] Eastern Sichuan and western Hunan are the places the choicest Chinese bristles are produced, and these are the best in the world, although they are all black.[21] Both parts of table 3.2 show that from 1930 onward the production and export of Sichuan bristles began to decrease, probably due to the same causes—civil wars on the highlands and heavier taxation to finance them.

Making preserved vegetables or salt, gathering herbs or fungi, and mining or quarrying were handicrafts the highlanders sometimes did side by side with farming. These and other nonagrarian productive activities should have provided a livelihood for over 28 percent of the inhabitants of western Hubei, 31 percent of those of eastern Sichuan, and 13 percent of those of western Hunan.[22] Remuneration for such activities should have been at par with that of other handicraftsmen, such as builders, tailors, tinkers, and porters. An interesting estimate was published in the *Xinshubao* on November 27, 1935. In Wanxian, a port city, next in importance only to Chongqing in Sichuan, there were six weavers, five masons, four carpenters, three tailors, and two each of blacksmiths, wicker-makers, and clay-wall builders in every thousand inhabitants. Being a port city, it also had 1,400 quayside porters and 1,000 bearers, 2,000 sedan-chair carriers, 10,000 rickshaw pullers, 24,000 shopkeepers, and 30,000 shopworkers.[23] The rest of the

40 percent of nonagrarian workers in Wanxian must have included domestic servants and other laborers. Wanxian, of course, was not Sangzhi. In that remote little city, the reporter of the *Dagongbao* of Changsha counted only food processors, builders, furniture makers, tanners, garment makers, domestic servants, farm labourers, and a few weavers among the craftsmen and craftswomen.[24]

The pay scales of craftsmen in eastern Sichuan and western Hunan were remarkably similar. Skilled workers earned as follows: sawyer, 0.25 yuan a day; mason, 0.24; tile layer, 0.22; weaver, 0.21; miller, 0.21; oil presser, 0.21; painter, 0.20; winemaker, 0.17–0.19.

An unskilled laborer, such as a bearer or a porter, made only 0.05–0.09 yuan a day plus food. A man-servant was paid 2 yuan a month plus food and lodging; a maid-servant, only 1 yuan. Farm laborers earned considerably more for considerably heavier work. Their annual pay plus food and lodging was as follows:[25] Luxi, 10.80–21.60 yuan; Fuling, 16–20; Leiyang, 16–28; Chengbu, 20–37; Sangzhi, 25–50; Chenxian, 29–40.

The two biggest money earners in the highland were tong oil and opium. The enormous increase in their production and sales was the mainstay of the commercialization of the agriculture of this mountain area.

Tong oil had been used for centuries in China to mix paint and varnish for protecting wood, metal, cloth, and even paper against water; to make soap and ink; for lighting; and for other purposes.[26] But foreign traders in China did not see its wide marketability until after 1895. Neither the *Shangwu guanbao* of 1907 nor the *Nongshang gongbao of 1914*, both official papers of the central government, paid any attention to it. The first record of its export, worth $62, was made in 1869. At the beginning of the twentieth century, L. S. Wilcox, American consul at Hankou, drew business attention to its potential uses. Thereafter its export rose spectacularly, to 500,000 piculs at 5.8 million HG taels in 1912.[27]

In Sichuan the tong trees (*aleurites fordii* and *aleurites mantana*) grew well along the eastern rim from north to south, as recorded in the relevant local gazetteers. In Hubei, they flourished in the northwest and southwest, and in Hunan, in the Yuan and Li valleys.[28] Generally, a young shoot is transplanted when it is about one year old; it begins to bear seeds at the age of three; its productivity declines from the age of ten, but it continues to grow seeds even at the advanced age of thirty or forty.[29]

On average, when a tong tree is at the prime of its life it can yield 5 or 6 catties of seeds, which become ripe when the autumn harvest has been brought in. As it ages, its productivity shrinks to 1 or 2 catties a year. A hundred catties of green seeds can be dehydrated to 30 catties of dry seeds, ready for the press to yield 10.5 catties of tong oil (see table 3.3).

According to the report of the Central Agricultural Experiment Institute, each household devoted 1.1 mu of land to the tong on which forty-three trees were densely planted. The average yield of seeds per tree was 1.75 catties. The forty-three trees therefore yielded 76.97 catties of seeds, which after drying would weigh 23.09 catties. On the assumption that the average price of tong oil in the highland was 0.085 yuan per catty, the 23.09 catties of dry seeds would produce 8.08 catties of oil, which was worth 0.69 yuan to the grower. This seems too low for the grower to take the trouble.

From a different point of view, table 3.4, gives this picture: East Sichuan, from 1912 to 1930, received from selling tong oil a total amount of 64,875,579 yuan, or an annual average of 3,604,198.8 yuan. Assuming the number of the tong households remained constant at 567,000 (i.e., 63 percent of the total of 900,000 households that produced 63 percent of the total Sichuan tong oil output in eastern Sichuan), each household derived an annual income of 6.36 yuan from the oil. Furthermore, from 1930 to 1937, the annual average of 479,500 piculs at 7.50 yuan a picul produced a total income of 25,173,750 yuan, and for each tong household, 6.34 yuan per year. Therefore, the oil benefited the eastern Sichuan highlands to the tune of 90 million yuan, and each tong household made nearly 160 yuan from 1912 to 1937.

In the same manner, one can assume that the share of Li valley tong oil in the total export from Hunan was 24 percent.[30] From 1912 to 1930, the valley made 17,399,219 yuan from the 779,024 piculs it sold at the Shanghai price. Assuming that in western Hunan the local price was only 8.50 yuan a picul, the total receipts would be reduced to 6,621,707.40 yuan. Adding the receipts from oil sales between 1931 and 1937, the total benefit would be about 9 million yuan, and each of the 168,000 tong households should have gained some 55 yuan in these twenty-five years.

Western Hubei's share in the provincial total sales of tong oil was 43 percent. Assuming the local price was 8.50 yuan a picul, the

536,831 piculs produced in this part of the highland would have yielded 10,611,791 yuan from 1912 to 1930. Adding seven more annual averages of 598,544 yuan, the total benefit in the twenty-five years was about 15 million yuan, or 61 yuan for each of the 240,000 households.

What was exported from the highlands was unrefined oil produced at local presses. The grower must first take the seeds out of the hard shell after a process of fermentation and then dry them before taking them to the local oil press. A press would have cost about 1,000 to 2,000 yuan to establish and employed four or five workers.[31] At the press, the seeds were ground and then pressed. In three shifts of 70 catties each, some 20 catties an hour or 200 catties a day could be pressed.[32] Much of the oil is in the seeds (56 percent); the rest is in the skin and shell. For 100 catties (a picul) of dried seeds, the charge of the press was 1.50 yuan or 4 taels out of each peck of oil.[33]

There were four or five presses for one hundred tong households, which worked on tong oil from November to January and on other vegetable oils from April to September.[34] The worker was paid 5–7 yuan a month or 0.20 yuan a day plus food. After the oil was squeezed out, the remains in the shape of a round cake about two inches thick and two feet in diameter went to the grower to be used as fertilizer.[35] The unrefined oil was then shipped to the nearest central market, for example, Chongqing or Wanxian, Changde or Yichang, and finally to Wuhan to be refined.[36]

A business as profitable as the tong oil one was bound to attract modern entrepreneurs to invest in it, to enlarge its scale of production and improve its efficiency and profit. In 1929 Yirui Corporation acquired land in Wanxian and planted 8,000 tong trees; this was the corporation's first forest. Then it bought land in Bishan, west of Chongqing, and planted 100,000 tong trees on it; this was called the corporation's second forest. By 1933, the first forest yielded a pitiful 2 piculs of seeds or 80 kilograms of oil, while the second forest yielded 50 piculs of seeds or 1,263 kilograms of oil. In the following year, one produced 4 piculs of seeds and the other 60. The income from selling the rice on the corporation's land was needed to subsidize the forests. In the end both failed. So did attempts by Deyu Agriculture and Forest Company and Tongli Forest in Bishan.[37] It was generally assumed that these modern enterprises did not know what they were doing.

After the outbreak of the Sino-Japanese War, the future of tong oil was doomed. The Japanese occupation of Hankou spelled the end of the exports from southeastern Sichuan and the Li valley. The central market at Changde in Hunan had to be closed down. When Hong Kong fell, the destination for the transport of tong oil by land was lost. At the same time, the influx of migrants into the oil-producing provinces and the wartime inflation stimulated the price of grain. Peasants therefore abandoned tong trees and went back to growing food crops. Thus the great tong oil trade came to an end.[38]

No one knew how much opium was produced in these three provinces, not to speak of the highland areas there. Its growth in Sichuan probably dates back to the 1840s; there does not seem to be any reason to assume otherwise in Hubei and further to the west in Guizhou and Yunnan. It has been said that in Sichuan the cultivation of the poppy began in the south and then spread to the north and extreme west of the province.[39] By the time of the 1895 war it was found everywhere.[40] Therefore, it is difficult to share Sir John Jordan's belief that the growth of opium in Sichuan had been almost completely wiped out in 1911.[41] It is conceivable that Yuan Shikai's vigorous prohibition had attained some results, but the penetration of the Yunnan-Guizhou troops into Sichuan in the anti–Yuan Shikai campaign gave a fillip to opium production and consumption.[42] To combat the invaders, local commanders needed territories and revenues for financing the wars. They too gave a fillip to the drug. The situation grew from bad to worse until the triumph of the Communist revolution. But how much opium was produced in Sichuan, and how much additional income it brought to its growers, no one seems to know. Everyone is eager to offer an educated guess.

Total output of opium in Sichuan has been estimated as 177,000 piculs (1 picul = 1,000 taels) in 1881; 238,000 piculs in 1906; and the famous C. A. McAllum figure of 175,000 piculs in 1908.[43] These figures suggest that Sichuan produced more opium than any other province in China. But did the province dedicate 8.31 percent of its farmland to the poppy, or only a miserly 1 percent?[44] What does "farm land" mean? "Fields," or merely land divided into small squares with a ridge around them? "Dedicated," to the exclusion of other crops than the winter wheat?

McAllum divides his 1908 figure into 120,000 piculs for local consumption (69 percent) and 55,000 for export to other provinces (31 percent). If one assumes that in the 1920s the province's total annual output had exceeded 200,000 piculs, a figure close to Lu Pingdeng's estimate, in the 1930s it settled back to about 200,000 piculs. This assumption is backed by the recorded situation in Fuling, a major opium-producing and transporting center (table 3.5).

The accuracy of the figures may be open to question. For instance, in the introduction I calculated that if the price of opium fell below 350 yuan a picul (1,000 taels), the grower would find it hardly worth his while to take the risk and endure the toil of planting poppies. The prices per picul for 1934 and 1935 are therefore highly suspect. It is true that *Eastern Miscellany* reported the fall in the opium price in Fuling from 0.40 yuan to 0.20, and then to 0.10 a tael in 1934 because of the prohibition conducted by Generalissimo Chiang Kai-shek's Nanchang Headquarters.[45] At the same time, the *Shenbao yuekan* said that the price of opium in Fuling was 400 yuan a picul (or 0.40 yuan a tael).[46] The price would be double or treble that, including all the taxes paid by the smoker on opium distribution and consumption.[47]

Two observations can be derived from table 3.5: opium output, sales, and prices in Fuling declined in the 1930s due to official prohibition of planting, selling, and smoking of the drug. A great number of critical words have been said on the maladroitness and corruption of the prohibitive measures taken by the government in the nineteenth century and the first decades of the twentieth century, as if there was a general belief that any prohibition managed by any Chinese government was bound to be a farce. The case of Fuling tends to speak to the contrary. In Hunan, the prohibition of 1932–33, in my view, supports the Fuling case. It was fairly successful in curbing planting and sales, but not so in curtailing consumption.[48]

We know next to nothing of the production of opium in western Hunan. Local historians in Dayong and Sangzhi told me that it was grown everywhere.[49] We have no reliable statistics, however, to show the amounts of its production and sales. Being so close to Guizhou, the river valleys of western Hunan and southwestern Hubei were the natural routes for Guizhou opium to pass through, supplying the people on its way to Yichang, Changde, and Hankou. I shall say more on these opium routes in the next chapter.

Western Hubei along the Qing, Zigui and Junxian was the most important opium-growing area in the province.[50] If the amount of opium taxes was an indication of the size of the output, western Hubei, paying a quarter of the taxes on opium of the province, should have produced a quarter of the drug. Assuming each picul of opium bore 434 yuan of taxes, the annual tax bill of western Hubei—3,600,000 yuan—probably meant an annual output of 8,295 piculs there, and an annual output for the whole province of 33,180 piculs.[51]

The 8,295 piculs produced by 2,643,274 farming people in western Hubei at a price of 450 yuan per picul and a profit margin of 17.10 yuan per 100 taels of opium for the year 1934 should have brought a net benefit of 0.55 yuan to each peasant, or 2.75 yuan to each rural household. This rough guide can be applied to eastern Sichuan as well. In the early days of the opium trade, the prices were lower and output smaller. The tightening of the prohibition in the 1930s saw the prices again falling and output contracting. This information can be assumed to have held true for twenty years after the founding of the Republic or the death of Yuan Shikai. An audacious statement, I am aware, but what else can one do? I would say that each rural household in western Hubei and eastern Sichuan may have been benefited by opium to the amount of 55 yuan. Western Hunan peasants, I am afraid, were not so lucky.

If one considers tong oil and opium alone, an eastern Sichuan peasant household had been enriched by 215 yuan in the twenty-five years from 1912 to 1937; his counterpart in western Hubei, by 116 yuan; and one in western Hunan by 55 yuan. All the other extra-agrarian activities may have added another yuan to the peasant's income, or perhaps 25 yuan in the twenty-five years. Bold estimates for 1912–37 are given in table 3.6. By any standard, this was an enormously impressive amount of money. To use a hackneyed saying: the highlanders had never had it so good.

Table 3.1

The Highland Salt of Sichuan

| | Fengjie | | Wuxi (Daning) | | |
| | Output (piculs) | Tax (yuan) | Output (piculs) | Sales (piculs) | Tax (yuan) |
Year					
1920	30,028	41,624		101,566	128,468
1921	25,751	36,054		108,875	136,860
1922	31,353	44,454	120,000	118,168	151,882
1923	32,279	45,191	147,181	137,666	188,479
1924	27,219	38,106	151,170	157,439	193,427
1925	30,548	42,277	147,686	147,072	189,656
1926	26,941	37,718	114,291	113,339	144,977
1927	25,986	36,381	92,814	89,266	113,089
1928	25,828	36,159	18,136	17,954	22,776
1929	23,433	32,806	58,590	59,590	73,128
1930	26,085		101,460		
1931					
1932					
1933	42,000	138,000			
1934	42,000	127,000			

| | Yunyang | | | Pengshui | | |
	Output (piculs)	Sales (piculs)	Tax (yuan)	Output (piculs)	Sales (piculs)	Tax (yuan)
1920		192,388	242,685		37,382	44,480
1921	199,426	212,900	267,900	42,433	41,767	50,120
1922	278,994	216,182	262,568	39,560	40,148	48,177
1923	227,888	231,503	293,694	42,371	42,729	51,275
1924	295,074	306,787	395,384	45,346	43,147	51,777
1925	280,977	271,400	332,910	36,573	37,498	44,998
1926	274,058	270,424	340,679	35,956	34,826	41,792
1927	277,058	282,218	351,351	32,431	32,535	39,042
1928	307,114	292,230	359,586	33,952	33,104	39,724
1929	287,048	293,254	367,055	33,001	31,937	38,325
1930	304,703					
1931						
1932						
1933	401,000			29,000		
1934	419,000			31,000		

| | Zhongxian | |
	Output and sales (piculs)	Tax (yuan)
1920	2,842	3,382
1921	2,555	3,066

1922	2,598	3,117
1923	2,573	3,087
1924	2,633	3,159
1925	4,190	5,027
1926	4,262	5,115
1927	4,222	5,067
1928	5,674	6,089
1929	4,595	5,514
1930	4,524	
1931		
1932		
1933	8,000	
1934	8,000	

Quality of Highland Salt

	Sodium chloride	Water (percent)	Other (percent)
Fengjie	78.09	7.40	14.51
Wanxian	72.26	12.28	15.46
Wuxi (Daning)	67.12	5.94	26.94
Yunyang	77.05	15.57	7.38
Zhongxian	64.31	14.08	21.61
Fushun-Rongchang	91.74	2.56	5.70

Sources: Chuannan gequ yanchang, 13–15; *Yanwu gongbao*, no. 25, 166–68; *Jingji zhazhi*, 1/1, 42); *Jingji zhazhi*, 1/1, 39–40).

Table 3.2

Production of Bristles, East Sichuan (catties)

	1936		1910		1933		1934	
	pigs	bristles	pigs	bristles	pigs	bristles	pigs	bristles
Bazhong	26,000	3,250						
Chengkou	3,000	375						
Fengdu	29,176	3,647						
Fuling	53,000	6,625						
Guangyuan	5,800	725						
Nanjiang	15,000	1,875						
Pengshui	4,557	570	8,764	1,096	3,200	400	3,300	413
Qianjiang	3,929	491	4,417	552	1,964	233	1,920	240
Shizhu	6,100	763	11,883	1,485	6,052	757	6,134	767
Tongjiang	1,122	140						
Wanxian	75,279	9410						
Wanyuan	4,525	566						
Wushan	13,246	1,656						
Wuxi	19,200	2,400						
Xiushan	9,744	1,218	15,503	1,938	12,000	1,500	13,314	1,664
Youyang	14,688	1,836	11,737	1,467	13,049	1,631	12,403	1,550
Yunyang	35,850	4,481						
Zhaohua	2,263	283						
Zhongxian	18,101	2,263						

Table 3.2 *(continued)*

Export of Bristles from Sichuan

Year	Piculs	HG taels	Yuan
1928	11,391	1,812,648	2,289,375
1929	11,162	1,976,016	3,039,113
1930	12,248	2,221,090	3,416,036
1931	10,719	2,068,967	3,182,072
1932	9,536	1,695,022	2,606,944

Sources: Shi Daoyuan, 1945, 2, 4–5; *Sichuan nongye*, 2/4; *Sichuan wenxian*, vol. 84, 17; *Sichuan yuebao*, 3/4, 10–28; 9/3, 26–32; *Sichuansheng zhi shanhuo*, 1935, 2:97; *Zhonghua nongxuehuibao*, nos. 7–8, 154.

Note: Total = 425.27 piculs, about 3 percent of the total production of Sichuan. At the average Chongqing price in 1936, 324 yuan, the total value was 137,939.76 yuan. Each pig is estimated to produce two taels of bristles.

Table 3.3

Tong Households, 1940

Province	Households	Land for tong (mu)	Green seeds (piculs)
Sichuan	900,000	1,150,000	1,140,000
Hunan	700,000	650,000	810,000
Hubei	560,000	550,000	490,000

Sources: Zou Xupu (1944, 18--19); Zhou Kaiqing (1967, 3:8).

Table 3.4

Tong Oil Export—Shares of Sichuan, Hunan, and Hubei, 1912–31

Year	Total export (three-year moving avg.)	Sichuan share (piculs)	Hunan share (piculs)	Hubei share (piculs)
1913	495,339	133,742	128,788	49,534
1914	404,515	109,219	105,174	40,452
1915	421,691	113,857	109,640	42,169
1916	408,959	110,419	106,329	40,896
1917	468,462	126,485	121,800	46,846
1918	501,223	135,330	130,318	50,122
1919	547,341	147,782	142,283	54,734
1920	524,573	141,635	136,389	52,457
1921	568,610	153,525	147,839	46,861
1922	667,334	180,180	173,507	66,733
1923	826,163	223,064	214,802	82,616
1924	875,666	236,430	227,673	87,567
1925	846,098	228,446	219,985	84,610
1926	847,850	228,920	220,441	84,785
1927	914,582	246,937	237,791	91,458
1928	1,021,738	275,869	265,652	102,174
1929	1,110,401	299,808	288,704	111,040
1930	1,033,923	279,159	268,820	103,392
Total		3,370,807	3,245,935	1,248,446

Year	Average price (yuan)	Sichuan share (yuan)	Hunan share (yuan)	Hubei share (yuan)
1913	13	1,738,646	1,674,244	643,942
1914	13	1,419,847	1,367,262	525,876
1915	15	1,707,855	1,644,600	632,535
1916	17	1,877,123	1,807,593	695,232
1917	19	2,460,215	2,314,200	890,074
1918	19	2,571,270	2,476,042	952,318
1919	19	2,807,858	2,703,377	1,039,946
1920	19	2,691,065	2,591,391	996,683
1921	20	3,070,500	2,956,780	1,137,220
1922	20	3,603,600	3,470,140	1,334,660
1923	25	5,576,600	5,370,050	2,065,400
1924	20	4,728,600	4,553,460	1,751,340
1925	23	5,723,000	5,059,655	1,946,030
1926	25	5,723,000	5,511,025	2,119,625
1927	26	6,420,362	6,182,566	2,377,908
1928	33	9,103,677	8,766,516	3,371,742
1929	17	5,096,736	4,907,968	1,887,680
1930	34	9,491,406	9,139,880	3,515,328
Total		102,977,118	72,496,749	26,549,319

Tong Oil Average Annual Output in the 1930s (in piculs)

East Sichuan		West Hunan		West Hubei	
Fengdu	40,000	Baojing	17,746	Badong	4,776
Fengjie	20,000	Chenxi	27,200	Enshi	3,580
Fuling	10,000	Cili	4,800	Fangxian	23,880
Nanjing	500	Dayong	6,000	Jianshi	5,970
Pengshui	1,000	Fenghuang	16,000	Laifeng	5,970
Qianjiang	1,000	Longshan	4,000	Lichuan	2,390
Shizhu	10,000	Luxi	18,000	Xianfeng	5,970
Tongjiang	500	Mayang	7,300	Xingshan	2,388
Wanxian	80,000	Sangzhi	1,500	Xuanen	17,910
Wanyuan	3,000	Shimen	4,750	Yunxi	11,940
Wushan	5,000	Yongshun	40,000	Yunxian	17,910
Wuxi	10,000	*Total*	*147,296*	Zhushan	23,880
Xiushan	50,000			Zhuxi	23,880
Youyang	8,000			Zigui	2,390
Yunyang	100,000			*Total*	*152,834*
Zhaohua	500				
Zhongxian	140,000				
Total	*479,500*				

Tong Oil Exports from Wanxian, Sichuan

Year	Export (piculs)	Value (HG taels)	Price (per picul in HG taels)
1917	31,140	314,606	10.26
1918	64,765	582,885	8.24
1919	55,375	581,438	10.68
1920	45,496	439,036	10.37
1921	63,932	707,727	11.26
1922	230,290	3,539,626	15.63
1923	244,175	5,518,355	22.98
1924	263,638	4,745,484	18.31
1925	274,923	4,214,683	15.59
1926	178,366	3,567,321	20.74
1927	193,472	2,940,775	15.46
1928	324,492	5,480,856	17.18
1929	263,340	6,320,168	24.38
1930	312,555	4,688,326	15.00
1931	334,361	8,084,849	24.18
1932	292,010	6,491,382	22.23
1933	324,128	6,605,729	20.38
1934	265,868	7,260,855	27.31
1935	188,533	8,052,244	42.71

Sources: Chinese Maritime Customs, *Decennial Reports,* 5th issue, 1:1922–31 (Shanghai, 1933); *Tongji yuekan,* no. 38, 4; Zhang Xiaomei (1938, R77–78); *Zhongguo shiyezhi,* 1/5, 922; 3:11–13 [geng]; *Sichuan jinhji yuekan,* 6/2, 78; *Sichuan yuebao,* 7/2, 22–26; *Hubei nianjian,* 204; Tongyou (1941, 616); Li Changlong (1940, 49–50, 52–53); *Sichuan yuebao,* 2/2, 4344; 6/1, 87; *Zhonghang yuekan,* 1936/5, 28.

Note: Decennial Reports gives Sichuan share as 27 percent, Hunan's as 26 percent, and Hubei's as 10 percent of the national total.

Table 3.5

Opium Production, Fuling

Year	Local output (piculs)	Export (piculs)	Price per picul (yuan)	Price per tael (yuan)
1929	48,118	60,537	620	0.62
1930	36,413	48,118	800	0.80
1931	24,059	12,029	750	0.75
1932	24,059	12,029	400	0.40
1933	24,059	10,729	370	0.37
1934	24,059	7,153	320	0.32
1935	12,029	—	180	0.18

Sources: Chen Yanjiong (1935, 42–43, 49; *Sichuan yuebao*, 8/3, 144.

Table 3.6

Income from Nonagrarian Activities, 1912–37 (yuan)

Source	East Sichuan	West Hubei	West Hunan
Tong oil and opium	151,003,200	32,247,942	22,592,966
	51,907,350	29,076,025	
Other	235,400,775		
Grand total	*522,228,258*		

4
COMMODITY DISTRIBUTION

I MUST apologize for the tedious reading of this chapter, made so by the many place names, figures on the distances between places, and other details. In a sense, the tedium symbolizes the toil of transporting commodities in the highland. Even so, the goods had to be sent up and down, for they were extensively needed for survival and for comfort.

From the most central of the markets (Yichang, Wanxian, and Jinshi) to the remotest in the border regions (Liye, Chadong, and Yushanzhen), a common pattern of trade prevailed. It was an exchange of tong oil, herbal medicine, bristles, timber, and, of course, opium, for cotton yarn, cloth, paraffin (kerosene), salt, sugar, and cigarettes. There were indeed local variations, such as the *yiner* and *muer* of northern Sichuan, fine grain of Guizhou, and tea of western Hunan, but the general pattern remained valid throughout the highland in the period under consideration.

Transport

The commodities were brought down from and taken up to the mountains by traditional means. A waterway system and a road system were therefore absolutely essential for the highlanders' survival and development (see fig. 4.1). Heavy and bulky goods such as timber depended entirely on rivers. In western Hunan, logs were thrown into the Yuan to flow down to Xikou where they were gathered and tied into small rafts, and then to Hongjiang, where the small rafts were made into large ones. Eventually they reached Changde, where they were called "West Lake rafts." The logs of southern Hunan were allowed to flow down the Xiang to Quanzhou and then to Lingling, where the small rafts were enlarged. Finally they came to Hengyang and Changsha, where they were given the name "East Lake rafts." A similar way of transporting timber was found on the Furong, which cascaded down from Zhengan and Daozhen in Guizhou to Pengshui in Sichuan.[1] Passengers and breakable commodities, however, had to be treated more gently in traditional boats or steamers wherever available to operate on navigable rivers, as follows:

Western Hubei: (1) Han River (total length, 1,530 km; in Hubei, 979 km), the section flowing from Xianhekou to Jiahe (34 km) to Beihe (12 km) to Tianhe (30 km) to Yunxian (61 km) to Danjiangkou (100 km), taking the Du (285 km) into its course west of Yunxian; (2) Yangzi River (in Hubei, 1,200 km), the section stretching from Peishichang to Badong (44 km) to Zigui (55 km) to Taipingxi (62 km) to Sandouping (10 km); (3) Qing River (440 km), with eighty-eight rapids formed by enormous boulders, then unnavigable except for a short section between Enshi and Tunbao.

Eastern Sichuan: (1) Wu River (or Qian, total length, 940 km; in Sichuan, 247 km) the section flowing from Yanhe (Guizhou) to Gongtan (58 km), Pengshui, Wulong, and Fuling (189 km), taking in the Tangyan (68 km) at Gongtan; (2) the stretch of the Yangzi River courses from Fuling to Wanxian (147 km) to Fengjie (119 km) and to Yichang (203 km), incorporating the Daning at Wushan; (3) Jialing River (939 km), flowing from Chaotianyi to Guangyuan (47 km) and Zhaohua (30 km), taking in the upper reaches of the Dong, the Nan, the Tong, the Hou, and the Qian, all of which empty themselves into the Qu to join the Jialing at Hechuan.

Western Hunan: (1) Li River (388 km), especially the section from Sangzhi to Lixian (240 km), along which it accepts the Die, the Lou (61 km), and the Yongshun; (2) upper reaches of the Yuan River (800 km), from Chenxi to Pushi (30 km) to Luxi (30 km) and to Yuanlin (30 km) and its tributaries, the You (from Longtan in Sichuan to Baojing, 120 km, to Yuanlin, 120 km in three or four days downstream) and the Chen (from Tongren in Guizhou to Chenxi on the Yuan).

On the Han River, boats of different shapes and sizes sailed. Those that belonged to the Hubei boatmen's guild tended to be smaller and faster than those owned by Shaanxi crews.[2] Otherwise it is pointless to differentiate them, since many Shaanxi owners sold their boats in Hubei instead of taking them back. They did so because it took two months for the return journey from Laohekou to Hanzhong. At places a large boat needed one hundred men to pull it over a rapid like Huangjinxia. It simply was too costly and too slow.[3]

These boats carried from a few piculs to as much as one thousand. It is said that in the early years of the twentieth century there used to be more boats on the Han than the fifty thousand or so in the 1930s, the decline due to civil wars and banditry.[4] They sent down tong oil, lacquer, *muer*, hides, opium, and so on and brought back to Shaanxi salt, rice, paper, sugar, yarn and cloth, paraffin, and dyestuffs.[5] It cost three yuan to send one picul of goods from Ankang in Shaanxi to Hankou. On the return journey from Hankou to Hanzhong, one picul cost twice as much and took twice as long.[6]

As it winds its way chiefly through the red basin of Sichuan, the Jialing is not really one of our concerns. The section of the Yangzi from Fuling down to Yichang and back through the treacherous gorges was gradually taken over by steamers, which I shall discuss presently. In eastern Sichuan, the colorful river that is of interest here is the Wu with its tributaries. The 58 km from Yuanhe to Gongtan was littered with thirty-one rapids; the next 189 km from Gongtan to Fuling had ninety rapids. The Wu was navigable from Sinan down, but up only to Gongtan. The twenty-seven shipping guilds, each of which had eight solidly built large boats in operation, carried salt upstream and tong oil and foodstuff downstream. When the water was high, each could carry as much as twenty-five tons of cargo, but in the winter the load was reduced to under eighteen tons. A downstream journey needed only six to ten days from Yuanhe to Fuling, whereas an upstream journey took at least one month from Fuling to Gongtan. There were smaller boats, but even they could not sail upstream beyond Gongtan.[7]

The smaller rivers feeding into the Wu were the Yu, linking up Pengshui with Yushanzhen, a distance of 64 km, and taking on smaller boats carrying less than three tons of cargo; the Tangyan, whose small boats joined up Qianjiang and Gongtan; and the You of Youyang, Longtan, and Baojing, which was capable of having slightly larger boats laden with fifteen to twenty tons of cargo, but it was very hard going, for at places a boat required scores of pullers to drag it up the river.[8]

Although the sailing was laborious, the You River is important because it flows into the Yuan. Shen Congwen's description of these rivers in the 1920s and 1930s is delightful to read and is largely reliable.[9] The tong oil boat, with its high prow and square stern, was something like a home for its crew of twenty-six to forty under a Mayang captain. Sailing upstream, it employed temporarily from three to seventy pullers. It could take from three to forty-four barrels of tong oil, two hundred bales of cotton, or one hundred piculs of salt. Such

boats sailed only between Changde and Hongjiang, and between spring
and the onset of winter, they could make four or five round trips. The
trip Shen Congwen took was from Changde up to Chenxi. The boat
progressed at 30 li a day; it needed pullers often, and the whole journey of 440 li required eighteen days. Even this pace compared not all
that unfavorably with, say, the four-day trip down the Chen River from
Fenghuang to Chenxi, to cover only a quarter of the distance from
Changde. On the upper reaches, the waters flow rapidly. The boat had
to be solid and heavy to withstand frequent bumps against rocks. It was
punted or pulled rather than rowed.

The Li River laces up four fairly large alluvial basins—Sangzhi,
Dayong, Xikou, and Cili. It becomes navigable from Sangzhi and
could bear large boats from Cili all the way down to the Dongting.[10]
Like the Yuan, it is one of the four major rivers of Hunan. It is also one
of the major waterways on which tong oil and opium flowed.

Steamers could reach Laohekou along the Han during the summer,
Lixian from Dongting Lake along the Li, and of course between and
beyond Fuling and Yichang along the Yangzi.[11] Not only faster and
safer, steamers ran less risk of being robbed by river pirates or
requisitioned by soldiers.[12] I must hasten to add, however, that the
safety record for steamships over some thirty years (1909–39) between
Chongqing and Yichang left much to be desired. Fifty-five ships were
lost, compared with twenty-two ships between Chongqing and Xufu
from 1916 to 1939 and nine ships between Chongqing and Hechuan on
the Jialing from 1925 to 1939.[13]

The steamship service between Yichang and Chongqing dates back
to the end of the nineteenth century. The fifteen years from 1909 to
1925 was a period of intense competition between Chinese and foreign
enterprises, and therefore of growth. At the time of the May 30 Movement, a series of demonstrations and strikes against British and Japanese interests in China in 1925–26, this section of the Yangzi had 1,100
ships or 400,000 tons. The temporary withdrawal of foreign services
and the less inhibited behavior of the military toward Chinese ships
marked a decline to only 660 ships or 220,000 tons. The Sichuan-
Hubei service did not recover until the unification and reform of the
Sichuan administration in 1934–35. This entailed the establishment of
the Sichuan River Navigation Bureau, the stabilization of the turbulent
financial situation of the province, and progress in the campaign
against the Communists in northern Sichuan. Ships sailing Sichuan

rivers increased to 1,500 and then to 2,140 (tonnage from 500,000 to 750,000) in 1935–36.

Part of this advance was the contribution of Lu Zuofu and his Minsheng Shipping Company, which came into existence amid the 1925 strikes. By 1936 it owned sixty-two ships sailing as far as Shanghai, with a capitalization of 1,600,000 yuan.[14] With its faster and safer service, Yangzi steamshipping between Yichang and Chongqing drove the traditional boats out of business. The fleet of 2,900 traditional boats (100,000 tons) of 1899 was gradually reduced to only one (20 tons) in 1925.[15] Thereafter traditional boats were no longer seen on that stretch of the river.

Steamers monopolized the waters of the Yangzi, but they were hardly seen elsewhere. The short run between Jinshi and Lixian on the Li had only one solitary steamer of seventeen horsepower, carrying only six tons of cargo.[16] The rest of the waterway system of the highlands continued to be dominated by traditional shipping, which in turn continued to be dominated by its traditional regional guilds. These boats waddled upstream at a painfully slow pace and often had to stop before reaching the desired destination. Thus, passengers and goods had to get to the nearest port on foot before embarkation. As I have mentioned, even boatmen on the Han did not have sufficient patience to sail back to the upper reaches of the river; they sold their boats and walked. That is to say, roads were still important, and they were often cut along the valleys.

There were *dalu*, wide roads, often synonymous with *guanlu*, government roads for courier and military services. Wide enough for a sedan-chair or horse, they were paved with flagstones. But at places even government roads were so precipitous as to make travelers feel dizzy, such as the *zhandao* built along the cliffs, often overhanging, of Qinling and Dabashan at an altitude between 1,300 and 2,000 meters.[17] In contrast to the wide roads, the *xiaolu*, or narrow roads, were for ordinary people to use when going from village to village, town to town, and county seat to county seat. It took Shen Congwen seven days to cover a distance just over 100 km from Chadong via Songtao and Xiushan to Longtan.[18] In northern and southeastern Sichuan, a porter might walk 76 li a day, a sedan-chair 90, a beast of burden only 70, compared with the speed of courier service of 300–400 li a day from Chengdu to Langzhong in northern Sichuan, or 240 li a day in western Hubei.[19] The cost of overland transport was of course much

HUBEI
Yushanzhen

Qianjiang

Pengshui

GUIZHOU   SICHUAN
Youyang

× Gongtan
Longtan

HUNAN
Wu
Xiushan

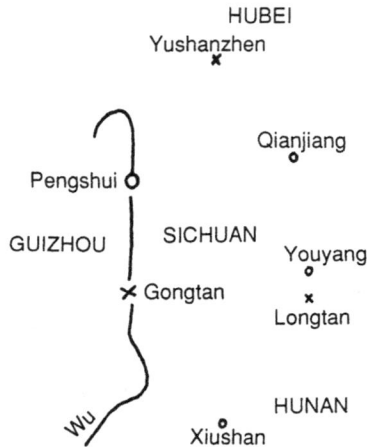

higher than river transport. The porter could carry 100 catties, for a pay of 1.50 yuan; the sedan-chair, just over 100 catties, for 4.00 yuan; and the beast and its drover, 200 catties, for 1.80 yuan. But a small boat could carry 2,500 catties, covering 60 li in eastern Sichuan for 0.80 yuan or 120 li in northern Sichuan for 0.50 yuan.[20]

Perhaps the most interesting arrangement of land and river transport was the one in the triangle of Pengshui-Qianjiang-Youyang, including also Xiushan, Longtan, Yushanzhen, and Gongtan. This was the golden triangle of tong oil, lacquer, gall nuts, salt, yarn, cloth, paraffin, cigarettes, and, above all, opium.

Goods were concentrated at Qianjiang, Xiushan, Youyang, Longtan and Yushanzhen either by land or by water, on their way to Gongtan and Pengshui. Once loaded on a boat in Gongtan, they were on their way down the Wu River to Fuling and wider horizons. Up the river the journey simply reversed the procedure: going from Shiye, Songtao, and Yuanhe, from Youyang and Qianjiang, they had to be carried, on a pole or on the back, to Gongtan.[21]

Opium has been mentioned, and this corner of four provinces (Guizhou, Sichuan, Hubei, and Hunan) was by no means the only route for Guizhou and Yunnan, and indeed Sichuan, opium to reach the eastern plains. It would have been unwise for the drug dealers and their backers to put all their eggs in one basket. Other routes were needed, and some of them were along the Yuan River from Songtao (50 li) to Fenghuang, Mayang, and Chenxi; from Tongren (70 li) to Fenghuang,

Mayang, and Chenxi; from Yuping (60 li) to Huangzhou and Zhijiang; from Tianzhu (60 li) to Huitong and Qianyang: from Liping (140 li) to Suining on the Wu and the Yuan; and from Songtao (120 li) to Qianzhou. Another route went from Qianjiang, Youyang, or Longshan to Lichuan, Xianfeng, or Laifeng in Hubei, then to Enshi or Xuanen, by the Qing valley to Yidu to join the Yangzi.[22] This simple fact of being on the opium transport routes made remote and dangerous places strategically and economically important.

As long as these and other routes were harassed only by local warlords and bandits whose interest lay in extracting as much money out of the opium and other goods as possible, but not in stopping them, it was a matter of sharing the proceeds to pay armed men commanded by tin soldiers of various sizes and various shades of legitimacy. They were, to put it cynically, birds of the same feather. Strategically, there was no need to exterminate anyone as long as a formula for compromise could be found. When the Communists rose on these mountains, the rules of the game had to be altered. Motorways had to be cut. They were gradually introduced in the middle 1930s (see table 4.1).[23]

I have discussed how much the ordinary people suffered when the motorways were being built, and how unpopular they became in the eyes of the users. Before the reorganization of the Sichuan Highway Board in 1935, only some twenty older machines were in operation.[24] The 140-li Santai-Mianyang Road, for instance, had only one bus that ran once every three days. A one-way ticket cost 4 yuan, compared with the open sedan-chair (*huagan*), carried by two men, slower but immeasurably more comfortable, which cost only 1.68 yuan.[25] The 350 new buses bought by the government in 1935 improved the service, but it remained as expensive as before. The parcel service was just as costly (table 4.2).

Economically, the motorways were no serious challenge to traditional land transport services; they were systematically introduced in western Hubei and eastern Sichuan, as in Jiangxi and Fujian, chiefly for military operations against the Communist soviet areas. Wherever the Communist menace was less intense—in western Hunan, for instance—the construction of motorways was pursued with less urgency and more ponderousness. Also in order to conduct a more efficient campaign against the Communists, telephone service arrived in the highlands in 1935. Telephone lines and receivers were installed along the Yangzi at such places as Wanxian, Fengdu, Shizhu, and Lichuan.[26]

Steamers on the Yangzi, a few trucks and buses, and some telephones did not make the transport system in the highlands modern. The majority of passengers and bulk of goods remained in the hands of the traditional transport systems.

Marketing

The marketing systems, too, remained predominantly traditional. Those for tong oil, timber, bristles, and cotton yarn are illustrated in figs. 4.1–4.4. The most important, opium, is also the most conspicuous absentee, however, for we know little of its marketing. But all signs suggest that it was also traditional. An attempt to form a private monopoly of opium distribution was made at Chongqing in 1935. The planned consortium would buy and sell as well as pay taxes to the authorities. It would have capital totaling five million yuan and be responsible for paying approximately one million yuan in taxes per month.[27] But the plan was never put into practice. The reason was that any concentration of purchase and sale would enhance the gains of some groups (regional, military, financial, etc.) at the expense of other groups. A large-scale private consortium like the one projected in 1935 could legalize and rationalize the existing marketing arrangement of opium, cut the cost, and make it more efficient, but it was utterly impracticable because of the irreconcilable interests of the various groups involved in this trade. By the same token, it was also impossible to rationalize and modernize the other marketing systems. One could merely tinker here and there and compromise in order to accommodate the growing volume of trade.

The systems were traditional because, with the exception of the timber trade, all of them began from the small producer and the independent small buyer. As soon as the volume swelled beyond the ability of the small buyer to cope with the guilds, both regional and specialized, stepped in, often with the backing of their respective regional political, military, and financial interests. At every stage, from their taking over the trade to handing over the goods to an exporter or a consumer, the guilds were tangled up in a web of conflicting interests badly in need of the services of a commissioned middleman. Take tong oil, for example. If all the regional guilds approached the exporter or were approached by him directly, they would cut each other's throat ultimately for the pleasure of the exporter. So they needed the

Figure 4.1. **Traditional Trading Systems: Hunan Timber**

A. Hunan Timber

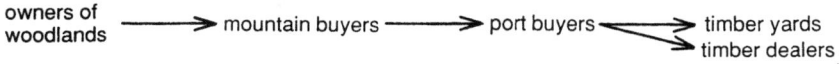

owners of woodlands ———➤ mountain buyers ———➤ port buyers ⇄ timber yards / timber dealers

Source: Zhongguo shiyezhi, 3: 197–98 *(ding)*

Figure 4.2. **Traditional Trading Systems: Tung Oil of Wanxian, Sichuan**

B. Tong Oil of Wanxian, Sichuan

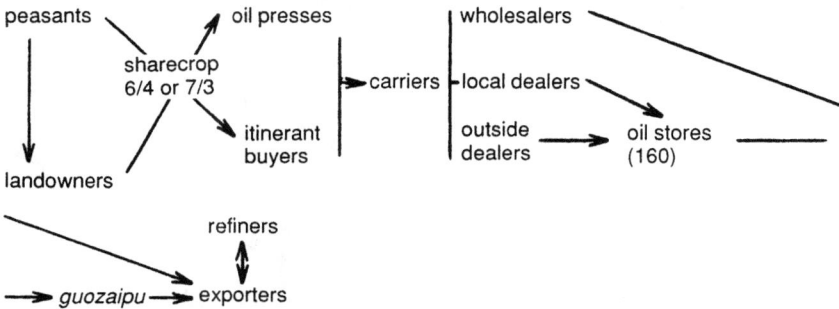

peasants / oil presses | wholesalers
sharecrop 6/4 or 7/3 ➤ carriers ⊢ local dealers
itinerant buyers | outside dealers ➤ oil stores (160)
landowners
refiners
➤ *guozaipu* ➤ exporters

Source: Zhang Xiaomei (1938, T1–8); *Sichuan yuebao*, 8/3, 13–4, 24, 26–27.

Figure 4.3. **Traditional Trading Systems: Sichuan Bristles**

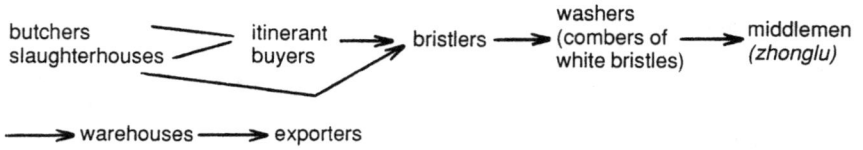

butchers
slaughterhouses → itinerant buyers → bristlers → washers (combers of white bristles) → middlemen *(zhonglu)*

→ warehouses → exporters

Source: Sichuansheng zhi shanhuo, 17–21; *Sichuan xuchan*, 1:20–21; Gu Gengyu (1980, 7); Shi Daoyuan (1945, 18–19).

Figure 4.4. **Traditional Trading Systems: Sichuan Cotton Yarn Imports**

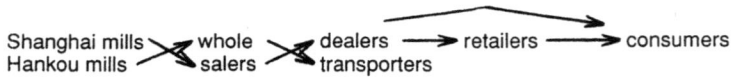

Shanghai mills
Hankou mills → wholesalers → dealers transporters → retailers → consumers

Source: Kanda Masao (1936, 447–49).

guozaipu, the last of a parade of middlemen, whose function was to act as the go-between between the guilds and the exporter; thus, they did not have to come face to face with each other until an agreement was ready for the seal, and goods and money ready for exchange. For this, he was thought to be worth his handsome commission from both sides.

Before the appearance of the *guozaipu* middleman in the tong oil marketing system, the wholesalers, local dealers, outside dealers, and oil stores were all regional in nature. Similarly, one finds local and imported medicine warehouses in the medicine trade, the need for the *zhonglu* middlemen in the bristle trade, and so on.

Big and small buyers and processors, wholesalers and retailers, middlemen and exporters and importers operated at all the levels of G. W. Skinner's markets. Wang Chengjing studied forty-three markets in six counties in the southeastern corner of Sichuan. Among them, eighteen had more than 100 households. The smallest had only 7 whereas the largest had 351.[28] All of them may have to be classified as standard markets due to the absence of wholesalers and financial houses. In western Hunan bordering on Sichuan and Guizhou, one finds places like Chadong, Liye, and Ala. Chadong, the *biancheng* border town described by Shen Congwen, lies on the right bank of the You River.[29] Its bustling dock area had several inns, restaurants, and of course prostitutes. Among the many shops there was the general store selling American paraffin lamps and paraffin. The raison d'être of this "intermediate" market was represented by a salt warehouse and the branch of an oil wholesaler. From here tong oil, gall nuts, and opium were exported while salt, cotton, yarn, cloth, and dried seafood were imported. Liye to its north and Ala to its south were similar but smaller.[30] I visited Ala on September 8, 1983. Situated to the southwest of Fenghuang on the northern bank of a small river on the border of Hunan, Sichuan, and Guizhou, it is a market that meets every five days. On the day I was there, some ten thousand people came to buy foodstuffs, seeds and herbs, cloth and clothes, farming tools, and other items. Normally, when people are less busily engaged in transplanting or harvesting, more than twenty thousand would turn up on market day. They buy miscellaneous goods and livestock—one hundred or so oxen, half as many sheep, and many times more pigs. A peculiar institution of this livestock market is the "bargainers" who are friends of the would-be buyers and discuss the prices of animals with the sellers. There are no wholesalers. Inns and restaurants cater to those

who come the day before a market day or who may stay overnight and push on to the next market on the following day. It is hard to fit markets like this into either the "standard" or the "intermediate" category.

Further up the Yuan River, Hongjiang is another interesting case. It is enormous, yet not in the same league with Jinshi, Changde, not to speak of Changsha. In fact, it is the first port down the Yuan where goods are assembled and dispatched to Changde and Hankou. In the 1920s and 1930s it exported the famous Hong oil and timber, and imported salt, yarn, cloth, a host of "foreign and Guang[dong] goods." It boasted a number of wholesalers and retailers (table 4.3).

Missing from the list were salt merchants and opium dealers. Bearing in mind their eminent presence, the oilers, timber merchants, and importers of goods from abroad and from the south were big players in the market. It was said that by 1934 the export of the Hong oil had fallen from seven milliion yuan a year to only about two million yuan as a result of heavy taxation, widespread unsettled conditions in western Hunan, and the burning of the tong forests by soldiers in their pursuit of bandits.[31]

The timber trade had two types of buyers: those who went up to the mountains, to buy from owners of mountains and those who sailed up the river to stay at a port like Hongjiang to buy from the mountain buyers. In the next stage, the timber yards and timber dealers were both middlemen who arranged business for the port buyers with the wholesalers and retailers down the river. They took a commission from both sides of the transactions. These wholesalers and retailers, like the importers of foreign and southern goods, were mostly Jiangxi and Hankou merchants. It was probably the regional differences and jealousies that made the services of middlemen indispensable.[32]

In the core area of Sichuan, many intermediate markets were to be found, especially at the end of the Qing and after the inauguration of the Republic. Shiyangchang of Guanxian, the market for Sichuan herbal medicine; Fangtingzhen of Shifang, the market for Sichuan tobacco; and Tangchangzhen now of Pixian, the market for Sichuan handicrafts, are examples.[33] Elsewhere in Sichuan, the cluster of famous markets along the Wu River was particularly relevant, significant, and interesting. There is not much information on the smaller markets there, such as Xiangkou, Jiangkou, and Baimachang of Wulong and Pingkaizhen of Xiushan, which had a couple of hundred households, dealing in timber, salt, tong oil, opium, cloth, paper, and so on.[34] There are, however, three well-known ones: Yushanzhen, Longtan, and Gongtan, the first under the jurisdiction of Qianjiang and the latter two under that of Youyang.

Located on the southern bank of the Yu River, Yushanzhen had between 566 and 1,000 households. Perhaps the smaller figure is more acceptable, as will be seen. It was a "hundred-day market town," that is, it conducted business all year round. The river is good enough for boats of three tons (deadweight) to sail up from Pengshui during the summer, but only of one ton during the winter. Above the town very small boats could sail into Hubei.[35] Otherwise, approaches to the town had to depend upon narrow roads. By land and by water, Yushanzhen was a market for salt from Sichuan up the river to Hubei and for tong oil and homespun down the river. Its business seems to have been rather limited; so do its market facilities—only ten inns, twenty eating places, and five teahouses. Even so, it was a more active place than the county seat, Qianjiang. In 1933 the city of Qianjiang had only five hundred households but no large-scale trade of any kind. It was the closure of China's sea coast and its increasing reliance on overland transport to Guizhou, Yunnan, and Burma during the Japanese war that brought prosperity to Qianjiang. Inside the city there sprang up a market that met every fifth day, conducting business in the traditional manner—in salt, tong oil, and cloth, but no reference to opium. By then, the city had more than two hundred families of temporary residents, fifty inns, twenty eating places, and a dozen or so teahouses.[36]

Longtan lies to the east and under the jurisdiction of Youyang. In the 1930s it had over 1,400 households or nearly 7,500 people. Later the war added some 500 families of temporary residents to it. Before the wartime boom it had sixty-eight inns, some of which ran a restaurant business downstairs. For some reason, we are told, people here quarreled and fought more ferociously than their brethren elsewhere in Sichuan, and so no teahouses operated for the denizens. In spite of its size, it was surprisingly not a "hundred-day market"; it met at intervals of five days. The You River passes by Longtan but not Youyang, and so the short distance between the city and Longtan had to be covered on foot. From Longtan the You flows down through Baojing to reach Yuanling on the Yuan. Another small river, the Mei, comes to join the You at Longtan, thus linking the town to Xiushan. On the You, there were three hundred to four hundred boats, each carrying fifteen to twenty tons; on the Mei, however, only small boats operated, carrying one and a half tons. Up the You, the boats transported Hunan cotton and yarn to Guizhou; down it, lacquer, tong oil, and so forth to Hunan. Both the tong oil and lacquer businesses were in decline after the outbreak of the Japanese war. It is said that in the decade after the fall of the Qing, some thirty thousand piculs of tong oil were sold by the thirty wholesalers of the town. Early in the 1940s, the amount of tong oil transacted here declined to less than ten thousand piculs. The story was the same for raw lacquer.[37]

At the junction of the Tangyan and the Wu rivers, the volume of water suddenly swells to make Gongtan, a town of 1,300 households in the 1930s, far more important than Longtan and Yushanzhen. This larger volume of water enabled boats to sail up to and required smaller boats to stop and reload at this entrepôt town. Yarn, paper, foreign imports, and Sichuan salt came up the Wu in exchange for tong oil, Guizhou grain, and opium. It is said that in the 1930s about 300,000 piculs of salt per annum were sent to Guizhou through this route, and 20,000–30,000 barrels of tong oil, including the well-known Xiu oil of Xiushan, were sent down from Gongtan. The Japanese war saw the oil trade at Gongtan, as elsewhere, decline to only 5,000 barrels. There were then some thirty wholesale establishments for the buying and selling of these important commodities.[38]

Local gazetteers published in the second half of the nineteenth century referred to the opium being grown in this corner of Sichuan. By the 1920s it was being planted almost everywhere, causing a food shortage.[39] Some reported that Xiushan was so poor that it had to grow a great deal of opium to make ends meet.[40] Pengshui was said to have produced 200,000 catties a year in the 1930s.[41] We know that opium shops (not smokers' dens) existed in four cities—Pengshui, Qianjiang,

Youyang, and Xiushan.[42] These bits and pieces of information do not add up to a coherent picture, except to show that opium was produced there, probably in sizable quantities to subsidize considerably the economy of the inhabitants.

Wanxian can be taken as an example of a central market. This port city of 811,465 people in the 1930s dominated the Yangzi trade from Fuling to Wuxi. Northeastern Sichuan and southwestern Hubei goods were assembled here by land for shipment to Wuhan.[43] For Sichuan tong oil, for instance, there was the Wanxian system, gathering the oil from Fengdu to Wuxi along the Yangzi and from Wanyuan and Chengkou in the north; the Chongqing system, accepting oil from the Qu and Jialing, which was then brought downstream to Wanxian; and the Fuling system, taking all the oil down the Wu, which again found its way to Wanxian.[44] In the 1920s Wanxian boasted no more than 10 tong oil wholesalers. This was to increase to more than 80 and then 150 in the 1930s, all of which were controlled by such regional guilds as the Zhongxian *bang* and the Yunyang *bang*. It was estimated then that no fewer than 100,000 people depended on this oil for living. After all, close to 335,200 piculs of it, at a value of approximately seven million yuan, passed every year from 1931 to 1936 through Wanxian to Wuhan and beyond.[45]

In addition, Wanxian had more than forty mountain goods wholesalers, dealing in bristles, gall nuts, hides, lacquer, and herbal medicine, which together were worth about one million yuan.[46] At the height of its salt trade, from the second half of the nineteenth century to the early 1920s, when Sichuan salt dominated the markets in western Hubei and Hunan, Wanxian exported four hundred to five hundred *zai* (1 *zai* = 90,000 catties) a year. Thereafter it decreased to less than half of that.[47] All imported goods were concentrated here before being distributed to various parts of the province. It would be most unusual if opium did not concentrate here before exporting to Wuhan.[48] Of this, however, very few details are known.

The enormous volume of trade naturally required the port city to become also a financial center. By 1934–35 it had eight branches of the national, provincial, and private banks, twenty-six money shops, and fourteen silversmiths.[49] It had grown to be so influential that its speculative operations caused a serious crisis in the province. The coming of the Red Army to northern Sichuan at the end of 1932 made nervous investors take flight to Wuhan and Shanghai. This was, however, only the first taste of what might follow if the government did not take measures to stop the market jitters. In January 1935, the province was encircled on the north, east, and south by Communists. The southern group, the First Front Army commanded by Zhu De, was obviously planning to invade Sichuan.

At this point, the Bank of Sichuan had been in existence for a year and had issued over 5.6 million yuan of paper currency.[50] The treasury system that was established along with the bank allowed private enterprises to borrow from the treasury, using government bonds and private securities as collateral. The government of course also had the privilege of borrowing by having the treasury underwrite its bonds and bills. The threat of credit inflation was there, to be touched off by the tense and deteriorating military situation.

Suddenly the amount of government bonds and bills leapt from a mere 300,000 yuan to 8 million, while their prices fell sharply. To cope with this, the government persuaded private banks and money shops to buy up 7.5 million yuan of these papers, following which the government issued more paper currency to redeem its bonds and bills. This inflation caused the premium of remittances to Shanghai in the autumn of 1934 to jump to 600, 700 yuan, and more for every 1,000 yuan. Holding devalued bonds, bills, and Sichuan paper currencies, the Wanxian money shops and silversmiths first speculated in the Shanghai remittances in the hope that the situation might improve, the premium would come down or stabilize, and they would be able to recoup the losses thrust upon them by the provincial government. When the premium continued to rise sharply, the money shops were caught between the devalued bonds and bills which they held and the increasing premium which they had to pay to finance the normal trade and to meet the demand of the capital in flight from Sichuan to Shanghai and Wuhan. The money shops and silversmiths lost some 8 million yuan. By September more than a dozen of them had gone out of business.[51]

From the above discussion it is apparent that one does sometimes face the basic difficulty of categorizing a given market. Was it a standard or an intermediate one? Was the presence of the wholesaler the only required criterion? Should its size be taken into consideration? Of greater practical significance was the relative importance of a sleepy mountain city compared with a bustling market under its jurisdiction. From the point of view of the traditional magistrate, perhaps the city or county seat and its surrounding fields were more important for the

settled livelihood of the population of the county and the more predict-
able revenue for the county government. But increasingly, especially
on the highland, trade grew to rival agriculture as a key economic
factor in the sense of being a source of livelihood and a source of
taxation. Consequently, to control the routes of transport and market
towns would mean additional revenue, which the magistrate may have
felt to be of little meaning to his governance of the county, but his
superiors may have thought differently. It was along the transport
routes, on land and on water, and at market towns that checkpoints
could be established, mainly for the purpose of collecting taxes on
goods in transit for the superior levels of government to use. It so
happened that in the period with which this study is concerned, the
superior level of government was that of the garrison region (*fangqu* or
zhenshoushi), and revenue was cherished by the garrison commander,
who used it to pay his men and for war.

Table 4.1

Motor Roads in West Hubei, East Sichuan, and West Hunan (kilometers)

Province	Year	Surfaced	Unsurfaced
Hubei	1937	2,023	2,030
Hunan	1937	2,787	—
Sichuan	1937	2,937	1,853

Province	Year	Route
West Hubei		Laohekou-Gucheng-Junxian-
	1935	Yunxian, 283 km
	1935	Badong-Enshi, 205 km
	1936	Enshi-Xuanen-Laifeng, 120 km
	1937	Enshi-Lichuan-(Sichuan), 129 km
Total		*737 km*
East Sichuan	1932	Sichuan-Hubei, completed to Wanxian
	1935	Sichuan-Guizhou, 640 km
	1935	Sichuan-Shaanxi, 412 km
	1935	Sichuan-Hunan, 704 km
	1935	Sichuan-Hubei, 515 km
Total		*2,271 km*
West Hunan	1936	Chadong-Yuanling, 200 km

Sources: Zhou Yishi (1957, 130); Hubei: *Hubei nianjian*, 633–34, 644; *Zhongguo jingji*, 3/8, 2; *Wuhan ribao*, January 19, 1935, February 12, 1936; *Sichuan yuebao*, 9/6, 162; Sichuan: Zhang Xiaomei (1938, G8–9, 11–12, 17–19); *Sichuan yuebao*, 9/3, 43–49; *Sichuan wenxian*, vol. 75, 10–13; Fang Xianting (1938, 2:1183–84); Hunan: *Jingji yanjiu*, 1/1.

Table 4.2

Parcel Service

Parcels by bus	Yuan (100 kg per km)	Parcels by other means	Yuan (100 kg per km)
First class	0.70	Wagon	0.003
Second class	0.42	Boat	0.023
Third class	0.26	Porter	0.040
		Donkey	0.026

Sources: Sichuan yuebao, 10/5, 232–35; *Sichuansheng nongqing baogao*, 3/5, 9–11.

Table 4.3

Hongjiang Wholesalers and Retailers

Business	Number	Capital (yuan)	Annual turnover (yuan)
Bank of Hunan			4,000,000
branch	1	460,000	(remittances)
Money shops	7	460,000	13,000,000
Tong oilers	7	510,000	1,800,000
Grocers	40	133,000	1,030,000
Drapers	30	247,200	976,000
Timberyards	13	33,000	680,000
Imported goods	28	16,000	570,000
Grain dealers	56	13,900	572,000
Stationers	6	18,000	211,000
Jewelers	10	104,000	200,000
Chinaware	12	36,700	150,000
Herbists	25	32,000	100,000
Clothiers	11	8,000	25,000

Source: Zhongguo shiyezhi, 3:159 [bing].

5
TRIBUTE MONEY (I)

ALTHOUGH this book deals with public finance only at the regional and county levels, brief references to provincial revenue and expenditure will undoubtedly be of help. One general trend in the three provinces during the period under consideration was the expansion of government functions leading to increases in income and spending. In that context, the importance of the revenue from land, in spite of the multiplication of its surtaxes, diminished in relation to currency manipulations, commodity taxes, and public loans. Another trend was the diminishing importance of administrative expenses whose traditional predominance was shared, even overshadowed, by loan services and defense expenses.

There were numerous institutional changes in government finance, especially during the Republican period. For instance, what used to be paid in terms of the treasury tael (*kupingliang*) was to be converted into the yuan after 1914. In Hubei, one tael equaled 1.40 yuan; in Sichuan, 1.60 yuan; in Hunan, 1.50 yuan.[1] Other significant improvements included the gradual introduction of a division between the incomes of the different grades of government. At long last, the heatedly disputed land tax became the mainstay of provincial revenue while its surtaxes went to the county treasury. Other provincial taxes developed in a similar way. This does not mean, however, that all surtaxes were county taxes; indeed, the 1927 and 1928 financial conferences left the division between provincial and county revenues undefined. It seemed to vary from province to province and county to county. To make the situation even more complex, there was yet another grade of government sandwiched between province and county after 1916. This was the garrison region (*fangqu*), presided over either more formally by a garrison commander (*zhenshoushi*) or less formally by a colonel or a brigadier general.

The garrison region system in Sichuan is well known.[2] Individual garrison regions came into existence with or without the approval of a higher authority, probably during the war of indigenous Sichuan troops against the expatriate Yunnan and Guizhou armies in 1917–18. They grew into a system of nine such regions in 1919,[3] lasting mutatis mutandis until the reorganization of the provincial administrative and military systems in 1935. In its stable form after 1928, eastern Sichuan as a great garrison region was under the jurisdiction of the Twenty-first Army commanded by Liu Xiang, and northern Sichuan was under the Twenty-ninth Army of Tian Songyao after 1930.[4]

It would be untrue to say that there were no garrison regions or only unstable ones in western Hubei. It had been the cockpit of various northern armies dispatched by Beijing, local troops, armed units from the neighboring provinces, and the "Divine Army" and bandits. They were fighting for the revenue from Sichuan salt and Sichuan and Guizhou opium, and for other reasons, such as provincial autonomy of this buffer province between the North and South.[5] By September 1920 a system of garrison regions was inaugurated, to recognize the fait accompli in the hope of stabilizing the regional situation. As it was excessively favorable to the northern forces at the expense of the southern, especially the Hubei ones, it did not work.[6] Another attempt was made in May 1931; it too failed.[7] Then it was not just a matter of reconciling national and local interests, but also a matter of coping with the threat from He Long's and Xu Xiangqian's Red Armies in the wake of the Li Lisan line, as reported, for instance, in the *Shibao* of Shanghai in 1930 and 1931.

Of the three regions, western Hunan had perhaps the strongest parochial traditions, including its garrison against the Tujia and Miao minority peoples. After a period of chaos in the second half of the 1910s, local hegemons emerged—Cai Juyou controlled the Baojing-Yuanling-Chenxi triangle, backed by his ambitious henchman, Chen Quzhen, to his west in 1920–22. Both opposed provincial autonomy, which was very much in vogue in the three provinces. Cai's defeat saw the growth of Chen in power and stature. It was he who stabilized western Hunan in 1927 and held the hegemony until a bout of impetuosity pushed him westward to fight his Guizhou neighbors. In so doing he ruined his finances and his Thirty-fourth Division in 1934.[8]

Chen and his contemporaries in western Hunan displayed an array of skills in financing their defense needs. Based on the reports in the *Dagongbao* of Changsha and the *Shibao* of Shanghai, they intercepted land tax and salt gabelle collections, planted opium and levied various taxes on it, issued paper currency and bonds, introduced their own taxes, borrowed from gentry and merchants, demanded money from the provincial government, and owed salary and pay to their men. This was the general pattern of gathering revenue and making it go far.

A few militarists did spend money on improving urban life and transport.[9] Nonetheless, it is fair to say that the basic objectives of the militarists' finance practices were to maintain and equip their men and to pay for war. They might rely on the provincial tax collection system for these purposes if they were in such a position, or they might depend on their own collecting agencies and the county governments under their sway.

The insertion of this level of government played havoc with the public finance system. As far as is known, no systematic records of revenue and expenditure were kept, except a few published by Liu Xiang's Twenty-first Army before he unified Sichuan. An unmistakable impression one forms is Liu's war government was created for defense against internal disturbance and external invasion; therefore, its finance policy was geared toward war. Like a ravenous beast, its insatiable appetite for more money, more men, and better equipment led to a continuous budgetary inflation and ever-increasing budgetary deficits.

I am not interested in analyzing here the budgets of the local governments as such. To quote from an Old China Hand, "No budget published since the establishment of the Republic has been other than a pious expression of hope that the revenues and expenditure would correspond with the estimates."[10] Rather, I would like to describe in more detail the circumstances of the financial inflation.

Land Taxes

Western Hubei

In western Hubei from 1912 to 1934, both the *diding* and its surtaxes had been increasing, but fairly mildly for all three types of land (see tables 5.1 and 5.2). The mildness may have been due to the ten years of relative political stability under governors Wang Zhanyuan (1916–21) and Xiao Yaonan (1921–26), a luxury neither Sichuan nor Hunan shared. Western Hubei, however, was less fortunate than the rest of the province as reflected in table 5.3.

The two sections of table 5.3 suggest that although both the land tax proper and its surtaxes were increasing, the momentum did not gather until after the end of Yuan Shikai's presidency. Looking at the *diding* alone, the total collection in western Hubei at the end of Qing was only 33,109 yuan; this decreased to 22,805 in 1915 and rose to 195,800 twenty years later. The series of three years is insufficient to allow one to detect a trend, especially as the figures for 1932 appear to be quite wild. Unreliable as they obviously are, these figures formed the basis of the analysis of *Tianfu wenti yanjiu* in the Hanxue series of 1936 (1:181–82). It is because of the contemporary attention they drew that I have reproduced them here. The figures for 1935 and 1936 should be read together with other reports. For instance, the Nongcun Fuxing Weiyuanhui spoke of unusually heavy surtaxes carried by western Hubei peasants. The growing trend of surtaxes convinced Jia Shiyi, the provincial treasurer and noted financial historian of the Republican period, of the need to put things in better order. Two attempts were made, only to cause increases in both the *diding* and the surtaxes.[11]

Sichuan

The higher productivity of Sichuan dry fields and dry land, as described in the previous chapters, coupled with a high rate of demographic increase, especially on the highlands, may have been responsible for the sharper rise in the *diding* in that province compared with Hubei and Hunan (see tables 5.4 and 5.5). The milder increase in Sichuan land surtaxes is, however, harder to explain. It may have been because the surtaxes had to be collected by the county tax agencies, whereas the military themselves could easily exact lump sums of the land tax in advance. In Sichuan, therefore, the frequency of levying the land tax rather than surtaxes increased

Sketchy as they are, the highland figures given in table 5.6 indicate a strong similarity between the development of eastern Sichuan and western Hubei land taxes—the land tax proper had multiplied several times, and the surtaxes on land had increased even more sharply. Perhaps the increase gathered speed after 1916, again similar to western Hubei. Much of the surtax was spent on the creation of militia units, officially encouraged since 1920. In the 1930s county expenses such as administration, militia, education, Guomindang (GMD) affairs, capital construction, and business operations depended almost entirely on the land surtaxes. "Some went to the provincial government and others went to the county. The latter were often several times greater than the former."[12]

Hunan

In the heartland of the Tujia and Miao minority peoples, the surtaxes were far lighter than in the riverine Han Chinese counties. Apart from this, the features of western Hunan *diding* and land surtaxes were no different from those of the other two highland areas. Cili and Linwu are the only two cases for which a more complete time series is available (table 5.10). There, as elsewhere, the increase in the surtaxes was also a gradual process that began after the end of the Yuan Shikai administration.

Thanks to Li Zhiping, more is known about the land tax payment in arrears in western Hunan (table 5.11). Take 1931, for example. The total amount of *diding* that should have been collected in the ten western Hunan counties was 121,114.51 yuan, and the payment in arrears amounted to 20,695.17 yuan or 17 percent of the total. Comparing this with the 10 percent in arrears on the plains,[13] and considering the relative inaccessibility of the highland counties, the percentage appears to be reasonable. Of course, it was a very serious matter.

Even more serious was the *diding* collected in advance or the widely and repeatedly reported *yuzheng* (tax collected in advance). Evidence of the imposition of the *yuzheng* was so overwhelming that I for one do not have the courage to regard it as either a hoax or a mirage created by left-wing propaganda. It is, of course, hard to imagine how, for instance, the Canadian government might collect the income tax a year in advance, or why it would be necessary to do so in the presence of so many other fiscal alternatives. The militarists' resort to *diding* in advance must have meant that (1) at the time of its introduction landowners were bearing a lighter tax burden than merchants and craftsmen; (2) it was neater and more efficient to collect it than to issue bonds, levy other taxes, or strike new and debased coins; (3) any resistance to paying would be futile or lead to dire consequences. In the 1920s such a circumstance could conceivably have existed in China.

According to Chen Hansheng, no fewer than eleven provinces indulged themselves in this form of land tax.[14] He does not mention Hubei, however, and I have not read a single reference to *yuzheng* in

Hubei either. The most systematic (but still very brief) treatment of *yuzheng* in Hunan is given by Angus McDonald, who says that in 1925, twenty-nine counties had collected *diding* to 1927, eighteen had collected them to 1928, five to 1929, and two to 1930.[15]

But it was in Sichuan that collection of taxes in advance was at its worst. Li Baihong stated that by 1932 the Twenty-first Army had taxed the land in its garrison region to 1962 and the Twenty-ninth Army to 1959. Liu Shiren said that the Twenty-first Army had taxed only twenty-two years in advance, and it was the greedy Twenty-ninth Army that had performed the feat of reaching to the year of 1998.[16] What had once been an annual tax rolled into a quarterly one and then a monthly one.

Perhaps a subservient people would agree to anything under duress, but what did this increase in tax frequency mean to the peasants if they were in the final analysis the bearers of the land tax? Take Fuling, a major port city in eastern Sichuan controlled by the Twenty-first Army, for example. According to my calculations, a person there paid 3.80 yuan (or 12.8 percent of his or her income) for *diding* in 1932.[17] The fixed amount of *diding* for Fuling was 5373.697 taels plus 806.054 *huohao*. In terms of the yuan, it was 10047.6. In 1932, each yuan of *diding* was actually collected at a rate of about 10 yuan. This fit in the county council's discussion on the keeping *yuzheng* for four more years in 1935. It was agreed to levy it, and the amount was estimated to be about 400,000 yuan.[18]

If the farming people in Fuling (85 percent of the total population) were to pay 400,000 yuan of *diding*, the share of each would rise from 0.12 yuan to 0.48 yuan, and consequently the total tax bill per capita would increase from 3.80 yuan to 4.16 yuan, or from 12.8 percent to 14 percent of the average per capita income of 29.40 yuan. How could this be done without provoking a popular protest or something worse?

We are told that the *yuzheng* was sometimes collected directly by sending soldiers to the payers with the advice and assistance of the tax police (*liangding*). Both soldiers and police enjoyed the work—exercising power and transforming power into pecuniary gain.[19] In the wide-open countryside, however, rich peasants and owner-cultivators could run away from home to avoid the collectors; they might not have enough cash to pay the *diding* of a household of five or more when the collectors were knocking at the door. The wailing wives would be unpleasant to deal with if the collectors had to wrest rings and bracelets from them in lieu of silver coins. I cannot document any of this, but to me it stands to reason. I remember on a summer's day in 1934 when father told me of his personal experiences as the magistrate of Yongchuan, a county west of Chongqing, in 1917. The province had just got rid of Yuan Shikai's men but came under the sway of the Yunnan and Guizhou forces. The provincial armies were growing, and a magistrate like my father was in fact a cat's paw, collecting taxes for his military boss. What the tax police collected—a heap of coins mixed with silver hair-pins, rings, bracelets, ornaments on children's headwear, babies' charms, and so forth—was so disturbing for my father to see that he sent it in together with his resignation.

Another way to collect *diding* in advance was to invite the big households (*dahu*) for a conference with tea, cakes, cigarettes, and perhaps even opium, to discuss the possibility of a loan from them with the *diding* in advance as collateral.[20] The service the host, a general no less, could perform for the wealthy guests was to control his soldiers, who could conceivably become uncontrollable. Indeed, the land tax in advance was often collected at a critical moment in a tense military situation—the county had just been taken by a victorious army, a defeated army was about to evacuate a city, or bandits or the Red Army were coming.[21]

If the second, less painful, and more efficient method was more often used, the question of the incidence of the *yuzheng* tax must be considered. Could landlords successfully shift the burden to their tenants? If not, the rich peasants and owner-cultivators, and indeed the tenants, would be better off than the landlords in this matter. One could use this as evidence to explain the phenomena of declining small landowners and prospering big military landlords who presumably could get away without paying. Even so, there remain many unanswerable questions and indeterminable possibilities.

Both methods would meet with strong resistance and end in a compromise. Inevitably, the amount originally requested would be whittled down through a process of bargaining. In my readings on this subject, I have not come across a convincing global figure of the *diding* in Sichuan paid in advance. Was it frightfully large? Take the garrison region of the Twenty-first Army of sixty-eight counties, for instance. In 1932 its total *diding* collection was reported at 9.5 million yuan.[22] This was a leap from just over 2 million in 1930, due probably to the army's recent victory against the Twenty-fourth Army under Liu

Fields terraced right to the top, on the way to Xuyong, Sichuan.

Fenghuang on the Tuo and ringed by mountains, Hunan.

A large valley floor green with late rice, Jiashang, Shaown, Fujian.

Ploughing for the second crop of rice, Hongjiaguan, Sangzhi, Hunan.

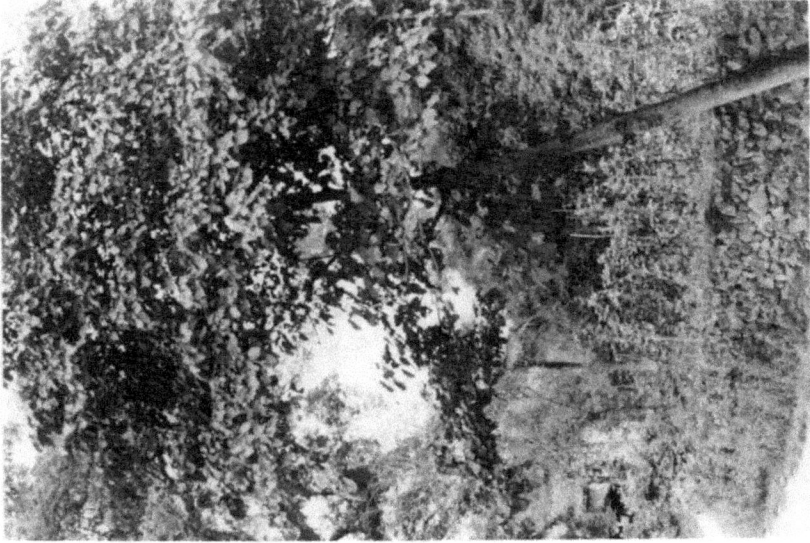

The Yongning flows into the Yangzi at Luzhou, Sichuan.

A *tong* tree.

Tea gardens, Jiashang, Shaown, Fujian.

An oil press, Fenghuang, Hunan.

Wangcun, the village where Gu Hua's *A Town Called Hibiscus* was filmed, near Dayong, Hunan.

A Miao woman in her wedding dress, Shanjiang, Fenghuang, Hunan.

Outside Guanwen—dwelling houses and summer crops, near Guliu, Sichuan.

Guanwen—a market town, near Ginlin, Sichuan.

The fortress–village, Shangjiang, near Fenghuang, Hunan.

The old fortress of Fenghuang ying, now called Huangshiqiao, near Fenghuang, Hunan.

The dry-wall houses, Shangjiang, near Fenghuang, Hunan.

The animal market at Ala, near Fenghuang, Hunan.

Wenhui. In the next year, it jumped again to nearly 16 million, and again in 1934 to 72 million.[23] Did these figures include the *diding* in advance? They probably did. From the beginning of the 1930s, the belligerent sides of the Sichuan militarists were preparing for a showdown in the name of unification. The war came in 1932, and hot on its heels the Fourth Front Red Army invaded the province. At the beginning of 1935, nearly all the Red Armies were converging on Sichuan, planning to turn it completely red. Understandably, the amount and frequency of the *yuzheng* increased by leaps and bounds.

Other Taxes

The major taxes in the miscellaneous category include the better-recorded revenues from title deeds, meat, and, for Sichuan in particular, salt. The *lijin* excise, later called the "consolidated tax" (*tongshui*), had been, right from its inauguration during the Taiping Rebellion, an exceedingly important source of income. Its importance grew with its amount of collection in the chaotic years of the rule of the militarists and civil wars; it came to be referred to as *keshui* (a nasty tax). No one in his right mind would have left behind a full record of "nasty" revenues. No full and reliable records were kept of the taxes on opium either. I shall try to give as intelligible an account of them as possible, however. Then there were lesser sources of government income—the stamp duties, brokerage tax, pawnshop tax, and so on—which were properly legislated in the fashion and through the procedure accepted at the time as well as *tanpai* (share-out) and wartime requisitions which were not.

Even in poverty-stricken western Hubei, both the deed tax and meat tax, introduced around 1915, had shown a tendency to increase, though the former did so less sharply than the latter. This observation agreed with the tendency of the same taxes in Sichuan. There the deed tax came to 2.3 million yuan for the province as a whole. In 1933 its surtaxes for the counties were 1.3 million, but in 1935 they rose to nearly 2.7 million. The meat tax was just over 1.1 million, and the surtax in 1933 amounted to 890,000, increasing to 2.3 million in 1935.[24]

Tables 5.12 and 5.13 should be compared with tables 5.15 and 5.16. The depiction of the county revenues in table 5.15 is by no means comprehensive, as I will demonstrate in detail in the next chapter. The juxtaposition of deed and meat surtaxes with those on land is meant to show their relative importance to the collecting governments. The budget figures in table 5.16 were a pipe dream and a warning to myself and those who are interested in studying the government finances of Republican China that budgetary figures were just dreams. In each italicized case, the actual revenue of 1933 far exceeded the budgeted figure for 1935, the year of Sichuan's financial reform. Needless to say, the reform did not succeed in reducing either revenue and expenditure or the people's burden.

The supply of table salt in this whole region and beyond (southern Shaanxi and Guizhou) depended on Sichuan. At the end of the Qing, the salt gabelle reaped some two million taels more annually than the land tax; it was the leading source of revenue for the provincial government. From the beginning of the Republic salt was taxed before it left the saltern. But this did not prevent other provincial authorities from imposing their dues, rates, and tolls on it. Before 1921, the governor of Hubei, in an attempt to curry the favor of the powerful Zhili clique of militarists, imported sea salt from eastern China while increasing the taxes on Sichuan salt. This policy was continued after him. For instance, in October 1928 a picul of Sichuan salt in Hubei bore 17.8 yuan of taxes; in 1931, other surtaxes amounting to 10.60 yuan a picul were added.[25] A similar development took place in western Hunan where in 1931 the local gabelle was only 1.50 yuan a picul, but the six surtaxes added up to 5.54 yuan.[26]

Take the salt produced in Pengshui, for example. In the early 1930s, it was sold at 9.50 yuan a picul in western Hubei, which included 1.50 yuan of the gabelle for the central government, 1.80 yuan of anti-Communist expenses for the provincial government, and 3.05 miscellaneous levies for the county governments concerned. In other words, 6.35 yuan was the total recorded tax burden contributing to the total cost of 9.20 yuan.[27] This agrees roughly with another report in the *Chuanyan tekan* (no. 178:3): the price of Sichuan salt comprised 25 percent in production costs, 25 percent in gabelle, 25 percent in surtaxes, 15 percent in the cost of transport, 5–6 percent in other expenses (insurance, wastage, interest), and 4–5 percent in net profit. There were of course local variations and deviations from this norm. It was reported that in Sichuan alone there were no fewer than nineteen different rates of the gabelle.[28]

As for the surtaxes, they ranged from 7.20 yuan a picul at Qianjiang to only 1.40 yuan at Shizhu and Zhongxian.[29]

The Shuiwu huikan (2a:2) aptly described the principle of taxing commodities: "When wars were frequent and military expenses enormous, many tax offices and collecting points were set up for the purpose of gathering additional revenue. The taxes were levied regardless of people's ability to pay, and their regulations were never carefully worked out. As a result, there were several taxes or collecting points in one district, and the same commodity was taxed [there] several times." Something had to be done about this; when the provincial treasurer, Jia Shiyi, was planning to reform Hubei finances, he meant to start from such port cities as Yichang and Shashi. There one found a host of levies—tea-merchant charges, fishery charges, public security charges, and so on—that had neither been recorded nor receipted. In western Hubei, there were also gentry's dues, oil-press dues, wealthy people's dues, bamboo-firewood dues, and other dues. But most of the "nasty" taxes on commodities in the form of *lijin* or the consolidated tax were imposed by the armies, militia, and even irregular armed groups. From Yichang to Laohekou on the Han in the 1930s, these people collected twenty-nine kinds of security tolls amounting to 280,000 yuan a year. At other places in western Hubei the tolls came to 2,200 yuan a month for Enshi, 1,600 for Jianshi, 800 for Laifeng, 1,600 for Lichuan, 600 for Xianfeng, and 800 for Xuanen.[30] When the Communists threatened to invade in 1931 and 1932, the security and defense tolls jumped by 8 million and 3.6 million yuan respectively.[31]

The situation in Sichuan was not much better. A few examples should suffice. To send seventy-six bales of dried rhubarb or seventy-five bales of dried *angelica senensis*, worth about 2,000 yuan, from Bikou in Pingwu along the Jialing to Chongqing in the war year of 1933, the commodity was taxed eighty-two times to the tune of 1,900 yuan.[32] To export a picul of tong oil from either Chongqing or Wanxian, the export duty proper was no more than 0.698 yuan, but it had to bear 3.532 yuan of taxes. After the financial reform of 1935, the tax burden actually went up to 3.8616 yuan.[33] To dispatch 100 yuan worth of bristles from Chengdu to Chongqing, the taxes en route were also 100 yuan.[34] All in all, the commodity excise of the 1930s had grown to be some twenty times that in 1912. It brought to the provincial government 22 million yuan, or to the garrison region government of the Twenty-first Army half of that amount. The irony was that in spite of the abolition of 120 kinds of "nasty" taxes and 50 collecting offices, even more money was being collected.[35]

Western Hunan tells the same story. Its tea had to bear four kinds of taxes on its way to Hankou in 1901. They were to multiply to twenty-six kinds in 1934.[36] The journey of timber from the mountains to Changde was even more exciting. After paying all the dues required to be paid before the timber could be shipped from its place of origin, merchants in Tongdao took a 3 percent commission; at Huitong, the next port of call, the armed escort collected 0.40 yuan for each yard of timber; at Hongjiang, the escort paid and was issued a receipt for stamp duties at the rate of 0.20 yuan for every 100 yuan of timber, an additional brokerage tax of 0.12–0.14 yuan, a landing charge of an indefinite amount, and two lots of militia dues at 1–2 percent each; the same stamp duties were repeated at Tuokou and Qianyang, but mercifully the escort fee, 0.50 for a yard of timber, was repeated only at Qianyang; further down the Yuan, more escort fees were required at Tantou, Chenxi, and all the way to Changde, at about 1 yuan each time; the stamp duties were repeated at all the port cities to Changde.[37] These taxes on commodities were often increased, especially along the upper reaches of the Li at Yongshun, Sangzhi, and Dayong. They were collected by both the civilian and military authorities for reconstruction, for maintaining a semblance of law and order, and for the survival of local administration and local armed forces.[38]

What was called *tanpai* in this region was not the *tankuan* of North China [39] It was not a sharing-out of the deficit of a county or a garrison region; it was a hybrid of tax and requisition, collecting money, goods, and labor service. It had neither a name nor a set of regulations, but was levied by any authority for any amount and at any frequency: it was usually needed in a hurry. For instance, it was imposed by the itinerant armies from Yunnan, Guangxi, and Sichuan that passed through western Hunan at different times.[40] Since it was an army taking things directly from the people in a hurry, the burden of it fell expectedly unequally on the different classes of the rural population. In Langzhong, northern Sichuan, landowners bore 8.8 percent of the tax; owner-cultivators, 48 percent; part-owners, 26.6 percent; tenants, 15.8 percent; and others, 0.8 percent.[41] This may well have been a general pattern throughout the mountain region. (Table 5.17 affords a glimpse of the share outs in the county of Fengdu.)

Now we come to probably the most lucrative source of government revenue, opium. Using the cost-of-production approach, an actual tax on the drug collected in Fuling in 1932 (434.80 yuan a picul), and an estimated annual output of opium in Sichuan (200,000 piculs), I came up with the impressive figure of 86,960,000 yuan of tax revenue per annum. Of this the garrison regions took about 60 million and the county government the rest. My estimates can be further strengthened by the tax revenues from opium in Fuling—in 1932, 775,200 yuan; in 1933, 11,035,046; and in 1934, 10,489,000.[42] The 1932 figure is arguably the best and most reliable set of county financial figures I have seen in my research for this study. The year was followed by two more of intensive campaigns against the Communists. The background of a worsening war situation makes the figures of 1933 and 1934 believable.

Fuling was a large and wealthy city in the Twenty-first Army garrison region. My view is that the amount for the whole garrison region should be well over 30 million yuan, leaving the rest, over 20 million, for the other garrison regions and their leaders to share. Having defeated the Twenty-fourth Army in 1932, the Twenty-first Army was supreme in Sichuan, which was on its way to reunification. It should have had the lion's share of this and other taxes, and its total income from the drug should of course have been far larger than that of Fuling.

Apart from Sichuan, western Hubei was reported to have an income from opium of about 300,000 yuan a month in 1923. This was considerably more than the opium tax revenue at Yichang in the same year and about 25 percent of the total opium tax for the whole province in 1924.[43] These figures were obviously too low. For western Hunan we have no figures at all. It was, however, the passageway for Yunnan and Guizhou opium to reach Changde or Changsha and Wuhan. The local warlord, Chen Quzhen, depended on opium and on the issuing of irredeemable bank notes to maintain his army and his power.[44]

Bonds and Currencies

Involuntary loans were first made in China in the second century, but voluntary domestic loans date back no further than the 1890s.[45] It was considered shameful for the government to borrow from the people or, even worse, from foreigners, and yet by the time of the European war, central and local government bonds came to be accepted as a normal way of raising money. In the mountain counties of western Hubei, however, I have found no records of bond issuing up to 1934. Although the provincial government of the 1920s and 1930s borrowed over twenty million yuan, it is not known how much of that came from western Hubei.[46] The general impression is that the sale of government bonds there did not make much headway.

In western Hunan the situation was very different. Local armed forces, both sedentary and itinerant, seem to have been more successful than those in control of the provincial government in raising loans. This was perhaps due to the compulsory nature of the borrowing. For instance, when the Yunnan Army was in Chenxi, it demanded a "loan."[47] Throughout the 1920s, local troops in Chenxi, Chengbu, and other counties made similar demands, from a few thousand to a few hundred thousand yuan from the well-to-do.[48]

Eastern Sichuan was different again, not only in reversing the situation in western Hubei, but in making both voluntary and involuntary loans an impressive success. The loans raised in the 1920s affected the plains around Chengdu; those of the 1930s were chiefly borne by eastern and northeastern Sichuan. There were pressing reasons for the success of the garrison region headquarters of the Twenty-first Army in the 1930s. First, the floods and the Japanese occupation of Manchuria in 1931 reduced the other revenues of the region, such as land taxes and the export duties on herbal medicine; second the 1932 war of provincial unification did the same. Therefore, from 1932 to 1935, the army issued fifteen kinds of bonds, secured on the *diding*, salt gabelle, and other taxes, amounting to some 54 million yuan.[49] By the end of 1934, 43.5 million yuan was still outstanding.

In the wake of the Twenty-first Army's defeat of the Twenty-fourth Army at the battle of Chengdu, the Fourth Front Red Army invaded Sichuan, necessitating further issuance of bonds for the war against the Communists and to consolidate existing loans. From 1933 to 1935 some 116.75 million yuan of bonds were sold for the war and 210 million for the consolidation, much of which was also spent on fighting the Communists.[50]

Inflation is the easiest but not the fairest way of defraying government expenses, but from the very beginning of the Qing dynasty a restrictive, almost deflationary monetary policy was established, purposely to avoid the mistakes of the previous dynasty. The internal rebellions and the external war from the 1850s to the 1870s put this tradition through its severest test. To pay for the mounting military needs, central and local governments had to resort to currency debasement and the issuance of paper money. Although in the last years of the dynasty the paper currency was largely redeemed, the debasement led to a messy situation that grew worse after the founding of the Republic.

In the mid-1890s Hubei decided to issue silver coins, to supplement and eventually to replace the *sycee* (tael), and paper notes in terms of the copper cash (*wen*). At the end of the decade it began to circulate another paper currency, silver-dollar bills. Both were fairly successful until the 1911 Revolution. At that time, the copper-cash notes in circulation amounted to 17 million yuan, and the silver-dollar bills to 1.6 million. They still commanded a great deal of respect. The next year saw a 10 percent fall in the market value of the copper-cash notes, which by 1926 were worth only 17 percent of their face values.[51] Meanwhile, the silver dollars remained strong as long as the new issues bore President Yuan Shikai's portrait. The other portraits, Xu Shichang and Sun Yat-sen, that followed in 1921 and 1933 were less respected by the market. There were also many other types of silver dollars from neighboring provinces and foreign countries.[52]

As the dust of the Northern Expedition settled, the Bank of China made an attempt to recall the much devalued notes and bills. Hubei, however, waited until the monetary reorganization of 1935. In the western mountain region of the province, local army commanders and merchants issued their own paper currency and minted their own copper coins. The reorganization of 1935 went a long way toward unifying the standard money, the dollar bill issued by the central banks. For a long time to come, the token money remained the same, for there was a dire shortage of it.[53]

Sichuan went through worse monetary chaos than Hubei. It also began to mint silver and copper coins in the mid-1890s, but its first issue of paper currency took place after the 1911 Revolution. These native monies, together fifteen types of copper cash and twenty-four types of silver coins, of different grades of fineness and different market values, from other provinces and countries, represented inflation through devaluation and debasement. Shroffery was not only a necessary trade but also an intricate study.

From 1901 to 1928, the provincial mint in Chengdu had cast 93,190,079 yuan of silver dollars and 193,138,030,600 wen of hundred-wen copper coins.[54] This ushered in a copper inflation from around the par of 1,000 wen to the dollar to nearly 2,000 wen in 1915, 4,500 wen in 1925, and 28,400 wen in 1935.[55]

From 1912 to 1915 the provincial government had to rely on "army notes," some fifteen million yuan worth, issued by the hurriedly established Bank of Sichuan. A change in the banking system in 1915 led to a corresponding change in the paper currency. The government recalled the army notes and replaced them with ten million yuan of bank notes. Another systemic change was accompanied by another issue in 1923. By the early 1930s the Bank of China, with its peerless credit, began to put its notes into circulation together with those of fifteen government and private banks in Sichuan.[56] I do not know how many of these notes were issued or what percentage of them was recalled. The situation was made even more confused with the minting and printing of money by garrison region commanders, other army officers, and local chambers of commerce in the highland and elsewhere in the province. One's impression is that the people of these three provinces, especially those on the highland, were not used to paper currency and tended to distrust it. It was largely their resistance that prevented the inflationary situation from growing out of control.[57]

Even so, the monetary chaos in Sichuan was far worse than in Hubei and Hunan, crying out for urgent remedies that did not come until the general reorganization of 1935.[58] As in Hubei and Hunan, the reorganization initially established a measure of unity of the standard money. One yuan of the new bank note (*fabi*) actually commanded one silver dollar. But the token monies of lesser face values were left as they had been. In 1936, new token monies of a total value of fifty million yuan were put in circulation. That meant only one yuan's worth for each person. The token money crisis and confusion thus continued in the highland counties.[59]

Table 5.1

Percentage Changes in the Land Tax Proper, Hubei (*diding*) (1931 = 100)

Year	Paddy fields	Dry fields	Dry land
1912	64	79	81
1932	110	108	102
1933	114	109	102
1934	116	109	108

Sources: Zhongguo nongcun, 1/7, 35–41, and several other publications.

Table 5.2

Land Surtaxes as Percentage of the Land Tax Proper, Hubei (*diding* = 100)

Year	Paddy fields	Dry fields	Dry land
1912	64	69	90
1931	95	91	99
1932	112	108	114
1933	124	119	116

Sources: Nongqing baogao, 1/11, 32, and other publications.

Table 5.3

Land Tax Proper, West Hubei

| Location | End of Qing | | 1915 | | 1935 | |
	Quota	Collected amount (taels)	Quota	Collected amount (taels)	Quota	Collected amount (yuan)
Badong	925.4	1848.3	818.2	818.2	19,200	9,800
Baokang	1,091.4	1,091.4	1,091.4	1091.4	9,700	6,800
Enshi	617.7	627.7	1,870.7	555.9	24,500	22,000
Fangxian	2,923.5	4,543.2	2,633.7	2,633.7	33,300	14,300
Hefeng	304.5	551.2	305.8	284.9	8,800	3,700
Jianshi	1,059.1	1,564.6	1,059.1	954.2	28,400	11,700
Laifeng	493	493	144.4	49	12,800	4,700
Lichuan	382.4	534.4	382.4	346.3	20,200	13,800
Wufeng			192.5	175.7	2,200	2,300
Xianfeng	379.7	862.4	440.3	343.4	20,000	12,500
Xuanen	130.5	130.5	117.6	117.6	20,000	19,700
Yunxi	1,935.6	1,935.6	1,735.6	1,743.8	24,000	16,400
Yunxian	7,624.7	4,605.7	4,155.7	4,167.4	36,000	27,000
Zhushan	1,747.3	3,683.6	1,574.7	1,574.7	15,800	14,100
Zhuxi	1,741.4	1,185.8	1,068.3	1,068.3	18,000	11,900
Zigui	857.5	891.8	706.9	711.6	5,000	5,100
Average percentage collected	106%		89%		66%	

Land Surtaxes as Percentage of the Land Tax Proper, West Hubei

Location	1932	1935	1936
Badong	1,918.18	128.57	237.5
Baokang	3,138.46	—	—
Enshi	142.37	111.11	244.44
Fangxian	29.79	87.5	264.25
Hefeng	150	100	200
Jianshi	—	128.57	126.52
Laifeng	150	111.11	224.99
Lichuan	8,600	106.67	271.42
Wufeng	50	50	270
Xianfeng	—	106.67	190.9
Xuanen	25	100	177.27
Yunxi	100.5	117.65	264.29
Yunxian	356.48	115.38	264.28
Zhushan	102.27	125	264.28
Zhuxi	92	123.07	264.28
Zigui	1,160	166.67	333.35
Average		111.86%	239.8%

Sources: Hubei caizheng jilue (1917, 2–6); *Hubei quansheng didingkao*, ms., n.d.; *Hubei quansheng zhouzian*, ms., n.d.; *Hubei tongzhi* (1921), and other relevant local gazetteers; *Wuhan ribao*, November 16, 1935; *Hubei nianjian* (1936, 510–11, 516–17); *Nongcun fuxingweiyuanhui huibao* (1934, 140–42); *Xu Zhengxue* (1934

Table 5.4

Percentage Changes in the Land Tax Proper, Sichuan (1931=100)

Year	Paddy fields	Dry fields	Dry land
1912	53	69	63
1932	120	131	127
1933	123	133	128
1934	130	148	107

Source: Nonqing baogao, 1/11, 3, and other publications.

Table 5.5

Land Surtaxes as Percentage of the Land Tax Proper, Sichuan

Year	Paddy fields	Dry fields	Dry land
1912	65	77	85
1931	108	111	115
1932	123	115	114
1933	113	110	102

Sources: Nongqing baogao, 1/11, 3, and other publications.

Table 5.6

Actual Collection and Accompanied Surtaxes to Each Tael of Land Tax Proper, Eastern Sichuan (yuan)

County	Date	Actual amount collected	Surtaxes
Fengdu	Jan. 1934	15.39	33.7
Fengjie	1930	8.62	12.28
	Dec. 1932	8.62	16.81
	Jan. 1934	8.62	23.08
	July 1935	8.62	32.00
Fuling	Jan. 1934	16.64	28.6
Nanchuan	Jan. 1934	19.22	38.29
Shizhu	Jan. 1934	18.43	76.51
Wanxian	June 1933	8.82	49.97
	Jan. 1934	20.98	49.97
Zhongxian	Jan. 1934	20.57	48.07

Sources: Sichuan yuebao, 2/7, 1; 4/5, 48; 5/1, 43–4; 6/6, 133; *Shenbao yuekan*, July 15, 1933, 20; 4/5, 48; *Zhongguo jingji*, 2/8, 3; *Xinshubao*, July 14, 1935; Lu Pingdeng (1936, 463–64; Zhang Xiaomei (1938, C144).

Table 5.7

Percentage Changes in the Land Tax Proper, Hunan (1931 = 100)

Year	Paddy field	Dry fields	Dry land
1912	47	58	53
1932	102	108	113
1933	108	111	125
1934	111	117	126

Source: Nongqing baogao, 1/12, 4; 7/4, 49, and other publications.

Table 5.8

Land Surtaxes as Percentage of Diding, Hunan

Year	Paddy field	Dry fields	Dry land
1912	90	82	84
1931	163	126	113
1932	161	131	113
1933	158	158	119

Sources: Nongqing baogao, 1/12, 4; 7/4, 49, and other publications.

Table 5.9

Land Surtaxes as Percentage of Diding, West Hunan

Location	1931	1932
Baojing	66	80
Chenxi	267	273
Cili	994	567
Dayong	112	158
Fenghuang	28	27
Longshan	42	99
Luxi	254	292
Mayang	77	202
Sangzhi	40	40
Shimen	457	459
Yongshun	288	376

Source: Li Zhiping (1934, 5548–55).

Table 5.10

Diding and Land Surtaxes, Cili and Linwu

Year	Cili	Linwu
End of Qing (diding + huohao)	8,610.4 taels	11,519.2 taels
1914 (surtaxes)	3,099.7 yuan	—
1921 (surtaxes)	8,610.3 yuan	—
1932 (surtaxes)	22,731.3 yuan	23,385.7 yuan

Sources: Cili xianzhi, ch. 8, 1–5; *Dongfang zazhi,* 31/14, 100; *Guiyang zhouzhi,* ch. 5, 7; *Zhongguo nongcun,* 1/8, 77–78; and *Zhongguo jingji,* 2/8, 3.

Table 5.11

Land Tax Payment in Arrears, Western Hunan

Location	1930	1931	1932
Baojing	192.27	312.36	119.30
Chenxi	8,460.89	8,907.08	10,406.12
Cili	—	—	651.01
Dayong	3,077.08	3,239.20	4,132.89
Fenghuang	60.45	84.44	134.97
Longshan	171.50	215.91	226.92
Luxi	1,724.73	1,935.27	2,696.27
Mayang	2302.05	2,976.96	3,659.62
Sangzhi	439.98	500.00	854.68
Shimen	—	1,079.84	886.68
Yongshun	1,248.28	1,444.11	1,819.91

Source: Li Zhiping (1934, 5656–58).

Table 5.12

Deed Tax and Surtaxes, Western Hubei (yuan)

Location	1915	July 1934–June 1935
Badong	3,890	3,211
Baokang	—	2,236
Enshi	7,065	15,212
Fangxian	4,952	9,425
Hefeng	887	641
Jianshi	3,428	2,890
Laifeng	2,073	4,288
Lichuan	8,071	9,020
Wufeng	784	2,890
Xianfeng	1,479	3,956
Xuanen	1,046	7,973
Yunxi	4,540	13,159
Yunxian	9,873	16,113
Zhushan	3,454	11,664
Zhuxi	6,854	17,929
Zigui	3,476	10,397

Sources: Hubei caizheng jilue (1917, 44–45); *Wuhan ribao*, November 18, 1935.

Table 5.13

Meat Tax, Western Hubei (yuan)

Location	July 1914–June 1916	1935
Badong	1,103	2,000
Baokang	—	3,400
Enshi	400	4,900
Fangxian	1,076	4,000
Hefeng	1,000	1,400
Jianshi	639	5,300
Laifeng	485	1,800
Lichuan	2,814	2,700
Wufeng	—	1,600
Xianfeng	—	200
Xuanen	416	2,000
Yunxi	3,017	2,800
Yunxian	2,180	2,100
Zhushan	854	2,300
Zhuxi	785	2,400
Zigui	432	1,800

Sources: Hubei caizheng jilue (1917, 58–61); *Hubei nianjian* (1937, 496–99).

Table 5.14

Salt Gabelle, Eastern Sichuan (yuan)

Location	1920	1921	1922	1923	1924	1925	1926	1927	1928	1929
Fengjie	41,624	36,054	44,454	45,191	38,106	42,277	37,718	36,381	36,159	32,806
Pengshui	44,480	50,120	48,177	51,275	51,777	44,998	41,792	39,042	39,724	38,325
Wuxi*	128,468	136,860	151,882	188,479	193,427	189,656	144,977	113,089	22,776	73,128
Yunyang	242,685	267,900	262,568	293,644	395,284	332,910	340,679	351,351	359,586	367,055
Zhongxian	3,382	3,066	3,117	3,087	3,159	5,029	5,115	5,067	6,089	5,514

Sources: Chuannan gequ yanchang, nos. 13–15; *Yanwu gongbao*, no. 25, 166–68.
*The Daning saltern.

Table 5.15

Revenues of East Sichuan Counties in the Garrison Region of the Twenty-first Army, 1933 (yuan)

Location	Land surtax	Deed surtax	Meat surtax	Others	Total
Fengdu	80,000	43,332	12,093	34,360	169,785
Fengjie	54,173	18,276	40,034	34,004	146,487
Fuling	150,937	48,302	8,000	71,370	278,609
Pengshui	53,000	2,400	4,250	6,585	66,235
Qianjiang	12,070	3,233	576	14,961	30,840
Shizhu	39,988	11,705	4,500	11,437	67,630
Wanxian	178,438	51,760	30,842	78,349	345,389
Wushan	47,807	5,815	11,426	20,037	85,085
Wuxi	71,503	5,396	10,342	31,503	118,744
Xiushan	101,461	990	6,980	3,462	112,893
Youyang	12,600	4,822	8,652	42,385	68,459
Yunyang	138,600	16,898	12,678	23,909	192,085
Zhongxian	167,865	15,994	10,692	33,534	227,585

Sources: Sichuan yuebao, 5/2; *Zhengwu yuekan*, no. 4; Zhang Xiaomei (1938, C143ff.)

Table 5.16

County Budgets, East Sichuan, 1935 (yuan)

Location	Land surtax	Deed surtax	Meat surtax	Other	Total
Bazhong	23,579	789	26,350	13,396	64,123
Chengkou	19,237	978	480	4,877	25,570
Fengdu	49,874	58,920	29,176	8,939	146,909
Fengjie	9,771	14,212	22,367	9,626	55,976
Fuling	62,582	75,500	41,100	51,868	204,485
Guangyuan	71,427	3,819	290	9,164	84,700
Nanjiang	20,920	—	5,000	1,725	27,656
Pengshui	38,669	2,099	1,600	13,939	56,307
Tongjiang	32,780	600	2,700	24,440	60,520
Wanyuan	42,187	2,880	5,700	1,952	52,719
Wushan	23,191	4,290	15,140	11,702	54,323
Wuxi	40,000	6,764	11,574	10,712	69,050
Xiushan	44,886	2,160	10,560	3,951	61,557
Yunyang	75,000	13,300	17,823	13,250	119,372
Zhaohua	30,023	71	455	7,443	37,992
Zhongxian	89,715	20,320	6,461	30,360	146,855

Source: Jingji zazhi, 1/1, 110; Zhang Xiaomei (1938, C21–26).
Note: Italicized counties may be compared with their actual revenues in 1933 in the table 5.16.

Table 5.17

Shareouts of Taxes, Fengdu County

Year	Use	Share (yuan)
1919	Commander Huang collected	30,000
1920	Commander Huang collected	30,000
1921	Military aid to Hubei	30,000
1922	To send off Sixth Mixed Brigade	10,000
1923	Division commander Yang	30,000
	Division commander Yang	76,000
	Commander of Seventieth Division	35,000
	Various army units	10,000
	Zhou Regiment of Second Division.	5,000
	Pacification Officer Li	30,000
1924	Rice for Sichuan armies	50,000
	Land tax in advance, 1926	35,000
	Land tax in advance, 1927	35,000
	Rice for Bai Brigade	40,000
	Stamp duties for Commander Yang	10,000
	Passing through of Wei Division	1,000
	Bai Brigade	4,000

Source: Sichuansheng yihui huikan, no. 10, 7–8.
Note: Four regular items that should not have been included in this table are omitted.

6
TRIBUTE MONEY (II)

THUS FAR I have delineated the general trends and patterns of the highland governments' revenues. The major proper taxes—on land, deeds, meat, and brokerages, the consolidated tax, and the stamp duties—went to the provincial and regional treasuries while the bulk of their surtaxes remained in the hands of the counties that had collected them. Most of the bonds and currencies were issued by the provincial government through its authorized banks. The income from all items had been increasing, but the overwhelming impression one has is that they increased much more moderately than the land tax in advance, opium taxes, and commodity taxes of the traditional *lijin* type, which people referred to as "the nasty taxes." These taxes were collected either by the military authorities themselves or by county government agencies on their behalf. They were chiefly for war and for the maintenance of the war machine. Their spectacular rise was *pari passu* with the rise in defense needs at the garrison region level. Since these monies were collected for neither the provincial nor the county government, and often not even collected by them, they did not appear in their records. The budgets and returns of these governments could be worked out as if no such taxes had ever been imposed. Since the civilian governments could not control the military, they might as well leave behind a clean and laundered book.

In this chapter, I shall try to establish the relationship between the increases in revenue and in military expenditures, especially after 1928 when the system of garrison regions in Sichuan reached its maturity. This date does not imply in any sense that the Northern Expedition commanded by Chiang Kai-shek had caused the military situation in this highland to deteriorate. That, in any case, is not my concern. The increase in the defense budgets at all levels had been a nationwide phenomenon since the founding of the Republic, especially after the demise of Yuan Shikai. The three buffer provinces under consideration were no exception (see table 6.1).

Throughout the period from 1913 to 1936, the percentage of the military budget in the total expenditures of the central government showed little fluctuation.[1] As Japanese aggression intensified side by side with the anti-Communist campaigns, the defense share incomprehensibly fell from 48.5 percent of the total budget in 1933 to only 32.2 percent in 1936. One thing was plain in the Nanjing budget: it did not include the provinces' military expenditures, aside from the regular needs of the units of the "National Army" (*guojun*) stationed in the provinces and probably grants-in-aid in times of military emergency.

Equally plain is that the provincial defense expenses of Sichuan, as shown in table 6.2, did not include those of the garrison regions, as shown in table 6.3. The provincial government paid for the regular needs of the units it had recognized. Should this be insufficient, as it often was, the garrison region and other commanding officers had to fend for themselves. In other words, only a small part of the provincial defense expenditure was covered by the central government and, likewise, only a small part of the garrison region needs was cared for by the province. What colonels and captains took from the people was never recorded anywhere.

One may object to my using the total revenue of the Twenty-first Army to compare with only the defense expenditure of the province (fig. 6.1). In fact, as I have indicated before, this and other garrison regions were created for handling military finances and other military affairs. The Nongcun Fuxing Weiyuanhui reported in its bulletin that of the army's total expenditures in 1933, only 1.2 percent was on administration, while the rest was on defense proper and on servicing debts incurred because of defense.[2] But tables 6.2 and 6.3 show only the relationship between the province and the Twenty-first Army. Admittedly, the Twenty-first was one of the two most powerful armies in Sichuan from 1928 onward, the other being the Twenty-fourth Army. Nonetheless, when the two giants, Uncle Liu Wenhui of the Twenty-fourth Army and Nephew Liu Xiang of the Twenty-first Army, fought for hegemony in 1932, the notable garrison regions in the province's 166 counties were as follows:[3]

Liu Wenhui, 24th Army (7 divisions, 12 brigades), in Chengdu, 81 counties

Liu Xiang, 21st Army (6 divisions, 46 regiments, planes, armored cars, and frigates), in Chongqing, 27 counties

Figure 6.1. **Sichuan Provincial Defense Expenses and the Revenue of the Twenty-first Army**

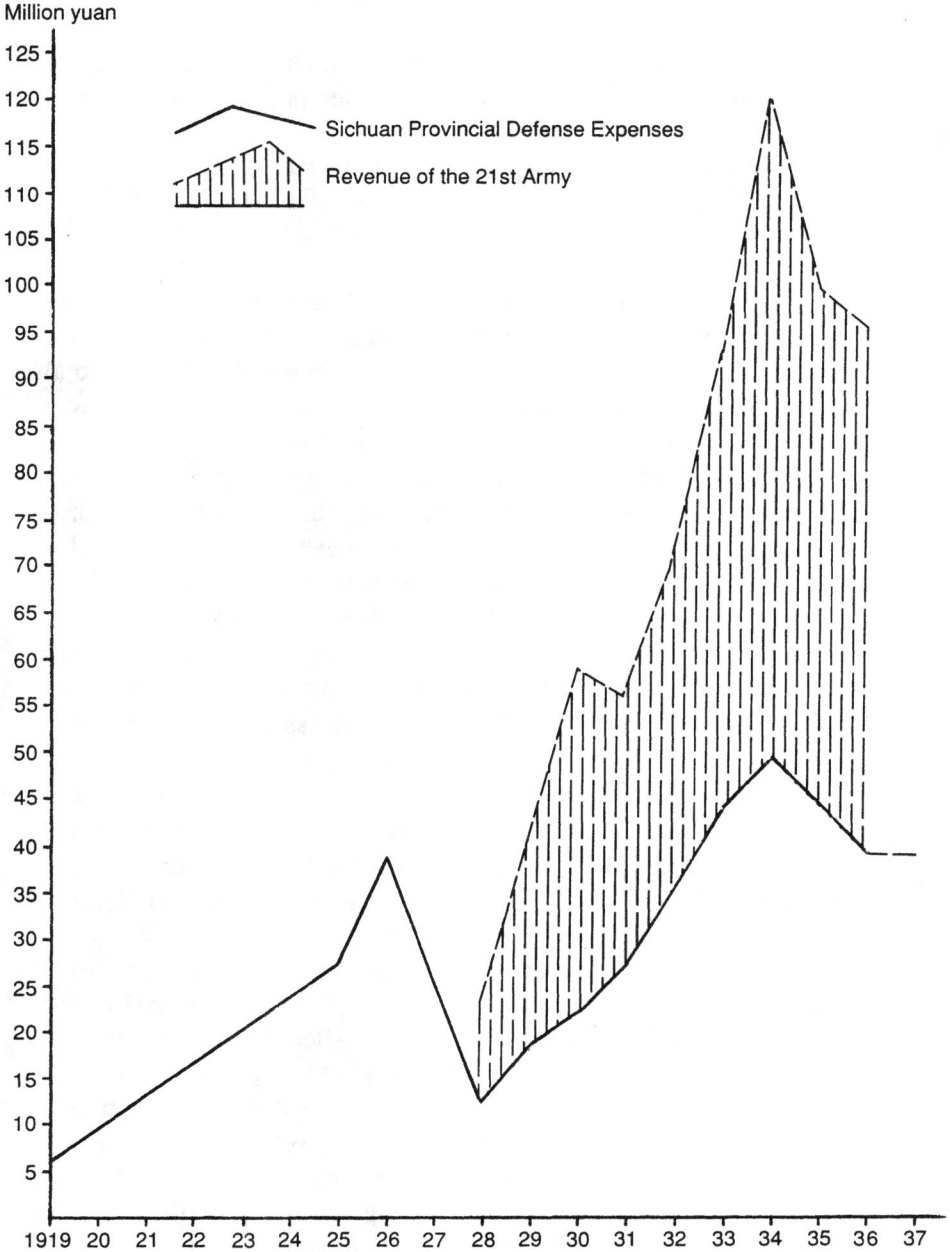

Tian Songyao, 29th Army (4 divisions, 4 brigades), in Santai, 26 counties

Deng Xihou, 28th Army (2 divisions, 10 mixed brigades), in Chengdu, 16 counties

Yang Sen, 20th Army (4 mixed brigades), in Guangan, 4 counties

Liu Cunhou, 23d Army (2 divisions, 2 mixed brigades), in Daxian, 4 counties

Li Jiayu, Sichuan Border Defense Commander (1 division, 5 brigades), in Pengan

Luo Zezhou, 23d Division (2 brigades), in Wusheng

Their strengths and their financial needs are variously assessed. The *Shenbao yuekan* estimated that some 500,000 men were involved, an average cost of ten yuan per person per month, for a total expenditure of 60 million yuan per year.[4] It was said that in the war of unification of 1932, some 120,000 soldiers were either killed or missing.[5] By 1935, however, after the campaigns against the Communists in northern and southern Sichuan, the strength of the provincial army had recovered to 540,000 men.[6] According to tables 6.2 and 6.3, the total expenditure on defense of the province and the Twenty-first Army was already over 60 million yuan in 1932. It would be too conservative to assume that either the Twenty-fourth Army or the weaker armies combined had spent less than the Twenty-first Army in 1932. A reasonable guess is that the province and its garrison regions had thrown no less than 120 million yuan into the war of unification. Immediately following this was the campaign against the Communists. Sichuan military expenses continued to mount: assuming that the Sichuan population in the early 1930s was about fifty million, one may assume that per capita defense expenses were 2.40 yuan per annum.

Far less is known about the army strengths and defense expenses in Hubei and Hunan, and practically nothing about the finances of the western Hubei and Hunan garrison regions. After the 1911 Revolution, Hubei embarked at once on a drastic disarmament program (see table 6.4). Strategically and economically crucial to whomever was in control of the central government, Hubei had always had more National Army units than the other two provinces under discussion. For instance, at least two divisions and four brigades of the northern armies and one division and one brigade of the southern armies were stationed there in 1917. In 1924, side by side with the provincial troops, there were five divisions and one brigade of the northern armies.[7] The northern or "national" units received their pay partly from the central government; the miscellaneous units roaming the western hills were not regularly maintained by any government at all. Whatever these expatriate armies took from the inhabitants was not recorded. The provincial government defense budgets and returns were kept neat and trim, but the actual expenses were far larger.

By the time Yuan Shikai's monarchical bubble was pricked in 1916, Hunan had four divisions of its own. In addition there were also northern units partly paid for by Beijing, as well as the irregulars who fended for themselves.[8] Following the expulsion of the prosouthern Governor Tan Yankai in 1920, the new strongman, Zhao Hengti, maintained at least four provincial divisions of unequal strength up to 1925.[9] But there were other beasts in the jungle—expatriate armies from neighboring provinces, the vengeful Tan and his southern troops, and the units under the garrison commanders. The total military strength of the province was estimated at thirty-four thousand by the *Huazi ribao* of Hong Kong, and at fifty thousand by the local historians who compiled the *Hunan jinbainian dashi jishu*.[10] Neither of these two figures could possibly include forces other than Zhao's provincial troops. Therefore, the two returns on defense expenses given by Jia Shiyi were much too low.

It may be useful at this juncture to remember a few landmarks in the military history of these three provinces. In all three, local army expansion came during the decline and after the fall of Yuan Shikai. In Hubei, the struggle to overthrow Governor Wang Zhanyuan was accompanied by the invasion of the northern army under Wu Peifu and troops from Sichuan and Hunan in 1921. The struggle to overthrow Wu and his henchman, Xiao Yaonan, ushered in the Northern Expedition, which meant expansion of Hubei armed forces as well as of the provincial defense budget. The fluid situation did not congeal until 1930. In Sichuan, Xiong Kewu made two failed endeavors at unifying the province in 1923, but it was Liu Xiang who succeeded in 1932. In the process, both the armies and their expenses increased. The unfortunate coincidence of unification and the Communist invasion continued the relentless demands on the province's resources. The various armies and their financial needs rose even higher when the war against Japan broke out in July 1937. In Hunan, the northern governor combined his own troops with those of Wu Peifu and Feng Yuxiang. Their with-drawal and expulsion in 1920 marked the coming of age of the provin-cial army, though Hunan continued to be harassed by expatriate armies. The provincial army itself had to be enlarged to cope with the intruders and irregulars. It was partly due to this that the Northern Expedition cut through the province to change the military situation. As in Hubei, stabilization did not arrive until late in 1930. Meanwhile, the defense expenditures of these provinces grew, eventually to the enormity of the 1930s.

To protect against bandits or against regular troops, to prey on the ordinary people for the benefit of the local elites, or to ward off the Communists, irregular troops below the garrison region were often used. There was, however, organizational as well as behavioral ambi-guity between them and the regular army, on the one hand, and be-tween them and the bandits on the other. A market town or village may have carefully considered the functional needs for creating a company of militia; it simply could not prevent them from harming its own interests.

In western Hunan the organization of militia seems to have come in two waves—in 1917 for defense against bandits and in 1927 for deal-ing with the Communists.[11] The first wave had the support of both local gentry and military leaders (Zhang Xueji, Tian Yingzhao, and later Cai Juyou). At the height of its development, the militia units of eleven counties were organized in four sections for training. Neverthe-less, they were not very effective.[12] With probably the same support, the second wave was believed to be about fifty thousand strong, equipped with forty-five thousand guns.[13] Hubei had about as many and cost the province some eight million yuan a year, according to the *Wuhan ribao*, of June 7 and 8, 1933. The sum of 160 yuan per militia-man per annum was 40 yuan more than the estimated cost of keeping a soldier.[14] This was obviously too high. In the first place, a militiaman ate and slept at home; second, he was less well equipped than a private soldier. I believe that 10–12 yuan would be a reasonable estimate of the cost of having a militiaman for a year. The militia force in Hubei should have cost 600,000 yuan a year instead of eight million. The units in western Hubei seem to have been particularly bad, according to the report of Xu Yuanquan, the field commander who conducted the campaign against the Red Army in the Hong Lake area.[15] Sichuan was said to have nearly ten times more militia units than either Hubei or

Hunan, just as Sichuan had ten times more soldiers.[16] Those that were organized in the 1920s aimed at defending villages and towns against marauding soldiers.[17] Those that came into existence in the 1930s tried to cope with the Communist threat. In the border regions these threats came thick and fast, and therefore militia leagues (*liantuan*) were formed between Sichuan and its neighbors after the devastation of the Communists.[18] Scattered reports indicate that they received regular pay from county governments as well as from the local gentry, and that they used their power to exact revenues from other available sources.[19] If each militia member cost roughly the same throughout the region, then the 600,000 yuan for maintaining some fifty thousand members in Hubei in the 1930s may be applied to Hunan. The ten times greater strength in Sichuan may have cost ten times as much. None of these figures is meant to be precise; they serve only to give an impression of the size of the defense expenditure. It may be concluded that much of the prosperity and additional income generated in the forty years between the Japanese wars was squandered in continuous civil wars. This is a point that deserves the most serious attention of historians of the Republican period.

Turning to government finances at the county level and the actual tax burden of the people, I can piece together the financial returns of only five counties: three in the highland region and two adjacent to it. Tables 6.5, 6.6, and 6.8 indicate clearly how different the tax systems were from county to county and how many taxes, dues, fees were collected. Their complexity contrasts sharply with the oversimplicity of tables 6.7, 6.9, and 6.10. The complexity does not mean comprehensiveness, however. None of the six tables refers to land tax in advance (perhaps an indication that it was not collected by the county tax agencies) or to the taxes earmarked for the central government (perhaps not collected by the county agencies either). Taxes on opium, opium dens, and opium addicts are conspicuous by their absence from the simpler tables. Also absent are the excise taxes on commodities in transit, the so-called nasty taxes, which were collected by the military authorities themselves. Historians would do well to notice these important omissions.

The most complete and reliable report is the one on Fuling, given in table 6.5. In order of importance, the taxes on land yielded 1,512,038 yuan (40.2 percent); on opium 775,200 (20.6 percent); on commodities 553,040 (14.7 percent); on salt 448,940 (11.9 percent); and the rest,

12.6 percent. Though the table is a report on revenues, it also provides some information on expenditures. The share of defense and security was no less than 28 percent, a high percentage of which was the county's contribution to the budget of the Twenty-first Army garrison region. The share on education and library was a miserly 2.3 percent. Fuling had 986,290 people, each of whom paid 3.80 yuan of taxes or 12.8 percent of their income.[20] Of this amount, 0.79 yuan came from opium, and 1.10 yuan went to defray military expenses.

Adding opium taxes, land tax in advance, *lijin*-type excise taxes, bonds and inflation, and requisition and corvée duties, the figure of 2.40 yuan as contribution of each Sichuan resident to the war in 1932 and the subsequent anti-Communist years was not, after all, outrageously high. Hubei and Hunan were more fortunate in this respect than Sichuan. Taking the highland as a whole, the governments' ability to mobilize financial and material resources for war and administration as well as for an occasional development project should be far higher than 3 or 4 percent of the people's average income; it was more likely to be 10 percent or more, when the omissions are considered also.

In chapter 3, I estimated that from 1912 to 1937 the two chief contributors to the prosperity of the highland region—tong oil and opium—had given eastern Sichuan nearly 203 million yuan, western Hubei 61 million, and western Hunan 22.5 million. Counting all the other benefits, the total additional income should have been approximately 522 million. One would do well to remember that the initial investment of the Hanyang Steel Works was under six million taels and that of the textile factory in Hankou was only five million.[21] Hunan wanted a railway to cut through the Xiang Valley, which, according to an early plan, needed only two million taels annually for five years to have the Hankou-Xiangtan section built.[22] Sichuan, too, dreamed of a railway running from Chengdu via Chongqing to Hankou. The Hunan-Guangdong line did not become a reality until September 1, 1936; the Sichuan project lingered until after the Communist revolution in 1949. These were basic industrial projects. If constructed, the railways, supported by networks of motorways, would have overcome the transport difficulties of the highland in exploiting its rich and profitable resources. Other projects were completed but were troubled by a serious lack of liquid capital for their normal operations and expansion.[23] On the other hand, the governments could mobilize some 10 percent of the people's income for administration and war.

Of course, no one can be sure that what captains spent on war could have been transferred to industrialists for profitable investment. Bungling soldiers wasted precious resources, as did bungling industrialists, bungling bureaucrats, and bungling engineers. The point here is that there were indeed resources. To make good use of them China and our highland needed competence, not just high-sounding moral standards.

Table 6.1

Defense Expenses (in yuan and as percentage of the total
provincial government expenditure)

	1919	Percent	1925	Percent
Hubei	4,226,507	59	8,130,415	74
Sichuan	5,805,518	61	26,296,358	87
Hunan	3,163,203	52	3,564,014*	51
China	76,534,924		181,867,927	

Source: Jia Shiyi (1932–34, 1:140–42, 148–52; 2:67–9).
*This figure is open to doubt. We know that Hunan was divided into twelve garrison regions in 1920. Two years later, five of them were still in existence. In addition, the province had four divisions of its own and a mixed brigade of the Hubei Army. A report in the Changsha *Dagongbao* (February 16, 1925) gives the following expenses for March 1925: 1st Division, 45,000 yuan; 2d Division, 39,000; 3rd Division, 75,000; 4th Division, 75,000. The Hubei Mixed Brigade and the Yueyang garrison region were worth 18,000 yuan each. Other expenses amounted to 19,000. This came to 284,500 and an annual total of 3,414,000, remarkably close to Jia Shiyi's figure.

What strikes me as odd is the omission of four other garrison regions in the report (see *Dagongbao*, April 3, 1922). Furthermore, the same newspaper reported on May 17, 1924, that the monthly military expenses of Hunan were 635,000 yuan and the annual total should have been 7,620,000 yuan. I cannot understand why in 1925, in the face of the growing threat of Jiang Jieshi's revolutionary armies in the south, the invasion of Xiong Kewu's huge army from Sichuan, and the internal dissension among the four divisional commanders, the defense expenses of the province should have been halved from the height of 7.6 million in 1924.

Table 6.2

Sichuan Defense Expenditures

Year	Defense expenditure (yuan)	Percentage of total expenditure
1919	5,805,518	61
1925	26,216,358	87
1926	38,603,853	98
1928	12,694,753	79
1929	16,901,681	73
1930	22,261,437	73
1931	25,859,692	80
1932	36,225,333	73
1933	45,269,702	71
1934	48,605,804	53
1935	43,876,708	61
1936	41,000,000	—

Sources: Jia Shiyi (1932–34, 1:140–42, 148–49); Zhang Xiaomei (1938, C17–19); Lu Pingdeng (1936, 26–27); *Sichuan yuebao*, 9/3, 63–65.

Table 6.3

Revenue of the Garrison Region of the Twenty-first Army   (yuan)

Year	Land tax	Salt gabelle	Opium taxes	Other	Total (mil. yuan)
1928	2,000,634	5,714,494	902,478	3,382,505	12
1929	3,354,976	4,509,932	3,193,410	8,063,449	19
1930	2,050,157	4,778,661	11,179,279	11,132,288	29
1931	9,987,517	3,609,604	8,352,144	9,644,901	27
1932	9,504,428	841,055	8,570,829	10,434,644	29
1933	15,990,645	7,418,500	9,277,849	13,650,687	46
1934					72
1935					53
1936					50

Sources: *Shenbao yuekan*, June 15, 1935, 52; Lu Pingdeng (1936, 17–24).

Table 6.4

Defense Expenditures, Hubei

Year	Army	Defense expenditure (yuan)
1911	8th Division and 21st Mixed Brigade	
1912	People's Army (8 divisions, 2 brigades)	30,238,173
1913	5 divisions, then 3 divisions, 2 brigades	7,855,295
1914	1 division and 1 brigade	5,121,782
1915 (six months)		2,616,855
1916		5,794,620
1919		4,226,507
1924	2 divisions, 3 mixed brigades	
1925		8,130,415

Sources: Ding Wenjiang (1926, 1:203, 208–11); Jia Shiyi (1932–34, 1:140–42, 148–52; 2:67–69).

Table 6.5

Fuling Tax Collections and Other Revenues

For Sichuan and other counties	Yuan	For Fuling	Yuan
Land tax	357,632	Land surtaxes	810,480
Consolidated tax (lijin)	450,000	Red Lantern (opium den) dues	61,000
Salt gabelle	232,500	Opium addicts' dues	11,000
Land-tax loan	89,408	Oil-press dues	4,640
Land deed tax	23,000	New Year gifts	4,000
Deed stamp duties	40,000	Militia, telephone, self-government	60,000
Opium sales tax	486,000	Salt readjustment	141,500
Salt stamp duties	610	Salt compensations	35,000
Mining tax	820	Salt inspection fees	780
Tobacco and liquor	24,000	Militia provisions	159,514
Meat tax	30,000	Deed surtax, education	33,300
Provisional military expenses	89,408	Deed surtax, reconstruction	9,000
Meat surtax, Chongqing University	6,000	Deed surtax, administration	19,350
Chongqing wharf charges	200	Meat surtax, education	12,000
East Sichuan colleges	11,000	Meat surtax, district school	12,000
Surtax for Jiangjin education	1,600	Meat surtax, administration	3,000
		Meat surtax, GMD	3,000
		Preserved cabbage surtax, administration	1,200
		Advance opium surtax	186,000
		Stamp duty surtax	32,000
		Opium surtax, education	12,000
		Opium surtax, special uses	8,400
		Opium surtax, Zhirentang	3,600
		Opium surtax, library	3,600
		Opium surtax, opium escort	12,000
		Salt and road surtax at Jingnei Bridge	32,300
		Treasury bills	240,000
Total	*1,842,198*		*1,916,918*
Grand total			*3,749,116*

Sources: Jinghi yanjiu, 1/7, 3639; Zheng Wanggu (1934).

Table 6.6

Taxes in Echeng County, Hubei, 1934

Tax	Unit	Yuan
Land tax	26,963.3 taels 37,748.63*	
Surtaxes	1.136 yuan for each tael	30,630.31
Grain tribute (caomi)	11,956.82 piculs	33,479.10*
Surtaxes	1.856 yuan for each tael	22,191.86
Huangwei garrison pay	228.252 taels 255.64*	
Surtax	1.053 for each tael	240.35
Qiquwei garrison pay	179.286 taels	209.23*
Surtax	1.066 yuan for each tael	191.14
Wuwei garrison pay	260.278 taels	
Reed charge	222.116 taels	
Lake charge	909.306 taels	
Surtax	1.108 yuan for each tael	1,542.14
Deed tax		18,000.00*
Surtax		9,200.00
Business tax	4 percent ad valorem	5,100.00*
Meat tax		2,100.00*
Brokerage tax		500.00*
Surtax for Guomindang		1,000.00
Stamp duties		12,000.00*
Cotton dues		1,000.00
Flax dues		3,000.00
Paper dues		3,000.00
Store charges		4,000.00
Construction charges		8,000.00
Recruitment of laborers		6,000.00
Firewood dues		3,000.00
Fish dues		585.00
Mu tax		100,800.00
Total provincial taxes (*)		112,211.55
Total xounty taxes		196,648.08
Total taxes		308,859.63
Number of households in county, 83,436		
Average tax per household		3.7

Source: Gongshang banyuekan, 6/13, 56-57.

Table 6.7

Taxes in Shizhu County, Sichuan, 1935

Provincial taxes	Yuan
Land tax	25,626
Deed tax	8,662
Meat tax	3,067
Salt gabelle	48,693*
Tobacco and wine tax	10,712
Consolidated tax	13,634
Total	*110,394*

County taxes	Yuan
Land surtaxes	30,907
Deed surtaxes	15,719
Meat surtaxes	6,300
Income from public property	1,236
Income from school property	3,380
Other revenues	3,500
Total	*61,042*
Grand total	*171,436*
Average tax per household	4.7
Total number of households, 36,496	

Sources: Zhang Xiaomei (1938, C23); *Sichuan nongye*, 2/4, these being figures for 1934.
Note: Calculated on the basis of the province's average consumption of salt at 0.264 yuan per capita and the total population of the county was 184,445. The next two items are estimated at 22 and 28 percent respectively of the salt gabelle which were also the provincial averages.

Table 6.8

Taxes in Nanchuan County, Sichuan, 1920s

Tax	Yuan
Surtaxes per tael of land tax	
Militia	6.00
Office of education	1.80
County Guomindang	0.60
Pacifying the county	10.00
Surtaxes per 100 yuan of deed tax	
Administration	2.00
Police	1.00
Justice	0.60
Accountant's office	2.00
Military corvée	1.00
East Sichuan Type A Engineering middle school	0.40
County education	5.13
Loans to county students studying abroad	2.00
Loans to county students studying in Chengdu	0.50
Office of industry public notices	2.10
Compiling county gazetteers	1.00
Meat surtaxes per pig	
County education	0.20
Accountant's office	0.10
Compiling county gazetteers	0.10
Village primary schools	0.10
Salt surtax per picul	
Chamber of commerce, 200 wen	
Tea surtaxes per bale	
Office of industry, 1,000 wen	0.125
Chamber of commerce	0.03
Oil surtaxes per picul	
County education, 200 wen	0.025
Accountant's office, 320 wen	0.04
Chamber of Commerce, 80 wen	0.01
Petition paper charge, 3,430 wen	0.428

Source: *Nanchuan xianzhi* (1926, 11–13).

Table 6.9

Taxes in Nanchuan County, Sichuan, 1935

Provincial taxes	Yuan
Land tax	318,000
Deed tax	13,010
Meat tax	7,105
Salt gabelle	81,116
Tobacco and wine tax	17,846
Consolidated tax	22,712
Total	*459,789*

County taxes	Yuan
Land surtaxes	94,248
Deed surtaxes	10,841
Meat surtaxes	9,112
Other revenues	3,286
Total	*117,487*

Opium taxes (estimate)	150,000
Grand total	*727,276*
Average tax per household	11.4
Total number of households, 63,819	

Sources: Zhang Xiaomei (1938, C61, 90); *Sichuan nongye*, 2/4; *Sichuan yuebao*, 4/5, 48; 8/5, 71–73.

Table 6.10

Taxes in Wanxian County, Sichuan, 1935

Provincial taxes	Yuan
Land tax	269,298
Deed tax	34,572
Meat tax	32,960
Salt gabelle	214,227
Tobacco and wine tax	47,130
Consolidated tax	59,984
Total	*658,171*

County taxes (1933)	Yuan
Land surtaxes	178,438
Deed surtaxes	51,760
Meat surtaxes	30,842
Income from public property	3,682
Other revenues	16,814
Total county revenues	*281,536*

Grand total	*939,707*
Average tax per household	6
Total number of households, 157,225	

Sources: Zhang Xiaomei (1938, C84, 89, 94, 144, 147–50); *Sichuan wenxian*, 80:18.

7
CITIES AND FORTRESSES

NOW let me change the subject from the economic to the socio-cultural aspects of life on the highlands, leading eventually to politics, wars, and revolutions. Perhaps a convenient way to do this is to start with a few cities before approaching the less-known fortresses and hamlets,* to make clear the continuum, and the "discontinuum," from city to hamlet, or the other way around, in terms of social organizations and their functions, and in terms of cultural sophistication. I have yet to find an account, however brief, of a western Hubei city or large market town in the 1920s or 1930s. The traditional gazetteers do exist, but they hardly meet our needs here. Therefore, I use Nanchuan and Fuling in southeastern Sichuan, and Fenghuang in western Hunan for illustration.

Nanchuan

It was due to the enterprise of its magistrate that we now possess the 1926 edition of the gazetteers of Nanchuan County, and to the innovativeness of its editor-in-chief that the edition contains the information we need. To make it more easily available to the reader, its erstwhile denizens living in Taiwan decided to publish a photoprinted impression of it in 1967. No portrayal of this border city can even be attempted without relying heavily on this gazetteer.

Throughout the Qing and the Republican periods, the geographic

---

*The Chinese word *cun* is used more freely than either "village" or "hamlet." It means a group of people living close to each other in a rural setting. Neither size nor the presence or absence of a temple matters. When E. C. Baber (*Travels and Researches in West China* [London, 1882], 9), F. von Richtofen (*Letters* [Shanghai, 1903], 181), and G. W. Skinner (1964, pt. 1, 6) speak of "no villages in Sichuan," their observation may startle a Sichuanese. On the other hand, when Hunanese speak of Miao *zhai* (Miao fortress), it may puzzle a Western visitor, for it looks indistinguishable from an ordinary village.

reach of Nanchuan County and its walled city, developed on the site of an old market, Longhua, had hardly changed. It measured 3,029.01 square km (4,543,500 mu). I cannot explain why its cultivated area ranged from the 622,000 mu reported in the 1930s to the 421,881 mu reported in the 1940s.[1] Using the larger figure, 14 percent of the land would have been under cultivation; taking the lesser one, only 9.3 percent. However, the *Sichuan jingji jikan* stated that the percentage was 20.5.[2] It is doubtless a very mountainous and remote place, but surprisingly, 83 percent of the cultivated area was paddy.[3] As shown by figures 7.1–7.4, Nanchang is a county of many hills and many well-irrigated valleys.

In the 1930s the population was 307,257, that is, 104.4 persons per square km, of whom 271,684, or 88 percent, were engaged in farming.[4] This means that at least 36,870 people resided in the county seat and market towns. The 1926 gazetteer and the 1944 Wang Chengjing survey assert, however, that the town dwellers numbered no more than 16,660, or a mere 5.4 percent. In my opinion, the cultivated area given for the 1930s of 2.3 mu for each farming person is a more acceptable figure than the one for the 1940s. By the same token, I believe that the higher percentage of town dwellers is truer than the lower one. The rural population was further divided into 30 percent owner-cultivators, 20 percent part-owners, 40 percent tenants, and 10 percent hired laborers. Landlords were few; those who owned more than 100 mu each numbered 362, and those who owned less, 5,847.[5]

Not until 1935 was the section of the Sichuan-Hunan highway with 80 km passing through Nanchuan completed. Its economic and social impact on the county remained obscure before the outbreak of the Japanese war. Since the main waterway, the Xiaozihe, had only a navigable stretch of 9 km, the county depended entirely on traditional roads and carriers for its trade with the outside world.[6]

The county boasted forty market towns in the 1920s, only five having more than one hundred households each, five more between fifty and one hundred households, and some pitifully small ones with only a dozen households or so which Sichuanese would call *yaodianzi* instead of "market towns."[7] The loss of the coastal provinces and the removal of the national capital to Chongqing redirected much of the trade southward through Guizhou and Yunnan to Burma, and only then did Nanchuan come into its own. The city grew to over six thousand inhabitants. The thirty-four inns, forty-six eating establishments, twenty-seven tea-houses (where business was normally transacted), and thirty opium dens made life more interesting than before.[8] Catering, herbal medicine, and paper making seem to have been the three major industries in the county. The first took account of the people who came thrice in every ten days for the market; employing twenty thousand, the second had one hundred firms scattered in all directions; the third manufactured paper for ceremonial burning and for wrapping.[9]

The county government's chief concerns were to protect the citizens, not so much against invading armies as against robbers and thieves, and to educate the young, if they were intelligent and from a good family. Its spending was normally for three purposes: to maintain itself, to support an armed militia force, and to aid the schools.

The 1911 Revolution in this remote county ended in the dissolution of the old militia (*tuanfang*) and the gradual formation of the new (*tuanlian*). This change was designed to deal with the chaotic situation at hand. The revolution saw the sudden emergence of a thousand or more "righteous" people's armies who had to be coaxed into keeping some sort of law and order. About eight hundred of them were organized into four militia detachments. They were obviously too big a force for the government to maintain. In cutting the militia budget, the government scaled down its strategic task from defending the county to defending the city only. The market towns had to be persuaded to defend themselves. Consequently, the *baojia* security system in the market towns was transformed into a militia. Through trial and error a system of forty-five militia-baojia units were brought into existence, corresponding to the division of the forty market towns. The militia's strength was maintained at 1,310, with a reserve of 15,000 young men to draw from in time of emergency.[10]

The efficacy of this militia force depended upon how strong its foe happened to be. When the powerful and ruthless Tang Zimo led his raiders into the county in 1914, or when the Guizhou Army came to "save" Sichuan from the clutches of Yuan Shikai in 1916, it would have been suicidal for the militia to resist. It did score successes against weaker law-breakers, however. As militarization of Sichuan grew steadily after 1916, the stakes of the war game grew also. Once it had been a matter of a battalion, without a penny to its name, that came to stay; now it was a regiment or even a division, also without a penny to its name.[11] The militia itself, as I described it in the last chapter, was

Figure 7.1. **Delong Township**

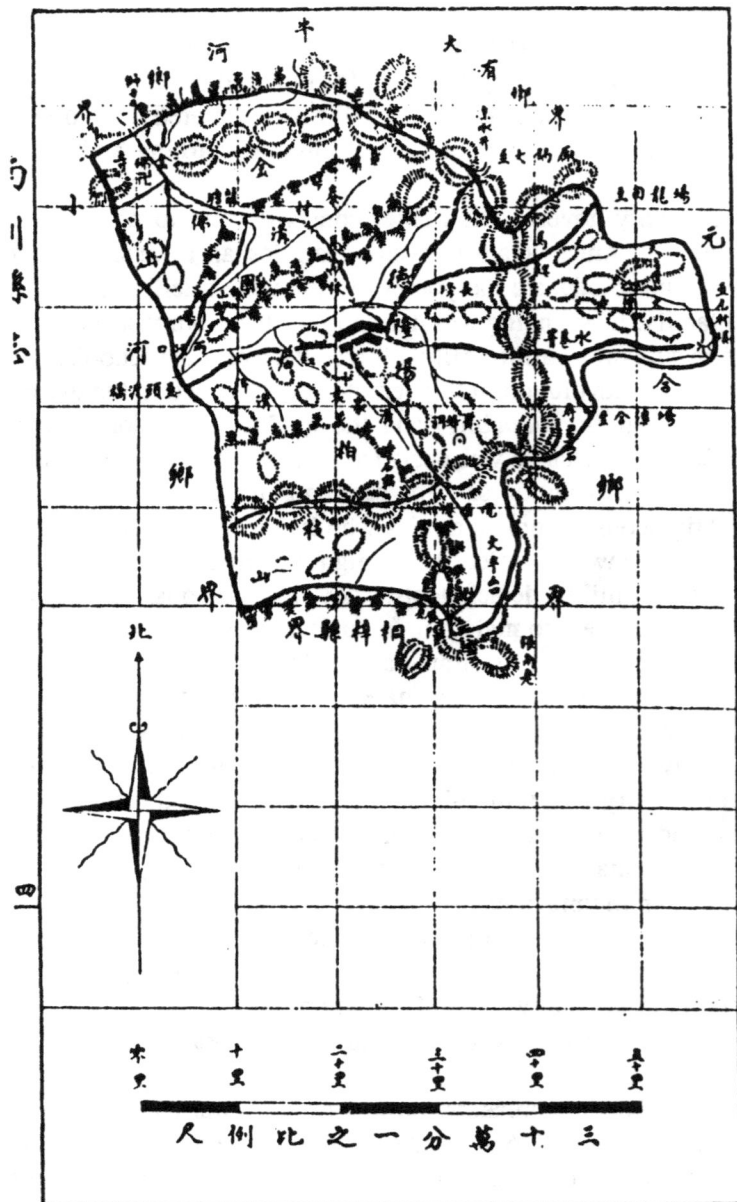

Figure 7.2 **Xiaohe Township**

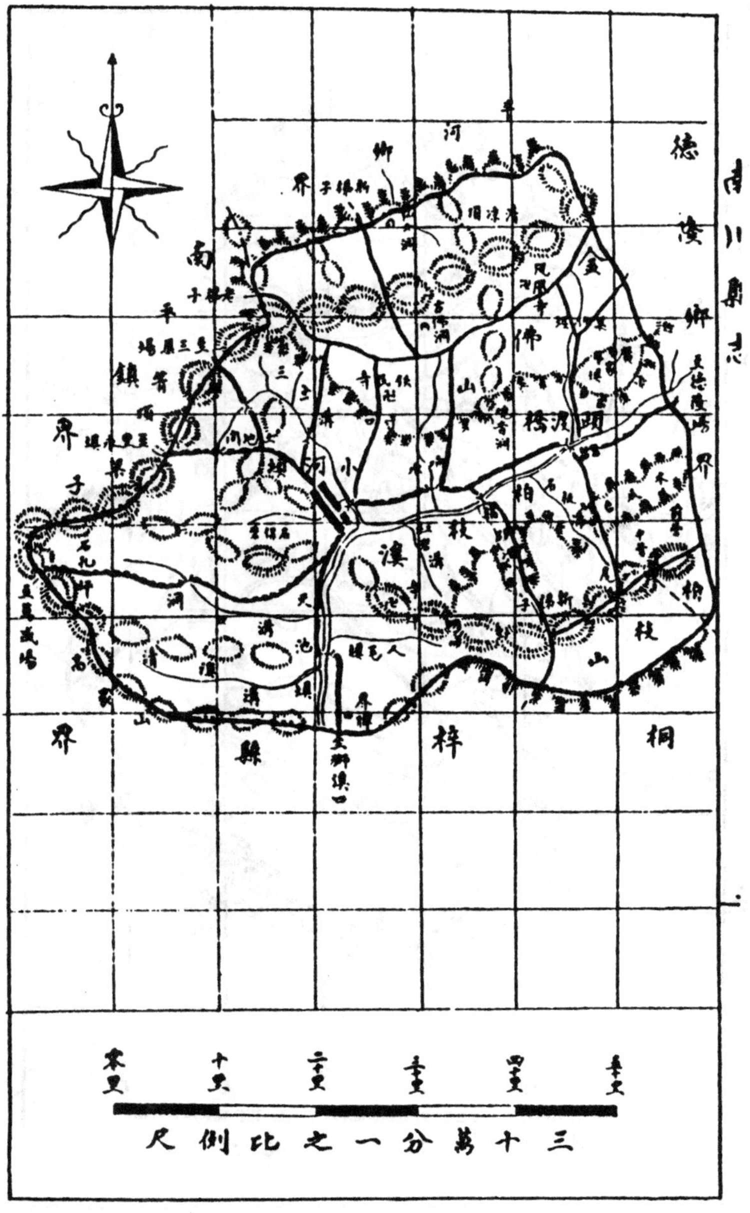

Figure 7.3. **Nanping Market Town**

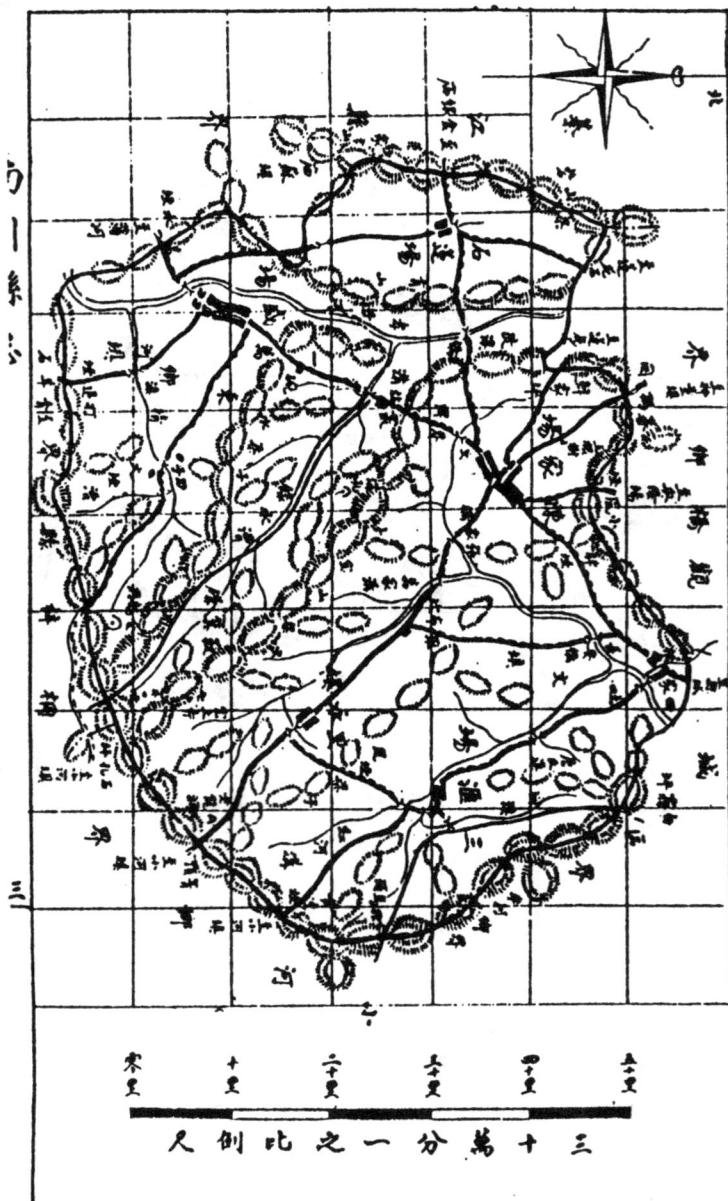

Figure 7.4. **Nanchuan City**

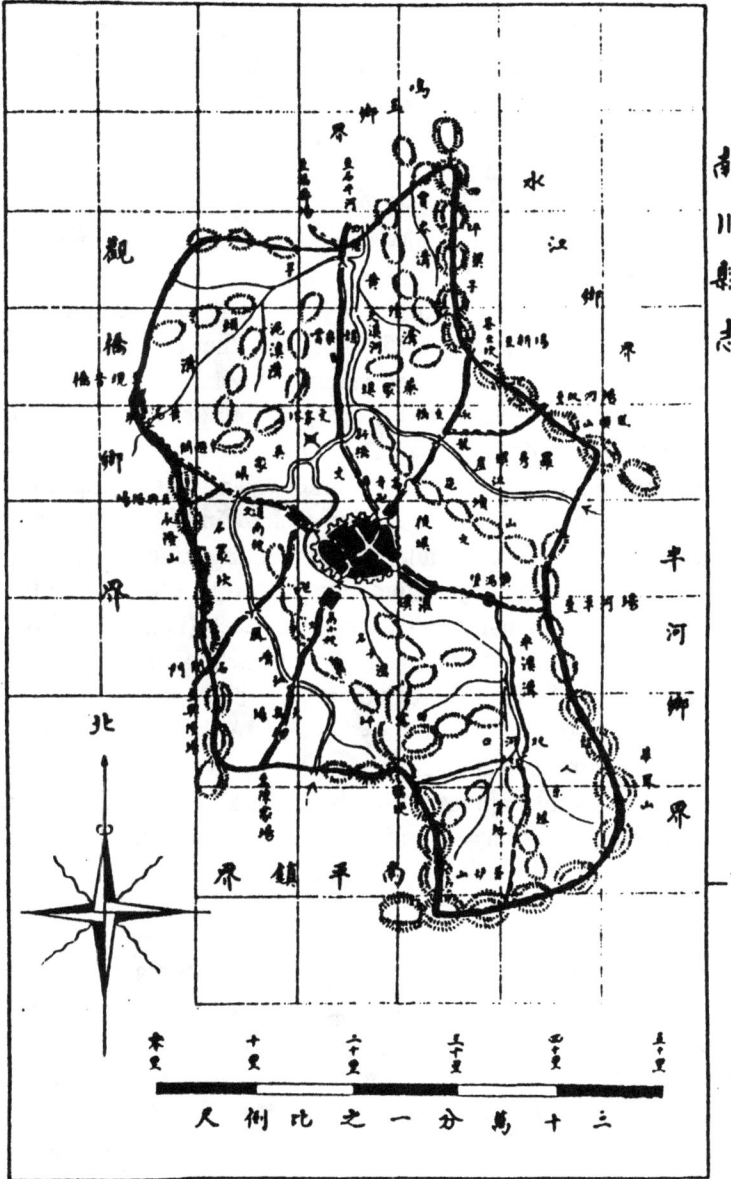

an ambiguous institution; it was not always what it was created to be. It could protect the people as well as prey on them.

The 1895 war made the Nanchuanese realize that modern education was the foundation of national strength, as the 1926 gazetteer stated (ch. 7, 12). But the first wave of establishing new schools did not begin until 1907. A four-year elementary school for some 15,000 children was founded in each of the five districts. Twenty years later, the number of four- and six-year elementary schools had increased to ninety—twenty of them, including three for girls, were located in and around the city. The thirteen in the city catered to a school-age population of approximately 1,600, while the seventy in the rural areas were for probably 90,000.[12] We do not know how many children were actually at school in these years. A 1935 report says that there were altogether 117 schools (none of them secondary schools), which taught 8,634 pupils, or on the average one for every 74 pupils. Then as before, the opportunity for a city child to go to school was much greater than for his contemporary in an outlying market town, whose opportunity, in turn, was much better than that for a child in a hamlet, who in all likelihood went to a private tutor for elementary education.

In the 1920s the county's education department had at its disposal a revenue of 32,500 yuan, 54,800 strings of cash (i.e., 54 million wen), and 4,970 piculs of rice from the county school land. It recorded a surplus in 1926.[13] This is hardly understandable, unless quite a few of the ninety schools were privately funded. Although it is not known how many were private schools and how the schools spent their money, the general impression is that, as in all the mountain counties, Nanchuanese education was uncomfortably backward.

Fuling

The important port city of Fuling is no longer a stranger to us. Its basic statistics were 178,720 square li in area, with a population of 986,290, a population density of 55 per square li, and 827,390 (85 percent) of the people engaged in agriculture in the 1930s. The farming people there worked on 28,943 mu of paddy fields, 77,224 mu of dry fields, 5,790,851 mu of cultivated slope land, and 67,560 mu of gardens of vegetables, herbs, and tea bushes for beverage and for oil. The total area under cultivation was close to 6 million mu, including wooded land and grazing land, giving an average of 36 mu per rural household, or 7 mu per rural person. The farming population was further divided into landlords (992, or 0.06 percent); owner cultivators (49,643, or 30 percent); part owners (24,831 or 15 percent); tenants (82,739, or 50 percent); and hired laborers (7,281, or 4.4 percent).[14]

The city was "modern" by Sichuan standards, for it was in the east, downstream of the most important river of the province, in touch with imported goods and ideas earlier than the places lying behind it. In the second half of the 1930s, it had 32,400 inhabitants. Like other riverside cities, it perches on a plateau with groups of houses on the slopes and row upon row of them on the flat land. Administratively it was divided into two wards (zhen) and thirty-seven bao (as in baojia), linked by macadamized streets, reminders of the two warlords who ordered their construction in 1924–28. Macadamization ushered in Japanese jinriki-sha, 120 of them, but, as reported, only 60 in regular service. By the 1930s there were cinemas, which probably used a "commentator" with a pot of tea and a hooka in front of him to explain the plot when a foreign film was screened, like most of their contemporaries in Sichuan and Yunnan. The city also had a broadcasting service and more than one hundred telephones.

Fuling was, and still is, a major export and import city, in those days dealing in foodstuffs, tong oil, opium, salt, sugar, the preserved cabbage called zhacai, and a host of mountain products carried thither by steamers. If the trade was more or less balanced, the total volume was probably over ten million yuan a year.[15] Necessarily, there were hundreds of inns, tea-houses, restaurants, and opium dens. These and other businesses were all controlled by guilds (gongsuo) among which the zhacai (see chapter 2) and salt guilds were the strongest, in spite of the lucrative opium trade.

I do not know how many market towns there were, but one of the better known was Linshi, with about 900 households, twenty whole-salers of grain, twenty-three of cloth, and eighteen of timber. It is situated on the river.[16] Seventy-five li to the southwest of the city, Dabozhen made a name on its opium; it was one of the great centers of opium production in Sichuan. It supported a population of over 1,000 households.[17] Handicapped by a lack of modern means of transport, Hanlongxiang had only 370 households, whose livelihood depended on growing rice, maize, timber, and, of course, opium.[18]

Nor do I know the strength of the local militia, except that in 1933 the county government had earmarked 219,514 yuan to be spent on it (see table 6.5). If it cost 10–12 yuan a year to keep a militiaman (i.e., one-tenth the cost of keeping a foot soldier), the amount of money would have been enough for a force of 18,290. It was considerably larger than the 72,900 yuan earmarked for education and culture at the same time. If this appears too low, then Lu Pingdeng's 24,981 yuan was minuscule for a population of nearly one million.[19] On the other hand, it was reported that the county had 1 secondary school, 2 junior teacher training schools, and 144 elementary schools. A large number of them must have been private. The secondary school taught 176 pupils, the teacher training schools (one for each sex) 206, and the elementaries, 10,194.[20] With probably 250,000 children of school age, it is amazing that only 4 percent of them were actually at school in the 1930s. Like Nanchuan, the opportunity for education within the city or a market town would have been immeasurably better than outside of it.

Fenghuang

Straddling the Tuo River, Fenghuang County was 8,849 square *shili* or 3.6 million mu in area, with a population of approximately 133,000. Among them, 74 percent were owner-cultivators, 8.11 percent part owners, 11.5 percent tenants, and 6.5 percent hired laborers. Households were considerably larger, having on the average about eight persons in the 1930s.[21] The average size of a family farm was over 26 mu, or about 3 mu per person.[22]

I visited Fenghuang in 1983. The account below is based chiefly on my own diary and observation, supplemented by my 1989 visit to Dayong and Sangzhi. The landscape is not all that different from the Sichuan countryside, chiefly because of the absence of large villages, the existence of only few *zhai* (fortresses), and the frequent presence of hamlets. I daresay that if one went further into the mountains, the fortresses would grow smaller, whereas they become larger villages as the terrain flattens out. In the fortresses as in the city, people of different cultures, if not of different races, live as neighbors—the Miao numbering more than the Han and ten other groups of peoples, such as the Tujia and the Tibetans.

The city lies on the valley floor of the Tuo, normally sleepy, but livable. I am tempted to describe it as charmingly quaint. Even today, the long shadow of General Chen Quzhen, the "king" of western Hunan whose headquarters were located in Fenghuang for nearly fifteen years before the Japanese war, can still be seen. Then the city had six thousand civilians and almost as many soldiers. There were offices, temples, residences of military and civilian leaders, schools, markets and shops, and *Landsmannschaften*. The last named were in the form of temples, such as the Wanshougong of the Jiangxi, the Tianhougong of the Fujian, and Chuanzhugong of the Sichuan merchants. Others who came here for business included those from Shaoyang in Hubei and Baoqing in Hunan. At the beginning of the Republican period almost 80 percent of the mercantile community was from Jiangxi. In spite of being Chen's headquarters and the location of his arsenal, the city had no electricity then. Even today there are no street lamps.

The government was manned by the Han in its upper echelon and by the Miao below. The army was commanded likewise, the majority of the NCOs and foot soldiers being Miao.[23] It was the Han elite in the government, army, and businesses who smoked opium, handled the trade, and collected taxes from it. The leading Han businessmen issued their paper currency which was later superseded by that of the West Hunan Village Bank, the de facto treasury of Chen Quzhen's army, the elephantine Thirty-fourth Division of thirty thousand men. The bank's notes circulated not only in the fourteen counties that were Chen's sphere of influence, but also in eastern Guizhou. In the city there were also Chen's arsenal, Chen's army blanket factory, Chen's police training college, Chen's police, Chen's mansions, and Chen's ancestral hall. With him and his armed forces there, there was no need for militia or other forms of protection.

General Chen was in his own fashion interested in education, like one of his predecessors, General Tian Yingzhao. Traditionally there were "tutors' fields" to finance the fifty-two old-fashioned schools—twenty-seven for the Han and twenty-five for the Miao. It was in 1905 that Jingxiu College was transformed into the Feng[huang]-Qian[cheng]-Yong[sui]-Huang[xian] Middle School, which took on fifty students. The old-fashioned schools, tuition free, were reorganized into sixty citizens' schools in 1912. Three of these were in the city, including the Model School from which the renowned writer Shen Congwen graduated. Continuing the efforts of General Tian and his family, Chen added more schools, encouraged private citizens to set up their own, and even sent his police and soldiers to compel children to go to them.[24] By 1924 the county boasted 33 schools. Unfortunately, the middle school was dissolved in 1926 for reasons unclear to me. In any case, it does not appear to have been due to a lack of money, for four years later, Chen had a rural teachers' training school established in Fenghuang, which recruited sixty students each from Fenghuang, Mayang, and Qiancheng. Further efforts were made to spread education among the children. For instance, fifteen tuition-free schools were added, six in the city and nine on the outskirts, and then twenty-seven more in the Miao areas. Still, by the time of the Japanese war, only about 1,000 children were reported to be at school out of a population of about 170,000. If this was true, many of the schools must have been defunct. Very few were for girls. Many children went to traditional tutors for instruction in Confucian classics.

The May Fourth Movement simply passed this mountained city by. One cause of this had to be the lack of any kind of mass media to link the county with the world at large, a malaise Nanchuan shared in the 1920s. Before 1937 the city had no daily newspapers, no periodicals except the ones for the army, and no regular theaters or cinemas. The occasional stage performances were traditional Han (Hubei) operas and the local Nuotang operas. Even the solitary bookshop in the city was not known to carry a meaningful stock of modern books. In other words, new ideas found no way over the mountain barrier that encircled the city except by individual agents.

Shortly after the 1911 Revolution, two members of Tian Yingzhao's family, Tian Xingliu and Tian Yingbi (a woman), returned from their sojourn in Japan. The former was appointed headmaster of the middle school; the latter began a girls' vocational training center. Then, in 1927–28, the misty serenity of Fenghuang was disturbed by the split of the GMD-CCP alliance. Young, educated radicals came from Changsha to stay and give performances of *wenmingxi* (dramas). An elderly gentleman told me in Fenghuang that he had seen a play on the May 1928 murder of Cai Gongshi, the Chinese negotiator, by the Japanese in Jinan, Shandong, soon after the tragic event had taken place. These people also made propaganda speeches on the street, organized peasants' associations, paraded "capitalists" like the manager of a herbalist shop and others through the streets. It seems that there was much propaganda but little organization. When Chen Quzhen came back, the movement was completely suppressed. The general did not want to have anything to do even with the Guomindang, let alone the Chinese Communist Party. Ideologically, he was a staunch defender of the traditional faith.

Ying Zhushi, the son of Chen's sworn-brother and chief of staff, was in Guangdong studying at the Institute for Training Organizers of the Peasant Movement when Mao Zedong was its director. Returning home, he joined Chen's secretariat, rose to senior adviser, and took up opium smoking. More distinguished citizens of Fenghuang there indeed were. They left their native place to seek a career in the wider world. In this respect, Fenghuang seems to have developed a trait different from Nanchuan, and even from Fuling. One recalls Xiong Xiling (1870–1942), premier of the Beijing government in 1913–14; Shen Congwen (1902–1987), a distinguished professor and writer; Huang Yongyu, a well-known artist; a number of high-ranking officers in the People's Liberation Army who were trained at the Anti-Japanese Political and Military University in Yan'an; a few high-ranking CCP cadres; and one or two who went to study in the United States.

Outside the city, I visited three fortresses—two Miao and one Han. Ala is now a huge market that meets regularly twice every ten days. Situated 28 km to the southwest of Fenghuang and only 18 km from Songtao across the border in Guizhou, with Sichuan not far away, Ala serves the needs of the frontier people of three provinces. When the market meets, twenty thousand turn up. Many of them are young, mixing business with pleasure. On the way to market they sing love songs in duet until they come to the green at the entrance to Ala. There stands a pavilion against the background of a stretch of paddy fields and an aqueduct. Such a green is called *malangpo*, and singing love songs in duet is known as *yaomalang*.[25] Before the day ends, the young man and woman have already made many promises to each other. They eat a snack at the market and leave together for their separate homes in different villages. Of course, the new fashions they wear and the nondescript grey brick buildings in Ala are new. They do not appear to fit into a scenario of essentially traditional courting and marketing practices.[26]

In chapter 3 I noted that the market was, and still is, divided into two sections—the smaller livestock section and the much larger section dealing in food, clothing, and an assortment of local products. People arrived at 8 A.M. and left at 2 or 3 P.M. They rose early, walked a couple of hours, and took their breakfast at the market. After business they returned home in time to prepare the afternoon meal before retiring to bed at dusk. They ate only two meals a day. Those who dallied usually were professional salesmen and buyers who had come the day before and would leave the day after the market.

Fifty km to the west of Fenghuang is the old Miao fortress called Shanjiang (mountain-river), now a market town whose market also meets twice in every ten days. A smaller market for local rather than interprovincial needs, the town has a larger and quieter section in which reside some three hundred households. The townspeople breakfasted at about 10 A.M. after a few hours of work in the fields; then they took a short break before going back to work until about 5 P.M. The afternoon meal was at 5:30 or 6:00.

Most of the houses, including the former residence of Long Yunfei, the leader of the great Miao rebellion of 1937, are built of stone. The tiny windows tend to make rooms dark. But the local people are highly skilled dry-wall builders. Tall buildings, such as watchtowers and blockhouses, standing there to remind people of more violent days, were themselves the institutionalization of violence. In this mixed Han-Miao region, there were more than 1,000 fortresses like this one—848 in Fenghuang, 188 in Qiancheng, 127 in Yongsui, and 69 in Baojing.[27]

Seven km west of Ala squats an eerie and ancient fortress of the Han garrison. Established in the reign of Empress Wu (690–704) and rebuilt for the last time in 1859, this walled community was formerly known as Fenghuangying and is now called Huangshiqiao. In an area of 4,000 square meters, one hundred garrison households lived; now there are only one hundred families of civilians. Since it is so close to Ala, it seemed pointless to develop a market here. Only a couple of general stores cater to the incidental needs of the inhabitants—cakes and incense, needles and thread, modern cigarettes and matches. A wall about fourteen feet high and four feet thick, a granary, vegetable patches, and wells allowed the fortress to withstand a siege of a few weeks before reinforcements arrived. Now it houses a community of farming people who have a school, a clinic, a single telephone, but no post office. What is remarkable is that it also has electricity.

If one pulled down the wall of Huangshiqiao it would be a village. Indeed, the so-called Miao fortresses, which I saw on the way from Fenghuang to Ala, are nowadays indistinguishable from ordinary villages. Then there were many clusters of houses among fields, reminding me of the Sichuan landscape. In the old days, a fortress had a number of gates, which were meant to be shut at night or in an emergency. The streets inside were as narrow and winding as those in

Shanjiang, and the houses were built face to face and back to back in the small lanes off the streets. Indeed, it was planned both for living together and for safety.[28] I saw Miao fortresses situated on the hills and surrounded by dry fields and dry land as well as those on the valley floor surrounded by paddies. Late in the Qing period, most of the garrison fields were in fact tilled by the Miao, who paid rent to the government. These were in most cases paddy fields.

In western Hunan more than thirty thousand mu of land were allocated to support the thousand-strong garrison and their families. Twenty thousand mu were in Fenghuang; the rest, in Mayang. The garrison fields came from appropriation of the land that once belonged to the Miao.[29] Not all garrison soldiers were Han, nor were all garrison fields by Han. In any case, some of the fields were given to officers and men as their entitlement; some, a smaller portion, were kept by the government for other defense expenses, such as the purchase of weaponry and repair of fortresses. Lying far away from a fortress, much of the latter category of land was leased to ordinary Miao to farm. The rent they paid helped defray miscellaneous defense expenses.

Unless a careful record of the changes was kept and no rapacious officials tried to alter or destroy it, a land system like this was bound to sink into incomprehensible confusion. It is a familiar story that Chinese cadastral registration made a habit of growing old, forgetful, negligent, and useless. The western Hunan garrison field records were no exception. Officers and men might be transferred elsewhere or die; pieces of land given as entitlement might be sold; when the able-bodied soldiers were fighting, it might be more profitable to rent out their land for income. Even after these and other changes, including three major Miao uprisings (1844–47, 1855, and 1879) against the rent of garrison fields, the system, which should have been drastically reformed to come in line with reality, remained.[30] The Miao's grievances were concentrated on the rent, which exceeded 50 percent of the yield in the Republican period.[31] The first serious warning was heard in Yongsui in 1935, but the provincial government did no more than grant remission of all rent in arrears.[32] Then came the great armed uprising of some eight thousand Miao led by Long Yunfei in Fenghuang in 1937. This ended He Jian's administration in Hunan. His successor, General Zhang Zhizhong, made the rebel leader a brigadier-general, ordered the county government to deal with the rent in light of the local situation, and started a series of reform measures that culminated in the privatization of the fields and the end of this ancient system in 1944–45.

In the struggle against garrison field rent, the Miao tried to rally the support of the Han by making a common front with them against the Manchus in the secret society called the Gelaohui (the Brotherhood). Its membership, both Han and Miao, included mostly low-ranking officials and officers, common soldiers, and transport workers. Because of this social composition, army commanders benefited by joining the Brotherhood and affiliating themselves with Miao leaders, thereby strengthening their command. Tian Yingzhao, who had led his men in the 1911 Revolution and the 1916 war against Yuan Shikai, and Chen Quzhen (who in a sense succeeded Tian) were both members of the Brotherhood. Han and Miao leaders could rise from the ranks. In Fenghuang there were eight "dragon heads" (*longtou*, or group leaders), seven of whom were Miao. But organizationally the Brotherhood did not regard the city as a "mountain," and hence no "mountain hall." In other words, no central county headquarters existed. When an acute situation developed, the society might exploit it and play a leading role in it. The 1937 uprising, for example, was led by an important member of the Brotherhood, Long Yunfei.

From the points of view of social welfare, protection, and education, the county city, market town and village, and hamlets clearly form a continuum. Soup kitchens, old people's homes, and orphanages were to be found only in the city. Granaries for famine relief, however, came mainly in three types: the county government ran two, one located in the city and another in market towns or villages; the village community ran the third in the village itself. Most of them were in the city, where they were perhaps safer and certainly more convenient for official inspection. Table 7.1 gives a few examples.

But officials were not entirely incorruptible. By the second half of the eighteenth century, what was kept in the granaries was well below the fixed quotas; a century later, "decay and degeneration" were widespread.[33] In spite of the efforts to revive this ancient system on the part of the Nanjing government, there were few visible results. Take the twelve counties in eastern Sichuan, for instance: six of them had nothing in their granaries, and the other six had eight thousand piculs in 1933–34. Two years later, only eleven thousand piculs were to be found in all the granaries of Sichuan.[34] Reports on western Hubei and Hunan were marginally more reassuring.[35] For the settlers in the hamlets on the slopes, no welfare arrangements of any kind existed, unless they went to the nearest market town. I discovered this in conversations with local archivists and historians in the Jinggang mountains in 1980, in Gulin, southern Sichuan, in 1983, and in Dayong and Sangzhi in 1989.

I have described the evolution of the Miao fortresses in western Hunan. During the decade of religious uprisings in western Hubei, eastern and northeastern Sichuan, and southern Shaanxi at the turn of the nineteenth century, many fortresses were built for local protection.[36] When Xiushan was threatened by the Taiping armies, for example, its inhabitants built fortresses.[37] The construction of forts continued whenever a place was threatened by bandits or unruly soldiers. There are reports on northwestern Hubei and northern Sichuan in 1927.[38] But it is difficult to explain what happened to these fortified market towns when peace returned. I have observed small blockhouses on mountain tops and at mountain passes crumbling away. Fortified market towns may have become open again as Skinner suggests (1971). Bambo's correction of Skinner applies to the hamlets and homesteads that were indeed exposed to natural hazards and human greed, and probably also to cases of irresistible invasions like those of the Yunnan and Guizhou armies in the second half of the 1910s and of the Communists in 1932.

The chief difference between a townsman and a country bumpkin, a plainsman and a hillman, lies in the realm of education and culture. I shall say a few more words on education here and leave cultural traits to the next chapter.

At the beginning of this century, when China was rethinking its education system, the viceroy of Sichuan was patently worried about the

> lack of education in the remote counties of the province. Nowhere is the mind more tightly closed, consequently nowhere is there more urgent need for talents, than in our peripheral prefectures and counties locked in myriads of mountains. The eyes and ears of the inhabitants are occluded. No one is farsighted; no one is able and wise. The uninformed regard school education as something strange and foreign. It is this attitude that gives rise to rumors and [other] difficulties.[39]

Under such official encouragement, local dignitaries began to donate money for the establishment of modern schools: Nanchuan, 3,000 taels; Fengjie, 2,000; Yunyang and Shizhu, 1,000 each. The sums were obviously not enough, however, for the elementary schools of Peng-shui in 1904 had to be housed in temples and had to have money diverted from railway construction.[40] Similar financial stringency was felt in Tongjiang, Guangyuan, and Qianjiang.[41] Some liked modern education so much that in Wuxi scholars over the age of fifty sought admission to the senior section of the elementary school; some hated it so much that they led strong-armed men to commit Luddism.[42]

In spite of this, modern schools sprang up willy-nilly in Fuling, Yilong, Yunyang, Zhongxian, and other highland counties. In 1907 Fuling went so far as to create a school for bureaucrats because they "understood nothing of public morality and justice."[43]

Another trend, encouraged in the viceroy's statement of 1903, was to send students to Chengdu and other advanced places for higher education. In the Chengdu Higher School, the 1905 class of 223 students had 18 from 13 peripheral counties.[44] In the same year the Chengdu Japanese Language School accepted 24 from 9 peripheral counties in a class of 100. It is noteworthy that among the 24, only one came from Yilong in northern Sichuan, while all the others were from the east or southeast.[45] The preponderance of students from the basin or the core continued to be evident in 1925 when, among the 50 Sichuan students studying at the Agricultural College in Beijing, only 5 came from Nanchuan and Fengdu.[46] What is unexpected is that in 1905, in a class of army cadets of 168 at the Chengdu Military School, only 4 were born in the mountain counties, none of whom was to develop a career comparable to their classmates from the plains, such as generals Wang Lingji of Loshan, Zhong Tidao of Chengdu, and Chen Hongfan, Liu Chengxun, and Chen Guozhu of the county of warlords, Dayi.[47]

In 1905 all the highland counties were advised to send students to Japan, the victor in the Russo-Japanese War. The twenty-four counties sent thirty-seven students.[48] On return, some exerted considerable influence in public affairs, such as the railway issue which ushered in the 1911 Revolution; others who were known to have gone back to their hometowns to initiate new ventures.

The highland had its own high schools, without which new ideas, especially cultural, social, and political ideas, could hardly take root and spread. For example, this was how eleven Communist leaders born in the highland became politicized:

Chen Youkui (1900–1928), Mayang, Hunan: Read Kang Youwei and Liang Qichao under the influence of a teacher at the Zhijiang High School, 1917, and studied at Mao Zedong's Self-Education "College" in Changsha, 1922.

Duan Dechang (1904–1933), Nanxian, Hunan: Influenced by Marxism-Leninism while attending Yage High School, Changsha, 1922.

Huang Dapeng (1908–1931), Badong, Hubei: Influenced by a Communist teacher at Yichang Teachers' School, 1926, and joined the party.

Kuang Jixun (1895–1933), Sinan, Guizhou: Under the command and influence of Liu Bocheng, Nanchong, 1925–26.

Li Jiajun (1902–1931), Wanyuan, Sichuan: Read *New Youth* and influenced by May Fourth Movement while in high school in Daxian.

Shi Yang (1889–1923), Zhushan, Hubei: Read Kang Youwei and Liang Qichao at Yunyang Agricultural School, 1907; read *New Youth* at the School of Law and Politics, Wuchang, 1914.

Wang Erzhuo (1901–1928), Shimen, Hunan: Politicized while at the Industrial School, Changsha, 1920, and at Whampoa Military Academy, 1924.

Wang Weizhou (1887–1970), Xuanhan, Sichuan: Involved in the railway protection movement in Chengdu, 1911, in the anti–Yuan Shikai war, 1916; influenced by the May Fourth Movement, 1919; studied in Moscow 1922.

Yang Keming (1905–1937), Fuling, Sichuan: Influenced by May Fourth Movement at Fuling High School.

Zhao Shiyan (1901–1927), Longtan, Youyang, Sichuan: Books sent home by his brother who was a member of Sun Yat-sen's Revolutionary Alliance; introduced to ideas of Rousseau and Darwin by a geography teacher at senior elementary school of Longtan; graduated from high school in Beijing and came under Li Dazhao's influence in 1919.

Zhong Shanfu (1899–1930), Fuling, Sichuan: Influenced by May Fourth Movement while at the Police School, Chengdu, 1919, and joined the Marxism Reading Circle there in 1920.

The pattern is clear. When these politicized people returned home to do educational and political work, they mobilized not their elementary school children but the peasants in and around their villages, just as did their contemporaries in southern Jiangxi and northwestern Fujian, the location of the Central Soviet of the 1930s.

Although nearly all these pioneering Communists embraced Marxism-Leninism when they were in a metropolitan city like Changsha, Wuhan, or Chengdu, the highland had its own high schools in the 1930s. There was one secondary school each at Fuling, Guangyuan, Qianjiang, Xiushan, Youyang, and Yunyang; two secondary schools each at Shizhu, Wanxian, and Yilong; three at Zhongxian.[50]

Longtan Secondary was the highest seat of learning in the golden triangle. It had four classes—three in the junior section, with sixty-two pupils, and one in the senior section, with twenty. Seven teachers, each of whom taught seventeen hours a week, received salaries ranging from 20 yuan to 50 yuan a month. Each junior secondary pupil had to pay 4 yuan a term, while a senior secondary pupil paid 6 yuan. The rest of the funds for running the school came from a county government allocation of 22,000 yuan a year. In 1936, the allocation was not paid to the school regularly.[51]

The report on Wanxian education carried in the *Xinshubao* of May 1, 1935, was considerably more detailed. First, at the apex of the bureaucratic structure was the Office of Education, headed by three inspectors who oversaw thirty-five school districts, each of which was a market town or village, which was, in turn, in the charge of five to seven commissioners of education. The budget of 1935 is given in table 7.2.

The surplus was probably fictitious, for the sake of face, honor, and fidelity to the principle of frugality. The county government's share of the budget came from various surtaxes; that of the district from land rent and donations, which were only another form of surtaxes.

There were under the jurisdiction of the county two secondary schools, one for boys and one for girls, with a total enrollment of 359 pupils under the care of 41 teachers; two girls' elementaries with 497 children and 19 teachers; ten complete elementaries (both junior and senior sections) with 1,750 children and 910 teachers; one women's vocational school; and one kindergarten—thus making a total of 2,769 pupils and 159 teachers.

Under the jurisdiction of the districts, 196 elementaries educated 8,532 children and employed 437 teachers. The mass education program included a conference hall and exhibitions, lectures, review shows, publications, public health, and other work.

Most of the teachers were trained at teachers' schools or ordinary high schools, but only 70 percent of them were certified to teach. At the high school, a teacher received 0.70 yuan an hour; at the county elementary, 36 yuan a month; at the district elementary, 8–20 yuan a month. Their pay compared favorably with that of a private tutor, who usually taught the children of three to five families and received 50–300 yuan a year. In 1935, Wanxian still had approximately 800 private tutors coaching some 20,000 children.

Lack of funds continued to plague highland education down to the 1930s (see tables 7.3 and 7.4). In October 1935, Zhongxian teachers went en masse to the county education office to demand their salaries in arrears.[52] The boys' and girls' schools of Guangyuan, under conditions just after the war, received only a fraction of their budgeted revenue and paid only a fraction of their salaries.[53] There is no doubt that the emphasis of highland education remained on the moral rather than intellectual development of the children. There was little difference between the training and outlook of the teachers at modern schools and private tutors who coached a few boys at home. In Shizhu, the traditional Four Books and Five Classics constituted the core of the curriculum of all the modern schools, whose teachers were often ill-qualified academically and smoked opium.[54]

As to girls' education, several highland counties did set up special schools, though they were far outnumbered by boys' schools. There were even coeducational schools, such as the one in Longtan, Youyang, where in 1936 among 406 pupils there were 136 girls. As elsewhere in the developing world, more girls attended lower than higher grades. They tended to disappear from school by their senior year.[55] On September 19, 1983, I met Madame Liang Yinlan in Gulin, southern Sichuan, and transcribed her story:

> Born in Hongjiang, Hunan, in 1902, I came to Gulin for the first time to visit my relatives in 1927. Then there were five elementary schools in the city—the senior, the northern city, the southern city, the model, and the girls'. The May Fourth Movement seems to have left very little impression here, awfully backward, not a whiff of modernity.
>
> I had a teaching post in Chongqing then. Here, I was regarded as an oddity, something like a "foreign" woman (*yang puozi*), because I wore short hair [neither a long plait nor a bun] and my feet were of the natural size while a large number of the pupils who studied at the girls' school had bound feet or semifreed feet. Fortunately, the principal of the senior elementary was an enlightened fellow, and the headmistress of the girls' school, Mrs. Zhang, had been to Chengdu, where her husband

was. They wanted me to stay and hired me as the teacher of music and physical education. At the senior elementary, Mr. Deng, a teacher and a member of the Creation Society,* also wanted me to stay. Although the gentry didn't like me, they didn't object either.

In those days, girl students customarily walked to their school by the back streets instead of the main street of the city. But when I did so, I deliberately used the main street. At neither this school nor the senior elementary were there sports and extracurricular activities. So I suggested that ball games should be introduced. Mr. Deng agreed. Therefore, for the first time we had basketball and volleyball games. I taught the girls to play on the playgrounds of the schools in public view. This was more than the gentry could put up with, because the girls were grown up and some of them were married. The leading citizens thought this display harmful to public morality, but they did not voice their objections.

The girls wanted to wear their hair short like mine. I not only agreed with them but also helped them cut it. This time, the gentry objected. I told the girls stories of the May Fourth Movement and the need for the girls to develop their minds like the boys. When their families tried to forbid them, some of the girls threatened to swallow opium to end their lives. Their parent relented. The fashion of short hair spread from school to the street. When that happened, the parents kept their girls at home instead of allowing them to go to school, for the fear that I would lead them even further astray. But this boycott didn't last long. In the first summer I spent there I even organized basket-ball matches between our school and the Gulin students who came back for the holiday.

The girls continued to be very nice to me. When the second term began early in 1928, Mr. Xu, a member of the gentry, hired people to shout dirty language at me when I passed by. I ignored them. I suggested to the school that we should organize an open day, to exhibit students' work and to explain to their parents what we had been doing. The boys' schools invited my girls and me to exhibit physical exercise at their schools. This provoked a tremendous uproar. The gentry sent people to see the magistrate, demanding my expulsion from Gulin. Mr. Gao, the magistrate, was a modern scholar. He defended me. And so my contract with the girls' school was renewed. By the end of the first year of my stay, girls could even go out on an organized trip with me. In the summer of 1928 three of my girls went to study in Chongqing.

---

*A well-known society for writers founded by Guo Muoro, Yu Dafu, and Cheng Fangwu in Shanghai, 1921. The man's claim might or might not be true. I have heard of a professor of English literature in China who is widely known to his colleagues and students as being a fellow of the Royal Society of London.

The old-fashioned scholars in the county education office, however, were threatened by the new style of teaching and also the new knowledge I had been introducing. The teachers of Chinese were the most threatened. They were still using twelfth century texts compiled by Lu Zuqian which the girls hated. They wanted their teachers to change; my colleagues also tried to talk the teachers into replacing their archaic syllabus. An elderly teacher therefore chose an essay on bidding farewell to friends going to study abroad. The sad thing was that many of the things referred to in the essay were beyond his ken. His explanation was so absurd that it provoked the girls into loud laughters. He made more mistakes when he graded and corrected their essays. The girls went on strike and the matter became the most talked about matter of the town. The education office had no choice but to fire him while the gentry and other teachers blamed me for have started the whole thing. Two weeks before the summer holiday I handed in my resignation.

On the eve of my departure from Gulin, the girls gave me a party; all of them turned up for it. The boys of other schools also gave me a farewell party. Then the head of the education office, having been made drunk by the gentry, came to look for me, carrying not one but two meat choppers. I fled to the home of Mr. Yu and slipped away from there. But the head of education was still looking around for me everywhere. His extraordinary behavior angered the boys of the senior elementary who went on strike and threaten to beat him up if he didn't stop. On the other hand, the commander of the local garrison, Pu Jianqiu, gave me protection.

To settle this ugly situation, the head of education, Wang Shaozeng, agreed to pay for a dinner party at which he would apologize to me. The place selected for the party was the County Institute of Culture (Wenhuaguan). Many teachers were invited; so were some members of the education office. Wang, however, did not turn up. The guests wanted to leave, if Wang insisted on being absent. Under such circumstances, he appeared reluctantly and shame-facedly. He sat there without uttering a word. The apology was spoken on his behalf by a school inspector.

Subsequently Wang sacked the headmistress and a number of teachers of the girls' school while I left for Chongqing where on the *Shangwu ribao* (Business daily news) I published a statement about the whole event. The dismissed teachers established a new school at Mr. Yu's residence. Nearly all the girls of our school went to the new school.

The secondary schools and elementary schools, teachers' schools and vocational schools, and the mass educational arrangements were either at the county seat or in the market towns and villages. Beyond these places if teaching was done, it was done by old-fashioned private tutors at their or their pupils' homes. The texts were traditional, for the inculcation of traditional values and primarily for the elementary skills of reading and writing. The years of schooling were normally short, and the lucky few who received this rudimentary education were few indeed. On the whole, the majority of the highlanders were hardly touched by either traditional or modern learning. Their's was a not yet literate society whose traditions and accumulated wisdoms were preserved and handed down chiefly orally.

Table 7.1

Locations of Granaries for Famine Relief

Location	City	Village
Enshi	7,485	70
Fangxian	2,939	4,900
Laifeng	2,316	2,600
Lichuan	3,134	2,620
Xuanen	2,781	500
Fengdu	8,457	1,938
Pengshui	5,520	6,461
Wanxian	32,150	3,418
Yunyang	26,730	1,043
Cili	10,246	6,000
Sangzhi	54,413	234
Shimen	3,230	6,872

Sources: Respective county gazeteers.

Table 7.2

Education Budget, Wanxian, 1935 (yuan)

Wanxian city	146,317
Districts	79,224
Total	*225,541*
Expenditure	
Administration	12,506
Secondary schools	35,443
County elementary schools	39,002
District elementary schools	79,224
Mass education	19,936
Total	*186,111*

Table 7.3

Education in Sichuan Highlands, 1930s (annual expenditure in yuan)

County	Population	Number of primary schools	Estimated number of pupils	Expenditure on education (yuan)	Number of pupils per school	Expenditure per school (yuan)	Expenditure per pupil (yuan)
Bazhong	644,247	603	10,391	86,666	17(?)	143.7	8.3
Chengkou	77,805	31	1,111	3,060	36	98.7	2.8
Fengdu	525,323	182	7,505	59,900	41	329	7.9
Fengjie	365,541	57	5,802	22,758	102	399.3	4.0
Fuling	1,041,688	139	11,973	96,665	86	695.4	8.3
Guangyuan	164,842	46	1,421	7,878	31	171.2	5.6
Nanjiang	218,270	39	1,505	3,500	39	89.7	2.3
Pengshui	210,162	56	2,840	21,321	51	380.7	7.5
Qiangjiang	115,461	47	1,215	3,000	26	63.8	2.4
Shizhu	189,445	33	2,025	13,205	62	400.2	4.7
Wanxian	811,465	308	16,905	66,117	55	214.7	3.9
Wanyuan	152,266	34	3,045	7,360	90	216.5	2.4
Wushan	150,492	42	2,090	15,221	50	362.2	7.3
Wuxi	150,633	61	2,430	28,040	40	315.1	11.5
Xiushan	314,112	81	5,682	21,940	70	270.9	3.9
Zhaohua	106,814	50	1,723	12,000	34	240.0	7.0
Zhongxian	505,889	228	10,539	44,135	46	193.6	4.2

Sources: Lu Pingdeng (1936, 69–72); Zhang Xiaomei (1938, B1–5, 7–11); *Sichuan yuebao*, 9/2, 397–406; *Sichuansheng zhengfu gongbao*, no. 16, 67–71.

Notes: In east Sichuan, one pupil in every sixty-eight people; average expense per pupil, 6.5 yuan. In north Sichuan, one pupil in every eighty-four people; average expense per pupil, 4.3 yuan. In southeast Sichuan, one pupil in every seventy-five people; average expense per pupil, 4.6 yuan.

Table 7.4

Education in Southern and Western Hunan, 1923–24

Location	Number of primary schools	Number of pupils
Anren	72	2,643
Chaxian	99	3,774
Chenxi	35	2,060
Zhenxian	69	2,736
Daoxian	164	5,880
Fenghuang	33	962
Guidong	89	2,892
Guzhang	2	30
Leiyang	109	4,375
Linwu	169	5,411
Luxi	27	923
Qiancheng	18	1,750
Qianyang	57	1,802
Rucheng	138	4,392
Tongdao	36	1,491
Xupu	65	3,406
Yongshun	31	1,245
Yongsui	39	1,750
Youxian	269	11,635

Source: Dagongbao, June 12, 1924.

8
A MARTIAL AND ROMANTIC TRADITION

THE COUNTY and prefectural gazetteers published in the second half of the nineteenth century describe the highlanders as being "unvarnished to uncouth," "ill-informed to uneducated," "quarrelsome to arrogant, even violent," superstitious for their belief in heresies and heterodoxies, and, the most surprising of all, "litigious."* These characteristics were noticed by the educated elite who participated in the compilation of the gazetteers and whose yardstick represented the values and norms of the genteel city dwellers.

Nonetheless, both the polished and the unpolished shared a great deal in common. Home was the center of life for both. The scions of the gentry, if successful in their careers, were likely to leave for greener pastures elsewhere, just as some young men of common stock joined the army. In time all of them would become heads of their families wherever they chose to live. The majority, however, remained; they worked and lived at home, which was at the same time a workshop, a store, or a farmstead, except for those few who spent part of the day in the magistrate's offices or in a modern school. The only other experiences of social life outside the home were the infrequent gatherings of the lineage association, local fairs and markets, and militia drills, and a chat over a cup of tea in a tea-house or a meal in a restaurant with one's associates. If one lived in a hamlet, one would be deprived of most of these social opportunities. Life would be even more centered on the family and the few neighbors for moral and emotional support, and for mutual aid in times of need. On such an institutional basis, the highlanders could hardly develop a communal ethos; they were, as Sun Yat-sen regretted, just "a tray of loose grains of sand" with no spirit to bind them together.

Whatever happened to be his pursuit—a craft, a trade, a farm, or an

---

*These cultural traits are shared by the mountain peasants of Jiangxi and Fujian whom I also study for purpose of comparison.

official career—wherever he happened to reside—a city, a market town, or a hamlet—a highlander developed himself not only in the context of home but also under the supervision of his father, the patriarch.[1] Home was where he loved and hated, felt happy and miserable, suffered the usual diseases, worked, lived, and died. Indeed, there were differences between living in the town and in the country, but they were not as sharp as oil and water, for as Braudel wisely points out: "the towns urbanized the countryside, but the countryside 'ruralized' the towns too."[2] I must hasten to add that the city we are concerned with here was not Braudel's city at the dawn of capitalism, but an "agrarian city," as Robert Lopez calls it.[3] The cities described in the last chapter had very little in common with, say, Genoa in 1300. Whereas the former were founded on agriculture and an externally imposed administration, unfree and undemocratic, the latter was founded on trade and self-government, free but still undemocratic. Both the twentieth-century agriculture of the highland in Central China and the trade and crafts in fourteenth-century Genoa were organized and controlled by the small producer, who was the patriarch. And so the home life, business life, and indeed sociopolitical life of the highland cities of China and the late medieval cities of Europe were permeated with paternalism.

What was known as the Confucian ethics of filiality, I believe, had its roots in this rural patriarchal life. Since everyone who was a Han Chinese was socialized on it and internalized it, it could easily be adapted and adopted by the office, the school, the guild, and even the armed forces. However refined at the metropolitan end or however crude at the market town end, it was recognizably Confucian. By it the Han Chinese could say to the Miao and the Tujia: "We are Chinese, you are not. It is you who should change to conform with us."

The official image of the highlander delineated his crudity, whose eradication represented progress toward "rites and music," as Confucius himself put it, or "rites and righteousness," that is, civilization, in a more recent expression, since the Confucian gentleman had long stopped making music. Even as late as the 1930s when he was governor of Hubei, Zhang Chun contemplated ways to reform the militant, violent character of the people in the western end of his province. In his words, they were the traits of "a people beyond the pale" (huawairen).[4]

Many of the gazetteers published in the second half of the nineteenth century contained a chapter on ethnography (*fengxi*). Their few successors published in the twentieth century quietly dropped it, however, as if to show that the users of these gazetteers need not pay further attention to it. The omission may have partly been due to the character changes that had taken place, particularly among the young men in eastern and northeastern Sichuan. Not rites and righteousness but opium addiction seems to have drained some of them of the vital energy to farm. It was women and the elderly who labored in the fields and on the hills.[5] Nevertheless, when it came to recruitment and fighting, the Red Army seized their addiction by its horns, coerced them to give it up, and organized and drilled them before sending them to the front.[6] Their Sichuan enemies, too, were opium sodden. On the other hand, Governor Zhang Chun still had enough reason to be concerned with the crudity of the western Hubei people and the tenants of the garrison land in western Hunan could still stage a mammoth uprising in 1937. The anger continued to burn in their chests.

The highlanders who lived in cities and towns, fortresses and villages were likely to possess the virtues and vices of the rural people the anthropologists have analyzed. They were conservative, conformist, distrustful, and untruthful. Often they resorted to the weapons of the weak—gossip, back-biting, and witchcraft, as we have learned from James Scott. But in Sichuan in particular, only a small percentage of them lived in this way—a mere 12 percent in the county of Nanchuan, for instance. The great majority scattered in the hamlets and homesteads had no institutional welfare or institutional safety protection to speak of. To them, not only the emperor and magistrate, but also the lineage association and temples were beyond their daily reach. Even if they had things to gossip and complain about, their words of grievance could hardly travel farther than the dozen or so pairs of ears in their neighborhood. What would be the purpose of gossip or back-biting? When a dozen families lived in close proximity, they knew each other so well that it would be pointless to conceal and lie, unless it was for the benefit of the outsider, the taxman, the bailiff, a traveling merchant, or an army deserter.

These homesteaders had to fend for themselves against a natural disaster, a roaming band of robbers, or a beast of prey.[7] They had to be physically strong. Shen Congwen, the novelist, referred to their martial spirit and martial prowess at several places—Zhijiang, Qianjiang, Fenghuang.[8] But he lamented the gradual loss of these attributes after

1916.[9] He Long, the commander-in-chief of the Second Front Red Army, about whom I shall say much more, was a native of Sangzhi. He agreed with Shen's observation of the highlanders' martial skills but did not notice any flagging in their martial spirit, perhaps because he was fighting with them and was a member of the local Brotherhood.[10] In violent action, their trust and distrust had to be as clear as day and night. They had to learn to trust or to distrust.[11]

Their litigiousness may have sprung less from their naive faith in the magistrate's justice than from the moral and organizational support of the local secret society, especially the brotherhood and sometimes the Divine Army. In a dispute between a landowner and his tenant, the tenant was not entirely without social recourse. In one between old and new immigrants to the highland, a settlement could be reached on an equal footing.[12] Neither the old nor the new immigrant was likely to be skilled in using words; neither was educated. The old immigrants were mostly garrison soldiers, tradesmen, refugees, and fugitives, sprinkled with a few physicians, fortune-tellers, and frustrated scholars. The social composition of the new immigrants was likely to be similar. They owed more to the esprit de corps of the secret societies than to the canons of Confucianism, the Three Principles of the People, liberal democracy, or even Marxism-Leninism.

Before their arrival, most of the highland was peopled by the Miao, Tujia, and other minorities. Needless to say, they owed little to indigenous Confucianism and imported foreign doctrines. Nevertheless, through the decades of interaction between the minorities and immigrants, they rubbed their cultural traits on each other, more out of necessity for being neighbors than for any high-minded reason. The Miao worship of Tudikong (or T'u Ti Kung) and the Goddess of Mercy, and the Han acceptance of the *wu* (witch), were just two of many examples.[13]

The Miao and Tujia had their religions—their worship of Nuo and the Three Kings (Sanwang), all of whom were heroic fighters. The *wu* witches were normally women in their thirties who could be possessed by gods as mediums. When so possessed once in a couple of months, they could exorcise evil spirits, bestow good fortune on believers, cure the sick, and enable barren women to become pregnant.[14] The *wu* was widely resorted to not only in western Hunan, but also in western Hubei (Badong, Laifeng, Yunxian, Yunyang, and Xingshan) and eastern Sichuan (Fengjie, Langzhong, Wanxian).

Han immigrants had their religions too. Fengdu was probably the most important center of popular Daoism whither all the ghosts were supposed to go. The famous Hall of the King of Hells and the Eighteen Hells of clay figures vividly portraying the evil doers through hundreds of tortures attracted many visitors and pilgrims every year; in 1935, no fewer than 3,519 went there from Changshou, Fuling, Chongqing, and other places. The city also had more than a hundred seances conducted by *wu* who claimed to be able to visit the hells and talk on behalf of clients with their deceased beloved ones.[15] In the eyes of the educated elite, these were disdainfully superstitious people indeed.

Militancy

In her *Warlord Soldiers*, Diana Lary describes "regions which produced soldiers as *by-products of the endemic violence*."[16] The violence was not just a matter of gnashing teeth and waving fists at each other and at outsiders. The militancy of the highlanders came from a long tradition of defiance of what they regarded as injustice and of institutionalized violence. We need not trace as far back as the rebellions led by the Buddhist White Lotus Sect on both sides of the Daba Range at the beginning of the nineteenth century. In the 1850s and 1860s the chapters on military affairs (*bingshi*) in the local gazetteers recorded wide-spread uprisings throughout western Hubei, southeastern Sichuan, and western and southwestern Hunan in conjunction with the Taiping rebellion, which nearly destroyed the empire. By the 1870s peace gradually returned, to stay until the 1911 Revolution. Then the invasion of warlord soldiers and Communist guerrillas set the highland ablaze again. Figure 8.1 shows the frequency of armed uprisings in western Hunan; the pattern can also safely be applied to the two other subregions.

In more peaceful times, between the recurring rebellions and uprisings, the Divine Army intervened on behalf of the oppressed. It would not admit anyone above the status of village security head (*baozhang*), and it appeared to be prepared to kill the head of any township (*xiangzhang*). It fought the officials, police, and people wearing army tunics. It objected to high rent and taxes, government policies responsible for the shortages in rice and salt, conscription of soldiers to fight in the Japanese war of 1937, and reregistration of land. Like so many pseudo-religious rebels all over China, the Divine Army did not seem

Figure 8.1. **Frequency of Violent Actions, Western Hunan**

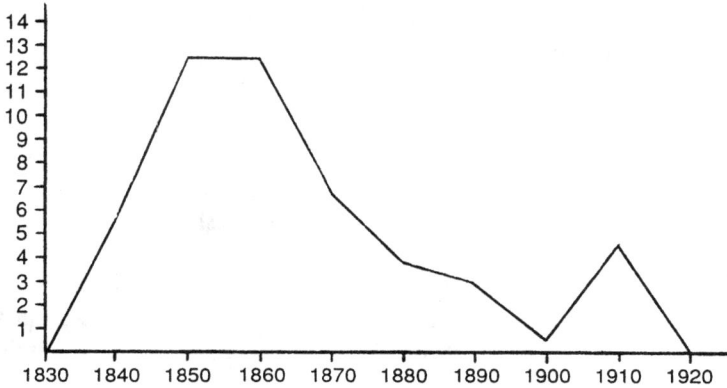

to have a unified organization from the Daba to the Wuling Range. Instead, it had only local bands. The mountainous terrain may have been partially responsible for this decentralization; food supply also may have contributed. If this judgment is acceptable, then it may not be fruitful to try to ascertain where and when the army began. It probably sprang up from among the peasants and woodsmen at several places.[17] According to an elderly gentleman in Gulin who had personally spent three or four days with a band of the Divine Army in 1929 when it attacked the city, it was about forty strong, led by one Hu Shangyao, and believed itself invulnerable. But like all the other claimants to invulnerability to knives and fire arms, this group was defeated and killed.[18] About the same time, some three thousand Divine soldiers assaulted Shizhu, because warlord Yang Sen had imposed a new monthly tax and the local militia sided with Yang. They had taken and kept the city in their hands for several months. In the meantime, Yang Sen was driven away by another warlord, Chen Lanting, who eventually quelled this spectacular uprising.[19] He Long, the colorful Red Army commander, himself a member of the Brotherhood, cooperated more than once with the Divine Army when he was in Hefeng (January 1929; January 1931), Lichuan (January 1934), northeastern Guizhou (May–June 1934), and Youyang (August 1934).[20]

The highlanders' militancy, useful in daily life and in an emergency, was fostered by an oral tradition of tales and songs. First, some tales of Herculean heroes and heroines of Miao, Tujia, or even Han origin came to be shared by all mountain peoples as their common legacy. Nu Wa's mending of the crack in the sky in order to stop the torrential rain that caused the great floods; Hou Yi's shooting down of nine of the ten suns so as to make the world cooler for human beings and vegetation; the impetuous Gong Gong's knocking down of the pillars between heaven and earth to cause the earth to tilt up in the west and the great rivers to flow eastward—these were the deeds of the ancient titans. In more recent times, legend had it that

> a woodsman [Han?] met and married a wild woman [non-Han?]. After the birth of their son, he stayed at home while she went out to hunt for food.
>
> One day the woodsman sighted a boat. He called and waved and it came to take him and the boy away. On returning home, the wild woman could not find them; she cried and cried. "I must search my heart and show it to you!" So saying, she hacked it out, fell on the floor, and died.
>
> Then the boy grew up to be an unusually strong young man. Even mountains had to yield to the might of his whip. He flattened all of them in the north on his way south in search of his mother's grave. When he found it, he knocked his head against the mountain on which she was buried. And he died.
>
> That is why there are so few mountains in the north and so many in the south.[21]

The way the western Hunanese interpreted the widely known Meng Jiang Nu story is indicative of their defiance. The story of Meng Jiang looking for her husband who failed to return home from his corvée duties of building the Great Wall plucked a sympathetic cord in the hearts of many Chinese in many provinces. It seems that all of them wanted to claim her as the "native daughter." In Guangzhou and Suzhou, she and her husband were described as Daoist immortals who descended to earth to save people from natural and other calamities. When this was done, they went back to the Paradise to live happily ever after. Guangdong people preferred to admire her not as a loving wife who committed suicide because she had failed to find her husband, but as a filial daughter who did what she did to please her parents.

Even the Miao of western Hunan claimed that Meng Jiang was one of them and worshiped her.[22] In Qiancheng they sang:

> When the grass turned yellow in October,
> Meng Jiang went to look for her man everywhere ...

She kicked and wailed
And the Great Wall crumbled.

Here there was no role for a Daoist immortal or filial daughter to play, only a wife who loved her husband and resented the cruelty of the governmental authorities so intensely that her tears and kicks undid the Great Wall, or perhaps the great wall between the Miao and the Han in western Hunan. Their interpretation harked back to that of Li Po, the famous "barbarianized" Han Chinese poet:

Her bitter tears made mountains collapse.
Her deep sorrow split open stones and rocks.[23]

Through the centuries, the Miao and Tujia had sung in praise of the rebellion led by Wu Bayue (August Wu) in 1795 in an epic of several thousand lines.[24] They celebrated that led by Li Yuanfa in 1849:

Big brother [Li] with 600 men
Fearlessly marched into the city.
They slayed the mayor
And shared out grain to the needy.
They burnt down the school
And then freed the jailed;[25]

They praised another led by Zhang Xiumei in 1855–72:

Come,
Unsheathe your sabers,
Push out your cannon,
Follow Zhang Xiumei and
Show your true color.
Be it red, be it green,
We, Miaos, are not to be bullied.[26]

Yet another was led by Prince Yi, Shi Dakai, of the Taiping Rebellion, to whose call to revolt Zhang Xiumei probably responded.[27] The anti–Yuan Shikai campaign of 1915–16, the Communist war of the 1930s, and the great uprising led by Long Yunfei in 1936–37 also received praise in song.[28]

The background to these songs of fury consisted of two important ingredients: the rent of the garrison land and the discrimination against the Miao and Tujia.

The *tuntian* garrison fields came chiefly from Han landowners. Taken by the government as such, they could not be transacted between individuals in order to prevent the recurrence of the concentration of landownership. These fields were located along the fortification line from Huayuan to Chadong as well as in Fenghuang. Elsewhere there were only the "feeding fields" (*yangkoutian*) of a yield of three pecks of grain to each adult male, one peck to each adult female, or eight pecks to each family of four. The recipient became either the head or a soul (*ding*) of a *tun*.[29]

Furthermore, in 1805 the old Great Wall of Hunan, some 300 li in length, was rebuilt with 1,100 blockhouses, checkpoints, and gates, manned by 7,000 garrison soldiers and 1,000 militia (see fig. 8.2).[30] Thereafter many Miaos and Tujias were transformed into tenants of garrison land who, according to the records, paid a rent of 78,218 piculs of unhusked rice on 103,223 mu of land.[31] The official rate of rent was fixed at 0.77 picul per mu. The tenant, however, actually paid more than 1 picul, or about 60 percent of the yield, higher than the prevalent rate elsewhere.[32] Bailiffs also collected rent in excess of the fixed rate. This alone would have driven tenants to give up the garrison fields, which were indeed being illegally sold to people who had enough influence and power to evade paying the rent. Thus, the rent-bearing garrison land decreased from the original 100,000 mu to about 70,000, and finally to about 40,000 mu in the 1930s.[33]

Another source of grievances was the general assumption that the Miao and Tujia were either genetically or culturally inferior to the Han. A policy of Hanification was adopted to teach them Confucian doctrines and force them to change their ways of living after the 1795 rebellion. The reconstruction of the Great Wall in western Hunan was seen as an insult. The culmination of these two factors was the outburst in 1936–37.

Born in Shanjiang near Fenghuang, Long Yunfei was an able commander who served under Chen Quzhen. When the Miao people burned down the garrison granaries in the Qinglong township of Yongsui and killed the official in charge, other Miao responded by demanding the abolition of the rent on garrison land and the dismissal of the official in control of it.[34] A Miao himself, Long Yunfei led an

Figure 8.2. **The Great Wall of Western Hunan. (Taken from Ling Chunsheng and Rui Yifu, 1947.)**

army of 1,200, took Qiancheng, and kept it in his hands for a fortnight.[35]
The provincial governor, General He Jian, offered his terms of reconciliation: cancel all the rent in arrears in 1933–35; reduce the rent of 1936 by
10 percent; and reduce the rent from 1937 onward by 20 percent.

This seems to have applied only to Qiancheng; the government
continued to collect rent as usual in Fenghuang. Consequently, Long
led the Fenghuang Miao tenants to join the uprising under the slogan
"Resist Japan, reform the rent system, overthrow He Jian!" The revolt
ended in He's departure from Hunan, Chen Quzhen's resignation from
the directorship of garrison affairs, the promotion of Long to brigadier
general, and the abolition of the garrison field rent system. All garrison
land thus became privatized.[36]

We know less of the folk expression of anger and protest in western
Hubei and eastern Sichuan because of a paucity of available printed
material. This paucity itself is a sign of the Hanification of the early
settlers of Miao and Tujia origins there. Another possibility is that
ethnographers and anthropologists as a rule do not choose to study a
people who live in relatively inaccessible mountain areas and yet possess scarcely any distinct, pronounced cultural traits to suggest a fruitful and meaningful inquiry. The gatherers of folk tales and songs from
Peking University and Sun Yat-sen University in Guangzhou in the
1920s were seldom natives of western Hubei or eastern Sichuan, and in
any case they did not go there themselves. But here are a few examples.

North Sichuan
Even the sea of a thousand ells
Is not deep as the people's hate.
For three generations we leased before sowing
And were left with naught but tattered clothing.[37]

Rocky, oh rocky Erdouping!
Yam and corn come out my ears.
The roads twist and turn,
The woods dark and dense,
My thatched roof rumble and crumble,
My bamboo gate shaky and rickety.
Dream of a bowl of rice, eh?
Never, never, never.[38]

East Sichuan
Police patrol,
You do us wrong.
Our wine for you to drink,
Our money for you to spend,
Our women for you to have fun,
As your women for the officials to enjoy.
Thieves and robbers, none of your business.
You bully only people like us.[39]

And two songs about the Communists, which may have been composed by the people themselves or by Communist song writers in the style of folk songs:

North Sichuan
Down with the dog, Liu Xiang,
It's Xu Xiangqian* we follow.
We'll join up with the Red Army
And have food, clothes, and all.[40]

West Hubei
Here comes He Yunqin**
Who camps at Lotus Pond Flats.
So many men, so many horses
Just for us poor folks.[41]

Romanticism

The Miao believed that if a man did not enjoy sexual pleasure with women (*wofie*), he would encounter two difficulties after his death. First, of his seventy-one souls, one would transform into a bird to keep him company in the nether world. But the metamorphosis could not be completed if he had not had experienced *wofie*. Second, he would not be able to travel across the Bushy Mound (Maosongshan) and the eleven hells to reach the souls of his ancestors.[42]

---

*Commander of the Fourth Front Red Army.
**He Long.

Wofie is not the *yaomalang* I referred to briefly in chapter 7. The former implies chiefly premarital sex; the latter, the entire process of courtship. At every Miao fortress or village, there was a *malangpo*, a hill where young people went to sing to each other. The boys came in a group to meet with beautifully dressed girls. They sang of their longing and love at a time when the autumn harvest was in and the weather was pleasant. They went from fortress to fortress, to sing and to croon, in search of a steady mate:

> *Come, singer, come.*
> *Don't stay away 'cause you're poor.*
> *I care not for your money,*
> *Only whether you're good fun.*

> *Come, together we sing*
> *Come, together we play.*
> *When we're old,*
> *We shan't have much fun.*[43]

The Miao also have a traditional story of the Deluge. When the water receded, only a boy and his sister were left. "Let's get married," he proposed, but she was hesitant. The brother suggested that each of them roll a stone down the hill. If the stones stayed together, they should then get married for the sake of continuing the human race. The stones did indeed stay together, but she remained hesitant. It was now her turn to suggest a test by throwing a needle and thread in the air. If the thread went through the eye of the needle, then they would get married. Miraculously, the thread did go through the eye.

Her first birth was a ball of flesh. Alarmed, they asked the gods to tell them what to do. "You should chop it up into small pieces and scattered them into the wind." So they did, and each small piece turned into a human being.[44]

Neither the belief in *wofie* nor the story of the Deluge, neither premarital sex nor incest under those circumstances, could be accepted by the prim and proper Han tradition. Indeed, when it came to love and marriage, the hillmen and plainsmen had very little in common. Zhu Ziqing of the Peking University is probably right when he says: "Because they [the highlanders] have hardly been touched by Confucian ethics, they dare to express [their emotions]

nakedly."[45] One may add that the highlanders had stronger, uncrip-
pled emotions, and the freedom to express them. They had no fear
of love or sex. After all, love songs are heard in villages and homesteads all over China. The point is that plains love songs differ radi-
cally from mountain love songs in mood, attitude, and intensity. The
former express more regret and frustration than happiness. Here are
three from the plains of Jiangsu:

> *A Widow*
> *Where can I find a lover in his twenties,*
> *To sleep with me just for one night,*
> *with his brand new water-wheel*
> *To irrigate this bone-dry field of mine?*

> *Love Suicide*
> *Last year you sang four lines in my backyard*
> *My young mistress killed herself*
> *And her sister-in-law jumped into the river.*

> *"Extreme" Obscenity*
> *I shake his shoulders to stop him singing,*
> *For my bright red pants are already sopping.*[46]

Tearful, unrequited love, the main theme of plains love songs, is almost totally absent from highland and desert love songs. Instead, the
highlanders sing of exciting expectations, tenderness between the
sexes, and the joy of love-making. Obscenity is a singularly inappro-
priate criterion to apply to folktales and folksongs, which are purely
for personal pleasure and never for monetary gain. I begin with a mild
one taken from Shen Congwen's short story:

> *In the skies, clouds are upon clouds;*
> *On the ground, graves are upon graves;*
> *In the kitchen, plates are upon plates;*
> *On your bed, a man is upon a woman.*[47]

A little stronger:

> *The sun sets behind the hills in the west,*
> *And the shadows of clouds cast on the walls.*

It's time for me to get the arena ready.
When it's ready, here my man will be.
His spear will thrust through my twin blades.[48]

Stronger still:

One thrust, two thrusts, three, four, and thirty-six thrusts.
Each pierces the heart of my peony flower.
Have mercy, oh please, have mercy.
I just can't go on any more.[49]

Highland Sichuanese, like the Jiangxi and Fujian mountain peasants, sing also, for protest as well as for love:

My lips are sealed,
But a fire burns in my heart.
One day the fire will erupt and,
Emperor and officials will have no place to hide.[50]

And,

Above my head, three knives hang—
Heavy interest, heavy deposit, and heavy rent.
Before me, three ways lead me to
Flee, suicide, or prison.[51]

In Fuling the peasants complained:

Guv, you have a strange abacus—
It makes a stone lion shed tears;
It gives me tiny wages
Enough for rotten food, but nothing for fire wood.[52]

Sichuan love songs were just as humorous and candid as their western Hunan counterparts:

Garden onions are not as tasty as wild onions;
My man is not as strong as wild ones.
The tone of his voice is as hard as he hits me;
But theirs is as sweet as honey.[53]

And,

> The sun sinks under the western hills,
> And I hold my love's hand who must go.
> How I want him to stay this night,
> But the door, like a sieve, has many eyes.
>
> The pomegranate blooms while its leaves fade.
> The young bride's bed is unshared by man.
> Like tender meat on the chopping board,
> Beyond the savour of the cat.
>
> By the gate of the wall I stand.
> My love sees me and leaves his heart.
> How he longs to become a mouse
> And creep through the wall up to my couch.
>
> The peony blossom is fragrant and sweet
> And is placed on my love's shoulder.
> Let me feel your dagger between my thighs—
> Eight inches long and eight in circumference.
>
> The pomegranate blossom is fragrant and red
> And I call my love, "dear heart."
> Let me wrap my legs around your shoulders
> When you caress my breasts.
>
> The fifth curfew has just sounded
> And my love must leave at once.
> He says: "My dearest. Don't forget me.
> Be patient, you must!" [54]

This kind of sexual frankness in songs and in behavior, the diametrical opposite of the shyness and timidity that characterized Han adolescents, came from childhood socialization of the Miao and Tujia in particular, whose traditions were orally transmitted through songs. Children began to learn to sing at the age of six or seven. Good singers, *bajiangsha*, were popularly admired.[55] It was believed that good singing surpassed good scholarship in expressing emotions and transmitting experiences. According to tradition, when Scholar Luo took a boatload of books to meet the Third Daughter Liu in a song contest, Liu sang these lines:

> *Everyone's mountain songs come from the heart;*
> *No one carries them in a punt.*[56]

She won the contest, of course, and her anti-intellectualism became a cherished part of the curriculum of socialization. Highland children also swam naked together in the river even after the onset of puberty. If a stranger came, young girls did nothing more than stay in the water while covering up their breasts with their hands.[57] Unlike the Han, they attached little importance to female virginity. Parents did not forbid their teenage daughters from social intercourse with young men; instead, they took pride in the their physical attractiveness and extended hospitality to the young man brought home by an unmarried daughter.[58] The courting couple could have premarital sex either in the seclusion of a forest (*wanshan*, play on the mountain) or at home for a period of several days at a stretch. There was no question of a patriarch beating or even killing his daughter for premarital sex, unless he, his relatives, and his neighbors were "Hanified."[59]

Courtship did not always lead to marriage as the young people reserved their right to choose before making a definite commitment. Then both went to their parents for consent, which was routinely given. The young man's parents would start the negotiations by involving a matchmaker, fortuneteller, and others. Even at this stage the negotiations could break down, and the young people could look around for another liaison.[60]

Marriage usually took place when the male was sixteen or seventeen years of age, but he could be as young as ten or as old as twenty. The younger he was, the richer his family. The female was often older, seventeen or eighteen, and could be seven or eight years older. The wedding ceremony was considerably simpler and therefore less costly than the Han norm. But singing was an essential component of it. At different places the arrangements for cohabitation after the wedding were different. At Gulin, the newlyweds did not spend the first night together. At some places in Guizhou, the bride went straight back to her maternal home after the wedding, then the groom came to invite her to his home, followed by a second separation until the first birth, following which the couple and the baby lived together as a family. At

Fenghuang the bride moved into the matrimonial home on the wedding day but refrained from having sex with her husband for the three days and nights immediately thereafter.[61]

The wedding marked the beginning of stricter sexual mores as long as the husband was alive. The couple had their own home of which the wife was the mistress, a person of considerable decision-making power as she was older than the man and did productive work.[62] Adultery was punished by paying a compensation to the injured party. Divorce usually ensued if there were no children of the marriage.[63] There was, however, an exception to this rule, if the adulterer happened to be the husband's father. In such a case, which was by no means rare, the adulterer just took his daughter-in-law as his wife or concubine while arranging a new wife for his son.[64] If a bride of a child-husband had an affair with another male in the household and gave birth to a baby, the family could accept the fait accompli with magnanimity and understanding. The two parties could get married and continue to live in the household; they did not have to die for their sin.[65] If a brother took a fancy for his sister-in-law, he could quite properly marry her when she was widowed.[66] The remarriage of widows was far easier on the highland.

In each of these cases the Han treatment would be drastically different, with far less tolerance and far more cruelty, so that the traditional, largely Confucian sexual morality could be upheld. Han Chinese of both sexes seldom developed the skills of singing love songs, and they abhorred premarital sex. The Miao and Tujia, on the other hand, disliked the Han style of arranged marriage between two total strangers; their girls were impressed neither by the timidity of Han young people (which was almost a Han virtue) nor by Han young men's attitude of making use of women for monetary gain or other kinds of convenience. To make things more difficult, few Han learned to speak the Miao or Tujia language, few took on the habit of frequent bathing, most Han girls bound their feet, and few of them treated the Miao and Tujia as equals. Not surprisingly, marriage between a Han and a minority was infrequent.[67]

Professor Wu Yunzhen at the University of Jishou, western Hunan, told me of his surveys, one conducted at Tuojiangzhen and another at the northern suburb of Jishou. Tuojiangzhen has 111 inhabitants, 50 males and 61 females, or 77 Han, 27 Miao, 3 Tujia, and 4 Muslims. The only known mixed marriages involved one Miao man marrying a Han girl in 1930 and one in 1937, and one Han man marrying a Miao girl in 1913, one in 1929, and one in 1948. The Jishou suburb has 102 inhabitants—47 males and 55 females, or 66 Han, 16 Miao, and 20 Tujia. Its known mixed marriages involved Miao men marrying Han girls in 1902, 1936, and 1942 (one each), and one Han man marrying a Miao girl in 1905. Professor Wu also told me that up on the mountains, mixed marriages with the Han were even rarer.[68]

Indeed, the highlanders' views on love, sex, and marriage were profoundly different from those of the plains peasants. Their love was purer and more romantic; their sex, freer and more satisfying; their marriages, less a matter of duty and more a matter of choice. They were at variance with the abstentionism of the Aztecs and the southern Italians, but in agreement with the absence of priestly chastity at Montaillou.[69] Unlike plains peasants, they did not seem to be aware of the need to conserve their energy for back-breaking work in the fields. They did not seem to have suffered from this negligence either, as the plainsmen were full of praise for their virility.

This does not mean, however, that there was in any sense sexual equality. Some women on the highland took part fully in farming; some did not, when, for instance, fiber for spinning and weaving was available. Some had their feet bound; some did not. Some enjoyed considerable freedom of dignified divorce; some did not. Some adulteresses were treated with humaneness; some were not. The patriarch was always present during a woman's social intercourse, although the highland patriarch had less power and appeared to be more magnanimous, similar to that in the Occitan Marriage Square described by Le Roy Ladurie.[70]

Not only toward women, but also toward other men, the highlanders' attitude and interpersonal relations were different. They did not entertain the prejudice or distrust of all other men in their neighborhood, because of mutual need in daily life and work and in an emergency. Since they lived together in small numbers and close propinquity, they knew each other intimately, making unnecessary lying truly unnecessary. This was probably why several gazetteers—Fenghuang, Nanjiang, Wushan, Fengdu, Enshi, Laifeng, Xianfeng, Xingshan. Zhixi—described them as being *pu*: blunt, straightforward, "rough diamond." They had not been civilized enough to become habitually false.

Less skilled with words than with their fists, the highlanders had a history of violence, of martial discipline and military action. It is not easy to establish which county of modern China had the highest frequency of violence. The propensity to resort to arms on these highlands was pronounced. This too made them different from the traditional image of the passive and cautious peasant. Instead, they were a group of peasants who dared to love, to tell the truth, to find the limits of the utility of lies, to take action against authority when the authority on the highland was, relatively speaking, always weaker than on the plains and the men of action were always stronger.

All this does not add up to a denial of paternalism, of the image of the limited good, of a serious lack of information and education, of a deficiency of vision and a shortage of organizational skills. Their action of protest and revolt, no matter how praiseworthy, was spontaneous, in need of outside help to be effective. Nearly all their uprisings were failures, yet they tried again and again. As peasants went, they were truly extraordinary.

9
THE CIVIL WAR BELT

IN AN EARLIER study on the warlords, I discussed the division of China between the northern and southern groups of military leaders.[1] The division was by no means simply a geographic matter—north and south of the Qinling range or of the Yangzi River. As a geographic expression of a complex of political, military, and economic factors, it could not possibly coincide with a range of mountains or a river. With Beijing as the center, the north extended its power and influence, in ebb and flow, westward to the western Sichuan plain and southward to the deltas of the Pearl in Guangdong and the Min in Fujian in 1915–16. Thereafter, the north withdrew a few steps, although it tried to maintain its control of the lowlands around the Mufoshan-Jiulingshan-Luoxiaoshan range, ringed counterclockwise by Nanchang-Jiujiang-Wuhan-Yueyang-Changsha-Hengshan in the shape of a hairpin. To lose it was to lose the south altogether, and to possess it was the first step toward conquering the north. And that was what the struggle was about in 1926–27.

Before that fatal contest, the stronger northern group bore down on the southern militarists, led either from Guangdong-Guangxi or from Yunnan, along the Daba-Wuling ranges and farther south along the Wuyi-Nanling ranges, each of which are shaped like an enormous boomerang and together a gigantic "S." Chinese call this the "civil war belt." The focus here is on the first boomerang, the Daba-Wuling ranges, the highland under inquiry. When the north was strong, such as in 1919–20 and 1922–24, it pressed toward these ranges and threatened to pierce through their passes. When the south was in an expansionist mood, it would push northward along the Xiang or the Gan to the Yangzi, as it did in 1921–22 and 1926–27.

Li Jiannong, under the nom de plume of Bansu, has estimated the frequency of civil wars from 1912 to 1928 (actually to 1930). Table 9.1 gives both his estimates and my own.

To put it differently, the provincial frequencies were:

Sichuan, 16	Jiangsu, 7	Zhejiang , 4
Guangdong, 13	Anhui, 6	Rehe, 3
Hunan, 13	Chihli, 6	Outer Mongolia, 3
Shaanxi, 12	Guizhou, 6	Suiyuan, 2
Fujian, 8	Jiangxi, 6	Fengtian, 1
Guangxi, 8	Yunnan, 6	Qinghai, 1
Honan, 7	Gansu, 4	Shanxi, 1
Hubei, 7	Shandong, 4	Xingjiang, 1

What is particularly noteworthy are the high frequencies in the three provinces of Sichuan, Hunan, and Hubei and in the other provinces on the civil war belt—Shaanxi, Jiangxi, and Fujian.

The highland actually experienced some kind of military operation every year from 1916 to 1933, except the peace maintained by General Chen Quzhen in western Hunan in 1930–34.

If one takes the Communist invasion into consideration, peace did not return to the highland until 1936 when He Long and Xiao Ke embarked on their Long March. Along this belt of high war frequencies, the militarists either fought for larger reasons than local interests, such as the unification of China and the preservation of the integrity of the 1912 Provisional Constitution, or for local issues, such as the autonomy of these provinces, the Sichuan salt markets in Hubei and Hunan, and often just the capture of garrison regions. All of these warring activities are listed in tables 9.2–9.4, at the end of this chapter.

Roughly speaking, the wars in western Hubei evolved chronologically from the anti–Yuan Shikai campaign in 1915–16 to the demand for provincial autonomy with help from Sichuan and Hunan in 1918–21, to the wax and wane of the northern and southern armed forces there in 1923–25, to the invasion of Sichuan troops on the bandwagon of the Northern Expedition in 1926–27; to the invasion of the Communist troops and bandits from 1928 onward. In eastern Sichuan, it all began with the anti–Yuan Shikai campaign and the invasion of the Yunnan-Guizhou armies which inspired the province to strengthen its own defense. After the campaign, these indigenous armed forces drove out the Yunnan-Guizhou armies and began an incessant series of wars against each other for the hegemony of the province. Liu Cunhou, Xiong Kewu, Yang Sen, Liu Wenhui, and Liu Xiang were the leading actors, and it was the last named who eventually unified Sichuan while the Communists penetrated into the north of the province. The pattern in western Hunan was different again, although it also began from the anti–Yuan Shikai campaign. This was followed by the growth of the local forces led by Tian Yingchao, Cai Juyou, and finally Chen Quzhen. Neither the provincial army nor the invasions of Guizhou and Sichuan armies, nor even the Communists commanded by He Long, did much damage to the core of this indigenous force, which was the cause of both war and peace in western Hunan.

For whatever reasons, these highland wars were fought largely on local resources. Transport of food uphill or upstream to the belligerents, as indicated in chapter 4, was slow and costly, if not impossible. Billets naturally were requisitioned, and coolies with their wagons and carts pressed into service.[2] Once a place was taken, the army kept it until it was driven away or found greener pastures. It depended on the place for recruitment, provisions, billet, corvée labor, and money, or in short, for survival.

These needs and a consideration for them made a garrison different from an army passing through or a roaming band of armed men. In fulfilling their needs, the former was less cruel than the latter. By the same token, the indigenous army was more likely to be so than the expatriate army. Between the two, the inhabitants normally preferred the former to the latter. No matter how impoverished, some units of Yang Sen's Twentieth Sichuan Army seldom behaved so ruthlessly as they did traversing western Hubei in January and February 1928. Their main purpose for going there was to grab as much money as they could before returning to eastern Sichuan. Their demand for 300,000 yuan to buy straw sandals in a fairly large city, Shashi, was inconsiderate; that for 352,000 yuan in stamp duties without a declared reason in a much smaller and poorer city, Badong, was outrageous.[3]

In western Hubei, the struggle was among the north, the anti-north forces of Hubei, Hunan, and Sichuan, and banditry before 1927. After that, the north was a spent force and the struggle became a dispute among Sichuan and Hubei armies, bandits, and the Communists. Eastern Sichuan, however, had to be divided further into three subregions: the northeast, the east, and the southeast. Before 1925, the fight for control of the northeast was between the pro-north Liu Cunhou and pro-south (i.e., pro-Sun Yat-sen) Xiong Kewu. This was followed by a period of interregnum until the rise of Tian Songyao, commander of the Twenty-ninth Army, in 1930. Two years after that, the Fourth Front Red Army arrived. The east along the Yangzi was first the bone of contention between Xiong Kewu and the Yunnan-Guizhou coalition. From 1923 to 1925, Yang Sen's Ninth Division, with the support of Liu Xiang's Second Army and the backing of the redoubtable Wu Peifu, had held sway. Yang was not completely ousted by Liu Xiang's Twenty-first Army from the east until 1928–30. The southeastern situation had never been truly stable after the collapse of the domination of the expatriate armies from Yunnan and Guizhou. Even the suzerainty of the Twenty-first Army was more nominal than real. Protected by precipitous mountains and treacherous rivers, the fight for the control of western Hunan, like that in eastern Sichuan, was not a direct north-south confrontation, but an indirect manipulation of local armed forces. Immediately after the anti–Yuan Shikai campaign, Tian Yingzhao tried to keep both the Guizhou and the northern troops out; then the pro-south Cai Juyou tried to keep the pro-north provincial armies of Zhao Hengti out; and finally Chen Quzhen tried to keep out the Northern Expeditionary armies to achieve a measure of peace and tranquility (see tables 9.2–9.4).

In the process of consolidating his control over a garrison region, a commander could try one of five methods.

1. He might simply pay a sum of money to an unwelcome army and ask it to leave. For instance, in April 1926 Liu Xiang and Yang Sen offered Yuan Zuming, commander of the itinerant Guizhou army, 1.2 million yuan as the transfer fee for his army to go somewhere else. At the same time, the former Hunan governor, Tan Yankai, who was then in Guangzhou planning for the Northern Expedition, tempted Yuan with half a million yuan to invade western Hunan and fight against Ye Kaixin, a protégé of Hunan Governor Zhao Hengti, Tan's sworn enemy.[4]

2. If the problems of his garrison region had far-reaching and complex implications, the commander and others might hold a conference to settle them. One such conference was called at Chenzhou in December 1919 by Tian Yingzhao and attended by the representatives of no fewer than nineteen army units to discuss the problems after the death of Zhou Chaowu—unity, protection of commerce, separation of the military from the civilian administration, and educational reform.[5] But the most spectacular one took place at a remote northern Sichuan town, Shunqing, in May 1931. At stake were the seven counties under Luo Zezhou and another seven under Li Jiayu. Both these garrison regions lay in north-central Sichuan overlooking Chengdu and Chongqing, and

both commanders were becoming too independent. To their north were Deng Xihou's Twenty-eighth Army and Tian Songyao's Twenty-ninth; to their south, Liu Xiang's Twenty-first (Chongqing) and Liu Wenhui's Twenty-fourth (Chengdu). Their strategic importance and the military maneuvers to destroy or contain them threatened the security of the whole province. Consequently, the conference was attended by the representatives of all the powerful commanders, for the purpose of redrawing the map of the garrison regions there, fixing the strengths of Luo's and Li's armies, and fixing the subsidies to these two garrison commanders, to preserve the peace in northern Sichuan.[6]

3. When there was a way to ensure compliance, an order from a superior authority might be able to transfer an unwelcome army elsewhere. For instance, the once powerful Twentieth Army of Yang Sen had been reduced to the sorry existence of having "no fixed abode" in 1929. Its First and Second divisions were ordered by the Nanjing government to depart from the southeast, and its Third Division was sent from Fengdu to western Hubei. The counties they evacuated were to be taken over by the Twenty-first Army.[7]

4. The most humiliating way was to run in front of a *force majeure*, like the flight of Liao Xiangyun from the lucrative Hongjiang before the arrival of Cai Juyou. Once a commander had done this, he was unlikely to recover his respectability and assume command again.

5. More often than not, the way adopted by garrison commanders was an old-fashioned fight, which might turn out to be the most convincing and effective. The way the Twenty-first Army expanded its domain proved this point. In 1926 it defeated the Guizhou army and captured Chongqing; in 1928–30, it routed Luo Zezhou and Yang Sen to take a firm control of eastern Sichuan; finally, in 1932–33 it drove the enormous Twenty-fourth Army west into Xikang, to achieve its hegemony and a nominal unity of the province.[8]

It is difficult enough to estimate how many men bearing arms there were in these provinces; it is even more difficult to agree on the numbers of the legitimate army units stationed on the highlands from 1916 to 1937. Indeed, one can pertinently ask what was a legitimate army unit. Take western Hubei in the years following the anti–Yuan Shikai campaign, for instance. The three so-called armies commanded by Li Tiancai, Lan Tianwei, and Wang Tianzong, altogether about 30,000 strong, were "legitimate" because they were recognized as such by the southern authorities in Guangdong, Hunan, and Sichuan, but reliable sources claimed that they consisted of a large number of bandits.[9] From 1921 onward, the south stepped up its support of these armies by sending no fewer than fifteen thousand Sichuan troops to western Hubei.[10] This led Wu Peifu to dispatch at least one division and four brigades, or about thirty thousand men, to strengthen its defenses.[11] When Wu ceased to be a key player in the affairs of China, there were as many as seventy-five thousand Sichuan troops, not counting the Guizhou and Hunan units, stationed in western Hubei.[12]

In the three subregions of eastern Sichuan, probably fifteen thousand indigenous and expatriate troops were stationed in 1918–19.[13] Ten years later, when the situation became clearer, only four armies had a stake in the subregions: Liu Xiang, Tian Songyao, Yang Sen, and Liu Cunhou, with a combined strength of nearly one hundred thousand men. Assuming that half of these were garrisoned in the highland, it represented a threefold increase. Although the total strength of the four armies had doubled again by 1932–33, the great war of provincial unification must have attracted them to fight in the core area. In the wake of it, the invasion of the Fourth Front Red Army pulled these troops up to the highland again. From 1933 to 1935, with the Communists in the north and southeast, the devastation and the concentration of fighting forces were so awesome that the Sichuan highlands had never seen the likes of it before or since.[14]

In western Hunan the pattern of growth in armed forces was similar. The Gan Army commanded by Tian Yingzhao at the end of the Qing was to increase from four or five thousand to about twenty-five thousand in 1918 when the northern troops led by Wu Peifu left the province.[15] In the great war of western Hunan, Zhao Hengti mobilized four divisions and Tan Yankai, five, with two other sitting on the fence— perhaps a total of some one hundred thousand troops stationed there. When the dust settled, Chen Quzhen's Thirty-fourth Division, thirty thousand strong, lorded over other armed forces in that region—Ye Kaixin's provincial division, Guizhou troops, local militia, and bandits, probably of an equal strength.[16]

The records of Nanchuan County as contained in its revised gazetteer lend support to the picture of increasing militarization on the highland. From 1912 to 1916, a contingent of only about 450 men was garrisoned in the county. This was to enlarge to 1,000 from 1916 to 1920 and to 2,000–3,000 from 1921 to 1926.

In addition to the army units, the mountain counties had to have local security forces, the militia (*tuanlian*), since both the traditional *baojia* security arrangement and the modern police were woefully deficient.[17] The militia units were created by the local elite to ward off predatory armies and bandits,[18] but not surprisingly, they were not often successful when the odds were against them. Their leaders, like the leaders of army units and bandits, were susceptible to corruption, to serving their own purposes.[19] Nonetheless, their existence might have had some justification.

As briefly mentioned in chapter 6, Hubei had about 50,000 militiamen in the 1930s, Hunan 45,000 late in the 1920s, and Sichuan 500,000 in the 1930s.[20] It is not known how much each militiaman cost the local elite and the county government. Since he lived and worked at home and fought for the defense of his village or city, he should cost much less than a common soldier. A detailed report of the militia units in the garrison region of the Twenty-first Army for the year 1934 was published in the *Zhengwu yuekan*, 2/10,[21] but it makes very little sense. For instance, since the per capita expenditure ranged from 1.34 yuan per annum in Zhongxian to 215.16 yuan in Kaixian, one naturally suspects its estimated number of militiamen or estimated expenditure. An interesting derivation from the report is that the twelve counties in eastern and southeastern Sichuan had a total of 116,495 militiamen maintained at 1,071,805 yuan, or 9.20 yuan per capita for 1934. At the same time, the total garrison region was estimated to have 535,472 militiamen who cost the local governments as well as the elite 5,312,063 yuan, or 9.90 yuan per capita. If these estimates are not too far removed from reality, the cheapness itself was a good reason for the maintenance of this scarecrow force.

A great deal has been said about the banditry in China in this period, but little is known for certain. There seem to have been more bandits and robbers in mountainous and hilly regions than on the plains, more highwaymen and market raiders than river pirates.[22] The metamorphosis from bandits to militia did not seem to be as easy as that from bandits to legitimate army units. Every province had bandit-armies (i.e., bandits legalized and reorganized by the government) as well as army-bandits (i.e., defeated army units that survived willy-nilly as bandits). President Li Yuanhong noted in a formal statement on June 6, 1922, that "Demobilized, soldiers turn into bandits; recruited, bandits turn into soldiers."[23] No one knows how many bandits and robbers there were in the highland. An estimate made before 1916 gave these figures: Hubei 4,500, Sichuan 4,300, and Hunan 1,300.[24] This was the time when the Sichuan bandit-army divisions—commanded by Yang Chunfang, Lu Shiti, Yu Jitang, Shi Qingyang, and Qiu Huaiyu—were being formed.[25] In Hunan at about the same time, the so-called people's armies were emerging on the western hills (see tables 9.2–9.4). Evidently, Zhou Gucheng's (or, more precisely, He Xiya's) figures were far too low. As bandits, they received no regular pay like militia, but they did damage to the persons and property of the local people. It is impossible to assess the amount of the damage. Here and there one finds records of the frequency of robbery,[26] but they are of no help in estimating the social cost of banditry.

Equally impossible to estimate is the social cost of the secret societies and religious sects that existed in the highland. Particularly powerful and widespread was the Brotherhood, which attracted many from the armed forces, the transport workers, the urban and rural poor, and merchants and landowners.[27] It was further divided into five nominal but only three actual hierarchical "generations" (bei)—kind (ren), for the landowning and educated; righteous (yi), for the merchants; and polite (li), for the lower castes. The two higher "generations," more the trading than the landowning, often quarreled with the lower and numerically strong one, for it absorbed many "murky" (hun, criminal) and violent elements.[28]

Apart from the Brotherhood, Yilong in northern Sichuan had the Red Lantern Sect; Nanjiang, also in northern Sichuan, had the Sect of the Allied Heroes; Qianjiang, in southeastern Sichuan, the Sky Cover Sect; Sangzhi, in western Hunan, the Family Protection Sect; and of course the ubiquitous Divine Army on these mountains. Their social usefulness ranged from spiritual healing to antitax, antirent movements; their chosen means ranged from religious meetings to the use of violence. Like the Brotherhood, these sects benefited and harmed the highland peasants at the same time.[29]

The murder of Ma Boyuan's father and the kidnap of his mother by a bandit group illustrates the delicate and complex relations between bandits and lawful authorities and organizations. The sad event took place in the county of Xiangyang in western Hubei on January 10, 1925. The bandits carried their victims, the mother and two of her grandsons, to the Nanyang-Tanghe area in southern Henan. If the bandit leader, one An Jianghu, was, as he was believed to be, an officer who had served under General Ma Wende, commander of the First

Mixed Brigade of the Third Army of General Feng Yuxiang's Guominjun (National People's Army), his decision to flee from the scene of the crime to Henan was brilliant. Ten weeks earlier, Wu Peifu's Zhili Army had been routed. Although Wu's trusted lieutenant, General Xiao Yaonan, was still in control of Hubei, Henan had been taken over by General Hu Jingyi of the Guominjun. The two military governors had not had enough time to conceptualize their personal and official relations; nor had the garrison commanders of Xiangyang and Nanyang, generals Zhang Liansheng of the Zhili Clique and Ma Zhimin of the Guominjun.

A former member of Sun Yat-sen's Revolutionary Alliance, a leading member of the YMCA, a friend of Governor Hu Jingyi, and a cousin of General Ma Wende, then the garrison commander of northern Henan, and General Ma Zhimin, Ma Boyuan mobilized all his social connections in a bid to save and free his mother and nephews at a ransom named by the kidnapper of thirty thousand yuan.

He approached, either by writing or in person, Feng Yuxiang, Hu Jingyi, and Xiao Yaonan as well as the garrison commanders concerned; using his former membership in the Revolutionary Alliance, he also approached Dr. Sun Fo, who was preoccupied by the deteriorating condition of his father, Dr. Sun Yat-sen, and Yu Youren, because of Yu's influence in the so-called people's armed forces in Shaanxi and Henan. He even talked with people who were believed to know An about the possibility of meeting with him. A few others volunteered their help—such as Zhang Qun, then the police commissioner of Henan, and David Z. T. Yui (Yu Rizhang) of the YMCA.

Ma Boyuan's own account of the affair is not clear as who was actually successful in getting his mother released on March 2 and his nephews a week later. His ambiguity was his tact. What is clear in the account is the sacred principle of respecting other officers' jurisdiction unless one meant to ignore it by defeating the others and annexing their territories. In this case, neither governor could send his troops to chase the bandits in the other's province; by the same token, neither could the garrison commanders. The result was passing the buck between the governors and garrison commanders while the bandits watched and waited, until the money was found by the magistrates of Tanghe and Nanyang, not that of Xiangyang, on Hu Jingyi's orders. Had this sacred principle been violated, however, there would have been war and anarchy, to the detriment of the legitimate authorities.

The principle that was respected for the benefit of the armies and the inhabitants turned out to be a blessing for the unlawful armed forces also. Bandits could survive by moving from one jurisdiction to the next; so could other antigovernment forces, such as the Communists.[30]

In the final analysis, all the armed forces, on the mountains as well as on the plains, were at the same time protective and predatory, sometimes more inclined to be one than the other, other times just the reverse. Principally, there were the armies and the militia, about one hundred thousand of each in eastern Sichuan, about one hundred thousand of the former and ten thousand of the latter in western Hunan, perhaps fewer of both in the poorer western Hubei. A common soldier might cost as much as 120 yuan per annum to maintain; a militiaman, only one-tenth of that. As to the bandits, perhaps they lived at a basic level, no better and no worse than a private soldier. If they numbered only about one-tenth of the strength of the regular armies, the prosperity of the highland in these years should have been able to pay for their existence. More than that, the highlands might even have surplus tax revenues to subsidize other armed forces on the plains of these provinces.

Table 9.1

Frequency of Civil Wars, 1912–28

Year	Bansu's estimates	My estimates
1912	1	2
1913	6	8
1914	1	5
1915	—	8
1916	9	10
1917	5	8
1918	9	8
1919	2	1
1920	7	7
1921	7	7
1922	10	13
1923	6	7
1924	8	17
1925	13	17
1926	15	9
1927	14	7
1928	16	7

Source: Li Jiannong (1929), cited in Zhang Youyi (1957, 2:609–10).

Table 9.2

West Sichuan Military Activities

1915–16	During and after the anti-Yuan Shikai campaign, units of the Jingguo (Pacifying the Nation) Army, Hufa (Defending the Constitution) Army, and Zizhu (Autonomy) Army carve out their satraps in western Hubei. Prominent among them is the 9th Kiangsu Division commanded by Li Tiancai. (Wen Gongzhi [1932, 1/2, 7])
1917	Li and Shi Xingchuan, Jing(zhou)-Xiang(yang) garrison commander and commander of the 1st Hubei Division, advocate western Hubei autonomy. The commander of the Northern 3d. Division, Cao Kun, sends Wu Guangxin to quell them. (Ding Wenjiang [1926, 1:204; *Guomingemingjun zhanshi*, 1:31–32])
1918	Cao Kun is ordered to attack Li and Shi; Yang Sen's Sichuan troops invade western Hubei; Li flees to Xingshan. (*Zhengfu gongbao*, January 30, 1918; *Huazi ribao*, February 16, 1918; *Shibao*, January 12, 1918)
	Li and Wang Tianzong retreat into eastern Sichuan while provincial troops led by Liu Zuilong are stationed at Zigui. (*Shibao*, May 1, 1918)
	Bo Wenwei, former governor of Anhwei, engages the northern troops in fighting in Xingshan and Badong. (*Shibao*, September 1, 1918)
1919	Bo Wenwei moves to Shinanfu where he is later joined by Lan Tianwei, a Manchurian army commander who supported the 1911 Revolution, and Li Tiancai. (*Shibao*, January 11, August 14, 1919)
	Xiong Kewu of Sichuan breaks up his relations with Li and Bo. (*Huazi ribao*, October 7, 1919)
1920	This motley collection of troops—Li Tiancai, Lan Tianwei, Bao Wenwei, Wang Tianzong—over 30,000 strong control the Enshi-Hefeng area until November when the provincial governor, Wang Zhanyuan, drives Li away. (Fan Chongshi [1962, 3–5]; *Shibao*, April 11, August 15, October 7, 17, November 22, 1920) Li Liejun's Yunnan troops are also there. (*Shibao*, November 3, 1920)
1921	The year of giving aid to Hubei from Hunan and Sichuan and from Wu Peifu's Northern Armies. The Hunan troops are easily defeated while the Sichuan troops occupy Badong, Xingshan, and Zigui for a short period, but Yang Sen's army stays at Lichuan and Jianshi from October 1921 to February 15, 1923. (Tao Juyin [1957–58, 6:46–47]; Ma Xuanwei [1983, 24–25]; *Huazi ribao*, September 1, 2, 1921; *Dagongbao*, August 22, 24, 1921)
1922	Yang Sen's army remains in Lichuan. (Ma Xuanwei [1936, 26]; *Huazi ribao*, December 15, 16, 21, 1922)

1923	Yan Sen rushes back to Sichuan because of the war there. The vacuum he left behind becomes a cockpit into which Kong Geng's division penetrates. (*Sichuan wenxian*, 131/3; *Shibao*, November 27, 1923) Meanwhile, the bandits led by Lao Yangren (the Old Foreigner) invade Yunxian, and the garrison at Xingshan mutinies. (*Yunxianzhi*, ch. 5; *Shibao*, November 4, 1923)
1924	The defeated armies under Xiong Kewu flee from the Wu valley to western Hubei, to join forces with the Divine Army in Enshi and Hefeng. (*Huazi ribao*, July 2, 1924; *Shibao*, July 5, 1924)
	Northern troops led by Wang Duqing and Yu Xuezhong and Hunan troops commanded by Hu Xiannian are dispatched to western Hubei to block Xiong's way. (*Shibao*, September 2, November 10, 1924; *Dagongbao*, October 25, 1924)
1925	Wang Ruqin's Northern troops are stationed in Xingshan, planning to overthrow Xiao Yaonan, the provincial governor; a small detachment of Wu Peifu's army is in western Hubei; the Guizhou expatriate army commander, Yuan Zuming, marches from Shizhu to Lichuan and Shinan to take Hefeng. (*Shibao*, January 11, February 13, March 23, 1925) Later in the year, Yang Sen is again in Badong. (*Shibao*, November 1, 1925)
1926	Song Dapei's Hubei 7th Mixed Brigade is sent to Badong and Zigui. (*Dongfang zazhi*, 27/6, 57)
1927	The defeated troops of Wu Peifu are incorporated into Yang Sen's army in western Hubei, which now controls thirty counties, and also into the Guizhou army under Wang Tianpei in Enshi and Hefeng. (*Shibao*, January 20, 28, February 12, May 25, 27, July 29, 1927; Xiao Bo et al., 1984, 42) Yang is defeated in June and Xia Douyin's army advances to Badong and Zigui. (Ma and Xiao [1983, 4446]) In July, Wu Peifu leads the remnants of his army through Xingshan, Baokang, and Zigui to Sichuan. (Ma and Xiao [1983, 60])
1928	Defeated by Liu Xiang, Yang Sen once again takes refuge in western Hubei—Badong, Xingshan, Lichuan, and Enshi. Lu Diping's Hunan troops are sent to western Hubei. (*Shibao*, January 10, March 2, 1928; *Huiyi He Long*, 311–12)
	Fanxian is captured by the Divine Army in November. (*Chuanyan tekan*, 16/23)
1929	As Sichuan armies are returning home, western Hubei is temporarily restored to Hubei troops. (*Shibao*, April 24, 1929)
	The Divine Army takes Lichuan and Baokang. (*Shibao*, July 10, 1929)
	The mutinied Northern armies in Yichang flee to Dangyang, Xingshan, and Badong. Soon they meet with Yang Sen's troops under Guo Rudong and the Divine Army. (*Shangwu ribao*, October 23, November 15, 16, 19, 23, 18, 1929)

1930	Henan and Shaanxi bandits invade Yunxi. (*Yunxi xianzhi*, ch. 5) Liu Xiang's Twenty-first Army advances to western Hubei, reaching as far east as Yidu. (*Shibao*, May 26, August 6, 1929) Lai Xinhui's troops march from the Wu valley to Enshi and Hefeng to Gongan and Shishou. (*Xinxin xinwen*, November 14, 1929)
1931	The Twenty-first Army occupies large areas along the Yangzi and the Qing. (Ma and Xiao [1983, 299–301])
1932	The invasion of Henan bandits into Yunxi in August is soon followed by that of the Fourth Front Red Army into Yunxian and Zhushan in October. (*Yunxi xianzhi*, ch. 5; Lin Chao et al. [1982, 15]; *Chuanyan tekan*, 158/12)
1933–34	Communists and bandits everywhere in western Hubei. (*Yunxi xianzhi*, ch. 5)

Table 9.3

East Sichuan Military Activities

1913	In the so-called Second Revolution, Xiong Kewu declares independence in Chongqing against Hu Jingyi, who represents Yuan Shikai's government. There are war activities in Fengjie, Wanxian, and elsewhere. (Wei Yingtao et al., 1985, 610–14)
1915–16	The anti–Yuan Shikai campaign draws northern and Yunnan-Guizhou troops into Sichuan. (Li Baihong [1962, 69]; Ma Xuanwei [1983, 7])
	At the same time, Sichuan people's armies spring up like mushrooms. (*Huazi ribao*, April 12, 1926)
1917	Sichuan-Guizhou war
	From April to August, the war has been waged around Chengdu between Liu Cunhou of Sichuan and Dai Kan of Guizhou. Liu's victory is quickly followed by his defeat at the hands of Tang Jiyao's Yunnan troops. (Huang Shou [1917, 10–23]; *Zhengfu gongbao*, August 8, 1917; Ma Xuanwei [1938, 10])
1918	Sichuan-Yunnan-Guizhou war
	In the Northeast, Xiong Kewu, supported by Yunnan and Guizhou armies, drives Liu Cunhou into Shaanxi. (*Shibao*, June 2, 1918; *Huazi ribao*, February 27, April 3, 1918)
1919	Xiong-Liu war
	Xiong drives Liu to Hanzhong, Shaanxi; Zhong Tidao and his 6th Division retreat to Nanjiang and Tongjiang where they are incorporated into Shi Qingyang's irregulars who are redesignated the 6th Division. (Feizhi [1933, 283–85]; *Shibao*, November 15, 18, 1919)
1920	Xiong-Yunnan war
	In July, Lu Chao of the 5th Division commands Shi Qingyang 's and Lu Shiti's troops (4th and 6th divisions), with the help of Liu Chengxun (3d Army), to attack the Yunnan units in northern Sichuan. After the defeat of the Yunnan armies, Xiong turns against Liu Cunhou in eastern Sichuan. Thus Xiong places the North under Yu Jitang and the East under Zhang Chong. (Feizhi . . . [1933, 283–85]; Fan Chongshi [1962, 5–6]; *Shibao*, July 1, 10, 23, September 30, November 3, 1920; *Huazi ribao*, November 6, December 16, 1920)
1921	Liu Xiang-Xiong war
	By March Liu Cunhou is completely routed. Soon Liu Xiang and Xiong Kewu are at each other's throat. (Fan Chongshi [1962, 6–9]; *Huazi ribao*, July 27, 1921)
	Xiong's 1st Army under Dan Mouxin is in control of eastern Sichuan along the Yangzi; Yang Sen is despatched to give aid to Hubei. (Xiao Bo [1984, 24–28]; Tao Juyin [1957–58, 6:58–59]; Ma Xuanwei [1983, 18])
1922	Revival of the Liu Xiang-Xiong war

July–August, Dan Mouxin, with the help of Deng Xihou (3d Division), defeats Yang Sen, then an ally of Liu Xiang, in eastern Sichuan. Liu Chengxun's army enters Chongqing and Fuling. Liu himself goes home in Dayi. (Ma Xuanwei [1983, 22–23]; *Huazi ribao*, July 19, August 2, 3, 11, 17, October 23, 1922; Fan Chongshi [1962, 21–23])

1923–25   War of unification of Sichuan by Yang Sen

February, Yang attacks Wanxian from Lichuan and Yang Chunfang of the Fourth Division in the 1st Army in Zhongxian surrenders to Yang Sen. (Ma Xuanwei [1983, 26])

The Northern army of the commander-in-chief of the Upper Yangzi, Wang Ruqin, invades Sichuan and takes Fengjie while Shaanxi army units come down to Zhaohua. (*Huazi ribao*, March 5, 1923)

After the seesaw battles at Chengdu, Chongqing, Yongchuan, and Wanxian, Liu Chengxun retires and Xiong Kewu leaves Sichuan. (*Huazi ribao*, May 18, June 23, July 5, October 23, 1923; *Shibao*, July 1, August 12, October 9, October 21, December 3, 1923; Li Baihong [1962, 70])

Yang follows up his successes by driving the rest of Xiong Kewu's army out of Sichuan. East Sichuan is shared between Yang's troops in Wanxian, Zhongxian, and Yunyang and the Northern troops in Chongqing and Fengjie. (*Shibao*, March 4, 13, 25, May 4, June 15, July 31, August 9, 30, 1924; Feizhi . . . [1933, 285–86]; Ma Xuanwei [1983, 35])

[The fall of Wu Peifu weakens Yang's position in Sichuan.]

February, Yang dismisses Liu Bin from the command of the 1st Division and Liu retreats from the north to Tongjiang and Nanjiang. Yang also tries to capture the salt gabelle at Ziliujing and this provokes an alliance of Liu Wenhui (31st Division), Lai Xinhui (1st Division), Chen Hongfan (8th Division), and the retired Liu Chengxun to defy him.

Furthermore, a brigade of Liu Bin's troops moves from Zitong to Zhaohua and Jiange without Yang's permission. Therefore, Yang, the governor of Sichuan, finds himself at war with his enemies at several places. (Tao Juyin [1959, 7:147]; *Shibao*, March 31, May 29, 1925; Ma Xuanwei [1983, 36])

The alliance of Liu Xiang (2d Army) and Yuan Zuming (Guizhou armies in Sichuan) defeats Yang. Yuan takes Chongqing, Changshou, Fuling while Liu Xiang captures the rest of eastern Sichuan. (Ma Xuanwei [1983, 47, 50]; Li Baihong [1962, 71])

1926   Liu Xiang-Yuan Zuming war

Defeated, Yang Sen is now in Hubei and Wu Peifu asks Yuan and Lai Xinhui to help Yang return to Sichuan. Yuan allows Yang to station his troops at Fuling, Zhongxian, and Fengdu. This does not induce Yang to support Yuan when Yuan is attacked by Liu Xiang in May.

Liu Xiang drives Yuan back to Guizhou while Yang decides to help defend Hubei against the Northern Expeditionary Armies. Yang is in Wanxian-Fengjie and in western Hubei. (*Jingbao*, March 10, 1926; *Shibao*, February 3, April 27, 1924; Mao Sicheng [1936, 8:116–17]; Li Baihong [1962, 71]; Feizhi . . . [1933, 285–86]; Xiao Bo [1984, 38–39]; Ma Xuanwei [1983, 78])

1927   May, Yang Sen gives aid to western Hubei once again, is defeated, and is forced to give up his possessions in each Sichuan by some of his erstwhile subordinates to move to the Wu valley in southeastern Sichuan. In June he manages to recover his losses in the east. By then Wu Peifu and his small retinue take refuge under Yang's wing. (Ma Xuanwei [1983, 82–88, 92, 104–6]; Xiao Bo [1984, 60, 66, 75–81])

1928   Yang's weakness continues to lure others to eastern Sichuan. His alliance with Lai Xinhui, Luo Zezhou (of the 6th Mixed Brigade), and Li Jiayu (of the Border Defense 1st Division) fights against that of Liu Xiang and Liu Wenhui in the Chongqing-Wanxian section of the Yangzi valley from June to December, resulting in Yang's final abandonment of eastern Sichuan.

The extreme east, Yunyang and Fengjie are occupied by the Divine Army. (Ma Xuanwei [1983, 111–13]; Xiao Bo [1984, 108–10]; Li Baihong [1962, 72]; *Chuanyan tekan*, 35/12)

1929   The two Lius, Liu Xiang and his uncle, Liu Wenhui, mop up the rest of Yang's and his allies' possessions. (Li Baihong [1962, 72–73, 80–81]; *Shibao*, October 28, 1929)

1930   The Yang-Lai-Luo-Li alliance fights Deng Xihou in the north and is defeated by Deng with the help of Liu Wenhui and Tian Songyao. (Li Baihong [1962, 73]; Xiao Bo [1984, 164, 168, 171])

1931   The core area of Sichuan is now divided between Liu Xiang in the east and Liu Wenhui in the west; the northern rim between Tian Songyao in the east and Deng Xihou in the west. In the gaps between their garrison regions are Yang, Lai, Luo, and Li, who continue to fight for the control of tax resources and lebensraum. (*Shibao*, March 19, April 3–10, May 21, 1931; Li Baihong [1962, 73–74])

The Lianyinghui secret society is active in Qianjiang and Pengshui until April 1933. (*Chuanyan tekan*, 170/11)

1932   War between the two Lius

It is fought in the basin of the province. Liu Wenhui's 24th Army is defeated by Liu Xiang's 21st, Deng Xihou's 28th, and Tian Songyao's 29th Armies. (R. Kapp [1973, 34]; Feizhi [1933, 109–24])

By the end of the year, Liu Wenhui retreats westward while the Fourth Front Red Army invades Tongjiang and northern Sichuan. (Xu Xiangqian [1985, 2:251])

Sichuan is now more united than any time since 1915. The civil war between the warlords is superseded by that between them and the Communists. (*Shibao*, May 11, 12, July 11, August 27, 1933; Chang Kuo-t'ao, 1972, ch. 5)

Table 9.4

The Growth of West Hunan Armed Forces

1916	Guizhou troops enter western Hunan in the anti–Yuan Shikai campaign, fighting at Jingxian, Huangxian, Qianyang, and Hongjiang. (*Huguo yundongshi* [1984, 220 and map]; Li Xin et al. [1987, II/1-B, 740])
	Emergence of people's armies: Yuanling militia, five battalions, under Zhou Zefan; Lizhou militia, four battalions, under Qin Heng; and Chenzhou militia, three battalions, under Liao Xiangyun(?) (Tao Juyin [1948, 32])
1917	Tian Yingzhao appointed western Hunan garrison commander (the Gan Army of 5,000 strong) with Cai Juyou and Chen Quzhen serving under him; Zhou Zefan, his deputy commander.
	Chang[de]-Li[zhou or Lixian] garrison commander is Wang Zhengya. (*Dagongbao*, September 10, October 18, 20, 30, 1917)
1918	Confused fighting among local, provincial, and Guizhou troops at Yongsui, Baojing, Chadong, Sangzhi, Shimen, Cili.
	Tian Yingzhao controls Fenghuang, Qiancheng, and Mayang and his army is strengthened (now 40,000 strong) by recruiting local bandits. Xie Guoguang commands provincial troops at Yongshun, Longshan, and Guzhang. (*Dagongbao*, June 17, October 5, November 14, 22, and December 8, 14, 1918)
1919	Tian Yingzhao made the commander of the Jingguo Fifth Army, proceeding to unite western Hunan. Zhang Xueji tries in vain to recruit armed units and bandits into his [Northern] army. Zhou Zefan assassinated by Liao Xiangyun. (*Dagongbao*, January 8, 18, March 25, 1919)
1920	Campaign against the provincial governor, Zhang Jingyao: Tian Yingzhao drives Zhang Xueji out of western Hunan; Chen Quzhen takes over Zhang's troops and Zhang himself is killed by bandits; Cai Juyou, now Yuanling garrison commander, defeats Liao Xiangyun; Qin Heng's militia forces attack and kill Wang Zhengya whose militia units are taken over by Zhou Chaowu. Zhou defeats Qin. Guizhou troops withdraw from western Hunan. (*Dagongbao*, August 2, July 19, 21, 1920)
1921	Wang Yuyin, Wang Zhengya's son, and Lin Xiumei fight for Hunan autonomy in Dayong, Shimen, Cili, and are defeated. Taking advantage of this, Li Liejun's Yunnan troops invade Hongjiang. (*Dagongbao*, October 19, 31, 1920–January 19, 21, 1921)

Cai Juyou's troops are ordered to give aid to the autono-
mous troops fighting in western Hubei. Cai himself and
Chen Quzhen show no personal interest in provincial autonomy. Instead, Cai unleashes an attack and defeats
Liao Xiangyun at Hongjiang. With twenty-five battalions
under him, Cai is now supreme in western Hunan. (January 29, February 4, August 3, 1921)

1922   Tang Rongyang's 8th Mixed Brigade stationed in
Lizhou, controlling Shimen, Cili, and Dayong;
Yuanling garrison commander Cai Juyou stationed in
Chenzhou, controlling Chenxi, Luxi, Qiancheng, Huitong,
Jingxian, etc.; western Hunan garrison commander Tian
Yingzhao stationed in Fenghuang; commander of west-
ern Hunan Mobile Forces Chen Quzhen stationed in
Baojing, controlling Yongshun, Baojing, Longshan,
Sangzhi, Guzhang, Yongsui, Mayang, etc. (*Dagongbao*,
April 3, 1922)

1923   Cai supports the Guangzhou government while Chen
Quzhen sides with the provincial governor, Zhao Hengti.
Zhao invades western Hunan, defeats Cai, who flees to
Guizhou; Cai's troops surrender to Zhao and Chen.
Chen is made a major general and the Yuanling garrison
commander, but he does not transfer his army to Yuanl-
ing.
Sichuan troops begin to penetrate into western Hunan from
the Wu valley. (*Dagongbao*, December 13, 21, 28, 1923;
January 17, February 3, 1924; *Shibao*, October 16, 1923)

1924   [The defeat of Marshall Wu Peifu weakens Zhao Hengti's
position in Hunan, and so]
Chen Quzhen attacks Tian Yiqin's troops in
Chenzhou, some of which surrender to Chen and others
to Tian Yingzhao.
Yunnan-Hunan allied troops reach Cili while, with Cai
Juyou's help, Xiong Kewu's Sichuan Army invades west-
ern Hunan. (*Shibao*, July 3, November 24, 1924;
Dagongbao,June 22, 23, 29, 30, July 11, October
18, 1924; Tao Juyin [1959, 7:150])

1925   Xiong Kewu has the help of several defeated erstwhile
Hunan warlords (Cai Juyou, Zhou Chaowu, Tian
Yiqin, Lin Zhiyu); he is stationed in
Chenxi, Lizhou, Cili, Shimen, recruiting bandits there.
Zhao Hengti attacks Xiong and retakes
Lizhou, Chenxi, and Changde. (*Dagongbao*, February
22, 1925; Tao Juyin [1959, 7:150–52])

1926   The Northern Expedition further weakens Zhao Hengti and
his commander in western Hunan, Ye Kaixin.
Cai Juyou, Zhou Chaowu, Quizhou armies, and He Long, together with He Yaozu, unite under Tang Shengzhi to
fight on the side of the Northern Expedition.
(*Guomingemingjun chanshi*, 2:23–24)

1927   Chen Quzhen dominates western Hunan. (My Fenghuang
diary, September 11, 1983)

1928   He Long returns to western Hunan to create a soviet area.

1929	Commanding an army of thirty thousand, Chen successfully resists the pressure from He Jian, the new Hunan governor, and Wang Jialie in eastern Guizhou. Zhou Chaowu's irregulars are active in the vicinity of Dayong. Zhang Faqui's Fourth Army is fighting with Hunanese troops in Changbu. (*Dagongbao*, September 10, 1929; *Shibao*, May 19, October 31, 1929)
1930–34	Peace in western Hunan under Chen Quzhen, except the activities of the Red Army commanded by He Long, who seems to have reached an understanding with Chen. (see Ch. IX)
1934	Chen expands his sphere of influence in Guizhou and is defeated. (My Fenghuang diary, September 11, 1983)
1935	Chen leaves western Hunan.

10
TWO RURAL SOVIETS

Western Hubei-Hunan

General He Long's decision to return to his native place, western Hunan, was taken at the first meeting of the Provisional Center of the CCP immediately after the important conference of the Politburo on August 7, 1927.[1] By the time he reached Shanghai at the beginning of 1928, the Center suggested to him that he should go to Moscow for a period of study. Without a word of Russian at his command, and with the urgent need for him to help create a soviet in western Hubei-Hunan, he thought he might be more useful in that part of China instead of Moscow. Traveling by boat, in February 1928 he and his companions called on the Communist guerrillas active in the Hong Lake area between Wuhan and Yueyang. Thenceforth they proceeded on foot via Lixian, Cili, and Shimen to the county of He's birth, Sangzhi.[2]

The Hong Lake area and western Hunan are connected by waterways, chiefly the Li and then the Yangzi, as well as a network of mountain roads across the Wuling range. They are as different, however, as day and night—the former being a lakeland, low and swampy, whereas the latter is rugged and hazardous. The reasons why these two regions, together with two other small guerrilla bases, should be combined to form a single soviet have never been explained, and they escape me. It is true that during and after the Autumn Harvest uprisings in September 1927, Communist activists tended to go back to their native places to stir up the peasants. Duan Dechang had grown up in Nanxian, and Duan Yulin was born in Shishou. They knew the lakeland well, and it was natural for them to return there. They were to become the leaders of the Hong Lake Soviet.[3] Another consideration might be its strategic location, which, if controlled by the Communists, would pose a serious threat to both Wuhan and Changsha, enhancing the political importance of the CCP in national politics. In this sense,

Figure 10.1. **Two Soviets: Northwestern Sichuan and Northwestern Hunan.**

the western Hunan highlands were merely the rear of the lakeland, offering a retreat to those who were exposed to danger and attack in southern Hubei. At this time, the CCP strategists had just begun to develop a system of highland guerrilla tactics; no one was aware of the need for another system of tactics for plains guerrillas.[4] Since the lakeland was exposed to danger and strategically more important than western Hunan, why was the mainstay of the Red Army paradoxically kept among the hills rather than among the lakes?[5] The reasons for this also escape me.

From April 1928 to February 1930, He Long and his army operated in western Hubei-Hunan. Although a soviet was created in Sangzhi in June 1929, it was soon abandoned.[6] His operations were guerrilla in nature, roaming all over the immense area of the Li and Qing valleys. When his troops and those of the lakeland met in February 1930, they formed the Second Red Army Corps and established the Hong Lake Soviet. The purpose was not so much to have a permanent soviet area and then to expand from it "wave after wave" outwardly, as Mao Zedong had been advocating, as to prepare for the summer offensive, to strike south on Changsha and north on Wuhan.[7]

After the fiasco of that summer, He Long retreated to western Hubei-Hunan, to be chased hither and thither, while the lakeland came under the heavy pressure of Chiang Kai-shek's armies early in 1931.[8] Unable to help his comrades there, He led his troops, now drastically reduced in strength, to northwestern Hubei.[9] Perhaps because of the frustration of his inability to create a stable soviet area in western Hubei-Hunan and the lakeland, the front committee of the CCP in his army decided to explore whatever possibilities there were in the Fangxian region.[10] The place was too poor to sustain a large army, however, and meanwhile he was relentlessly pursued by government forces.[11]

For the next year, He Long fought most of the time in northwestern Hubei while his comrades battled against very long odds in the face of the enemy and the devastating Yangzi floods in the summer and autumn of 1931. Both managed to survive precariously. In August 1932 the annihilation campaign against the Hong Lake Soviet began.[12] By September the soviet was abandoned.[13] Thus, the sorrowful history of the only lakeland soviet of the 1930s came to an end. It was beyond Duan Dechang's army to defend; it was also beyond He Long's army to protect both the lakes and the mountains. One wonders whether the original design of a western Hubei-Hunan soviet including the lakes was at all feasible.

For a while He Long tried to hook up with the oncoming Fourth Front Red Army, which was moving westward along the northern borders of Hubei. He himself was at Qujiawan in the Anlu-Yingshan area, with only about three thousand men.[14] The Fourth Front Army knew that he had formed a soviet there. When it arrived, he had left and his soviet was only a heap of rubble. The army turned north to Shaanxi; He turned south to cross the Yangzi at Badong.[15] At the beginning of 1933, he tried once again to recover his western Hubei-Hunan soviet area. He and his men hit and ran from the Qing to the Li and finally to the Wu valleys in the next fifteen months without being able to settle down anywhere. At Fengxiangxi, Yuanhe, Guizhou, on June 19, 1934, Xia Xi, He Long, and Guan Xiangying met to confer. Based on their estimate of "the fighting spirit of the masses" and "the war potential of the enemy," they decided to found a soviet at Yuanhe. After fighting in the Wu valley for a few months, they discovered that the available resources there could not sustain their efforts.[16]

Meanwhile, the Communist movement in Central China as a whole was going through a fateful change. In preparation for the eventual abandonment of the central soviet in southern Jiangxi, the Sixth Red Army Corps was instructed by the Central Secretariat of the CCP and the Central Revolutionary Military Commission on July 23, 1934, to join forces with He Long's Third Red Army and to develop a soviet in central Hunan. At that time the Sixth Army was about nine thousand strong and the Third Army had only some two thousand.[17] The two front armies, the First in southern Jiangxi and the Fourth in northeastern Sichuan, about one hundred thousand and sixty thousand strong respectively, were fighting for their survival. The party Center was planning to lay a stepping stone between the two front armies, to allow the First to move toward the Fourth.[18]

By the time the Sixth Army Corps actually made a junction with the Third Army at Songtao, northeastern Guizhou, their combined strength was no more than eight thousand.[19] They decided on several crucial issues: (1) to move back to western Hubei-Hunan to establish a soviet at Dayong; (2) to establish nine county revolutionary committees (provisional county governments), controlling 51 district and 230 township soviets, all of which (except that of Xuanen) were in western Hunan; and (3) more significantly, to menace the lower reaches of the Li, to draw the Guomindang troops thither, and thus to give aid to the First Front Army on its way to western Hunan.[20]

From October 1934, the beginning of the Long March of the First Front Army, to October 1935, that of Xiao Ke's Sixth Army Corps and He Long's redesignated Second Army Corps, the theater of operations was western Hunan, the Dayong-Sangzhi-Yongshun triangle, with Longshan-Laifeng as the rear. In the core of the soviet, the three cities in eleven or twelve months' time changed hands no fewer than six times.[21]

A pattern of the history of the Western Hubei-Hunan Soviet, which was very different from that of any other major soviet in Central China, has emerged, I hope, from the above description. None of the counties in this vast area had ever been held by the Communists for a long period of time. Their feeble control was due to a host of reasons, which I shall presently discuss. Because of it, the Red Army had to hit and run, looting from the rich and destroying or dodging whoever and whatever that was in their way. They appeared to be doing precisely what Mao Zedong and his comrades were trying to avoid. Periodically these wanderers would return to western Hunan, for the enemy was too strong in the lakeland or the resources in northwestern and western Hubei were too meager. They captured county seats here and there, in the final analysis, not for creating a permanent soviet but for carrying away whatever they needed and could take.

The official historiography of the CCP, even in the 1980s, attributes the obvious failure of the Western Hubei-Hunan Soviet to the Li Lisan line of summer 1930, which led the Second Army Corps away from the lakes and mountains to mount a futile attack on Changsha, and to the so-called Wang Ming line, which caused the destruction of the Hong Lake Soviet and He Long's ceaseless wanderings.[22] I am not sure that the impact of Li Lisan on the soviets was invariably harmful. The Oyuwan Soviet and the First Red Army were the creations of that period, and they were not demonstrably worse off after the summer of 1930.[23] The destruction of the Hong Lake Soviet was more a decision on the part of Chiang Kai-shek than of Wang Ming. He Long's wanderings were evidently not the result of carrying out the strategy of positional warfare attributed to Wang and his International Faction. An explanation of the history of the Western Hubei-Hunan Soviet has to be sought elsewhere.

When he returned to Sangzhi in the spring of 1928, He Long was a native son of a national reputation and considerable personal charisma. Physically strong and well traveled even when he was only a boy, he joined the army probably in 1918, rising to the rank of major in Chen Quzhen's army in 1921, brigadier general in 1923, and divisional commander in 1925. This rapid progress of his career was not entirely due to his bravery and martial skills. He had learned to survive as a commander of troops by manipulating both friends and foes alike, and by his ability to raise money for his men. Of course, he changed sides opportunistically: he was sometimes a Hunan officer, sometimes a Sichuan one, and sometimes even a Guizhou one for his personal and his soldiers' benefit. Whatever colors were hoisted on his mast, he remained in western Hunan, and the men under his command were western Hunanese.

In 1925 he was made the garrison commander of Lizhou, a landmark in his career, for the provincial governor, Zhao Hengti, recognized his ability and his importance as a military leader. Under his command were eleven or twelve regiments of foot soldiers.[24] In the autumn of 1926 he gave his support to the Guomindang and the Northern Expedition led by Chiang Kai-shek. This meant, among other things, the addition of a political department to his army, which was headed by one Zhou Yiqun, a Communist, and manned by some two thousand students.[25] This was another landmark in his career.

He attacked western Hubei, entered the port city of Yichang, and was transferred to Wuhan in January 1927. He was then the commander of the First Independent Division. June 1927 saw him fighting in Henan as the commander of the Twentieth Army.[26] The expansion of his army came after the incorporation of the workers' pickets and some armed peasant units. This accounted for the different nature of that famous army,[27] its participation in the Nanchang uprising on August 1, and its long march south to Shantou and subsequent destruction. He did not return home until March 1928, but his men had in the meantime found their way back to Sangzhi and other counties in western Hubei-Hunan. Within a matter of weeks he was able to gather a force of three thousand. No one else could have done it so quickly.[28]

Naturally, He Long depended on traditional and personal ties for his own safety and the success of his political plans. At Cili he found an old lieutenant in his First Division who was then managing a grocery. The police commandant of Linli had also served under him. Some of the militia units welcomed and protected him. When he reached home, a female cousin, He Ying, came with a contingent of troops; so did Wang Bingnan, formerly under his command.[29] The general's homecoming was exciting news. It might mean to his former subordinates the end of the doldrums and the revival of adventures. Had he depended entirely on these ties, the uprisings he led would have been more traditional in nature. The traditionality of these mountain counties was beginning to change, although they were far away from the center of the great peasant movement in the Xiang valley. Without secondary schools and with only a few native scholars returning from their studies at places like Changsha, whatever change that was taking place was bound to be slow. It depended on educated outsiders or enlightened natives like He Long.

Sangzhi people had a reputation for being tough and quarrelsome. Many of them possessed martial skills and had traveled on business trips as He Long had done. They either trusted or distrusted implicitly; they had little fear of officials or local ruffians.[30] In 1927–28 a few of their scholars studying in Changsha returned to Sangzhi to organize peasant associations, which were said to be six thousand strong.[31] It was probably due to their efforts that a series of small-scale uprisings on the lunar new year's eve broke out, coinciding with He Long's return to western Hunan. There were a number of them on both sides of the Jing, south of Shashi in Hubei. These Communist-led peasants fought the local militia and bandits for about a fortnight. In the end their strength swelled from four hundred to over one thousand, allowing them to wage guerrilla warfare in the Hong Lake area. Slightly later, in April 1928, the Communists in Shimen organized an uprising of some two hundred men on the southern outskirts, who incorporated many militiamen into their ranks but were eventually defeated by these militiamen who turned against them.[32] Evidently these uprisings demonstrated the peasants' support of the returned general. Further afield, a small guerrilla band operated in the Badong-Xingshan-Zigui area in the winter of 1927. Calling itself the Forty-ninth Red Division, it had survived until the winter of 1931. Further still, in the Xiangyang-Zaoyang area, another guerrilla band, about three hundred strong, created a base area simultaneous with the return of He Long. Ambitiously, these guerrillas called themselves the Ninth Red Army and fought on till summer 1932 when they moved south to the Hong Lake Soviet, where they were reorganized into the Ninth Division of the Third Red Army under He Long.[33]

Was it possible or easy for a man like He Long to draw a clear line of division between friends and foes in western Hunan, as Mao Zedong exhorted all revolutionaries to do in his essay on the classes in Chinese society of 1926?[34] Or must he make full use of his own equivocation to take advantage of an ambiguous situation without in the final analysis jettisoning his long-term goals? Without his extensive social connections, mostly traditional in nature, how could he gather a force of three thousand and take Sangzhi soon after his return in 1928? When he was driven out of the city shortly after that, fortresses and villages were in the hands of enemies of his guerrillas. It was true that they were divided—a local boss controlled one or two villages, a local warlord one or two counties, but they were all under the wing of General Chen Quzhen, who dominated about fourteen counties in western Hunan.[35] When He Long was not strong enough to challenge them, should he parley with them as he actually did?[36]

Then there were miscellaneous armed forces, from the "housecarls" (*jiading*) of a big landlord's estate to the militia, the Brotherhood, and the Divine Army. In the lakeland there were also buccaneers (*huba*) who cooperated with militia and an armed religious sect called Baijihui.[37] In the Xiangyang region of northwestern Hubei, there was even another Red Army unit, the Ninth Army, though it numbered only a few hundred, whose influence spread through Fangxian, Zhushan, Zhuxi, and Yunyang to Badong, Xingshan, and Zigui on the Yangzi.[38]

He Long had to fight them, especially the local ruffians, bandits and buccaneers, the predatory Baijihui, and so on. But from 1929 to the abandonment of his soviet, he had helped the Divine Army several times, just as they helped him. In his assessment, the Divine Army, wherever they happened to be, from western Hubei to eastern Guizhou, were more protective of the people, a type of social bandits. He could justifiably ally with them. More than once he absorbed defeated, *ronin*-type soldiers of former warlords into his own army, such as those under General Zhang Xuan in the Wu valley of southeastern Sichuan.[39]

The experiences of the other soviets in Central China showed that the key for mobilizing the rural population was the confiscation and redistribution of land, a subject all the memoirs and historical accounts of He Long's soviet years have avoided or at best have little to say on. From March 1928 to the end of 1929, no confiscation or redistribution of land was attempted in western Hunan and the Hong Lake area. One could probably argue that since the resolutions on the rural soviets and land problems adopted at the Sixth Congress in July 1928 were not known to He Long until the beginning of 1929, he simply did not include the formation of a soviet and confiscation of land on his agenda. But as for the rest of the year, Zhou Yiqun in the lakeland remarked almost nonchalantly. "Subjectively [we] did not notice this question."[40]

The first land laws of western Hubei-Hunan were introduced in January 1930. But before October 1930 He Long's and Duan Dechang's armies were busy preparing for an assault on Changsha, the first major target of the famous Li Lisan line. Before they resettled into their soviets, a new land policy was sent down from the party Center, to redistribute the land not only of the landlords and rich peasants but also of the middle peasants, and to give nothing but poor land to the rich peasants. Only the lakeland was held long enough for these changes to be implemented; only the lakeland was submerged by the great Yangzi floods of the summer of 1931. The Li Lisan adventures sufficiently alarmed the government, and the floods sufficiently weakened the Communists. Before the lakeland could be properly drained, Chiang Kai-shek launched an annihilation campaign that ended in the total destruction of the Hong Lake Base Area in September 1932.[41]

The paucity of reference to He Long's efforts in land redistribution may have been due to two reasons: He did not try hard enough, and he did not stay at a place long enough to make land redistribution worthwhile. Even the Eastern Guizhou Soviet, formed in August 1934, lasted only about eight weeks.[42] What would happen to the peasants who had received land from him after he left and the owners returned? He and the army led by Xiao Ke and Ren Bishi joined together in northeastern Guizhou in October 1934; they then decided to move back to the wealthier western Hunan. There, at Dayong, they declared the formation of the revolutionary committee of the Xiangechuanqian (Hunan-Hubei-Sichuan-Guizhou) Soviet on November 26, 1934.[43] A serious attempt was made to redistribute land in western Hunan according to the land law promulgated on December 1, 1934, and other laws subsequently. At Nanyaojie in eastern Guizhou, fifty-nine townships had redistributed their land, at about one mu or less per person. As discussed in chapter 2, this was far below the minimum requirement of land to keep a person alive. Since the Red Army was concentrated in the Yongshun-Dayong area, the land there must have been redistributed first, and with a measure of thoroughness. In Sangzhi, some 5,500 peasant households, or about 9 percent of all the rural households of that county, received a share of land. In Longshan, 25,000 mu of land was redistributed, or about 7.5 percent of the total cultivated land of the county. In Cili, a mere 4,000 mu or 0.5 percent of the cultivated land of the county was redistributed. These figures are simply too low to mean anything. In Dayong, however, 66 percent of the cultivated land was supposedly redistributed to 95,000 people. Based on the statistics in chapter 2, this meant 1.6 mu to each person.[44] Again, this was too small a plot to keep its tiller's body and soul together. One could argue that a plot of land, however small, was better than none, but one could hardly depict on that basis a glowing picture of peasant enthusiasm. Pushing the army to the lower reaches of the Li and trying to consolidate its hold there at the end of 1934 and the beginning of 1935, when the First Front Army was fighting in the south of Hunan and southeast of Guizhou and then northward to Zunyi, the Second and Sixth Red Army Corps were obviously giving aid to their oncoming comrades. Their land laws of December 1934 reminded one of the earlier land laws of the Hong Lake area in January 1930. Both were designed to serve military and political purposes. As socioeconomic measures, they were too half-hearted to be of any great significance. When a person needed some 4 mu to survive but was given only 1 or 1.6 mu as his share, the recipient probably appreciated the gesture of land redistribution in the western Hunan highlands. One must not forget that in western Hunan over 40 percent of the peasants were owner cultivators, and nearly 24 percent of them were part owners. They made up the bulk of the peasantry. Land confiscation and redistribution could benefit less than half of the rural population.

He Long began with about three thousand men in March 1928. In preparation for the summer offensive of 1930, his army, the Fourth, and the Sixth under Kuang Jixun were combined to form the Second Army Corps of some ten thousand men. By March 1931 the army corps's strength was reduced by half and it was downgraded to an army, the Third. As the army fought on, its losses were slightly more than being made up by the incorporation of other armed units, such as the Divine Army. In October 1934 when the Sixth Army Corps under Xiao Ke and Ren Bishi came up from the old Jinggangshan base, He had a little more than four thousand; Xiao, a little more than three thousand. Under whatever designation, He Long's army had remained at the same size from March 1928 to October 1934. In his mobilization of popular support, including recruitment, he had relied on neither land redistribution nor party-led recruitment campaigns. The constant size of the army, I think, goes a long way to explain its inability to hold onto a piece of land for long. It had to adopt either a hit-and-run or a driven-and-run tactic until Xiao Ke's army joined forces with it. Thereafter they conducted a land redistribution and recruitment campaign at the beginning of 1935. When they set out on their Long March in October 1935, He's Second Army Corps was said to have 9,200; Xiao's Sixth Army Corps, 11,000. They were probably far fewer.[45]

Northeast Sichuan

Having traversed wartorn Hubei and Shaanxi, the Fourth Front Army, then about nine thousand strong, descended upon wartorn northeastern Sichuan. General Xu Xiangqian, the commander-in-chief, recorded his first impression in December 1932:

> On both sides of the Tong, the overhanging cliffs and rocky stalwarts looked as if they threatened to pounce on us. The waters were rapid and white; the narrow pathways wiggled through the mountain gaps. Truly this was where one man could hold back a myriad. Although this was winter, the sun shone warmly on a landscape green with life as far as one's eyes could see. The scenery was completely different from the desolation of the Qinling range. As we beheld the ascents and descents and all the other things nature laid out to encircle us, we who had been so used to mountains and forests could not but feel enthralled. The commanding officers joyfully exclaimed: "North Sichuan is indeed a wonderful place. Now at long last we have found somewhere to rest our feet!"[46]

The pleasant surprise betrayed a general lack of knowledge of the place the army wanted to capture. In southern Shaanxi it had constantly been under the pressure of government troops, and there was no way for it to find winter tunics for the soldiers. On the other hand, most people had heard about the hackneyed image of Sichuan being a "paradise" (*tianfu zhi guo*) derived from "*tianfu zhitu*" uttered by Zhuge Liang in his conversation with Liu Bei in A.D. 207. Economically Sichuan was more resourceful than Shaanxi, and thus a better place for the army to found a soviet. The major warlords there, including General Tian Songyao of the Twenty-ninth Army, whose garrison region was in northeastern Sichuan, were engaged in a fierce power struggle on the plains around Chengdu. This left the northeastern part of the province open to external invasion. The army held two high-level discussions, one at Xiaohekou, Chenggu, Shaanxi, on December 10, 1932, and the next at Zhongjiagou, Xixiang, Shaanxi, five days later. The decision to enter Sichuan was made, and on Christmas Day the Fourth Front Army took Tongjiang, thus beginning the history of the Sichuan-Shaanxi Soviet.[47]

By the end of January 1933, the army had also taken Chengkou, Nanjiang, and Bazhong, while retaining some territories in Zhenba and Ningchiang in southern Shaanxi. Together with Tongjiang, this was the core of the soviet whose existence was inaugurated by an announcement early in February.[48] Hastily the warring generals patched up their differences and General Tian, insisting that he alone could comfortably deal with the Red Army in his own garrison region, was ordered to plan an encirclement campaign with the support of local and central government troops.[49]

The strategic pattern adopted by the Fourth Front Army was to abandon its less essential possessions, to concentrate its strength, and finally to counterattack. It was a strategy of deception that Xu Xiangqian executed with consummate skill. In May the first encirclement collapsed; the Twenty-ninth Army and its supporters were routed. The Red Army achieved more than the complete recovery of what they had occupied by pressing on westward to the Jialing and southward to the rim of the basin. The soviet now had an area of thirty thousand square kilometers and a population of two million.[50]

From June to the end of 1933 both sides were preparing for the next encirclement. The Fourth Front Army had increased its size with new recruits of peasants and surrendered soldiers, from just under ten thousand on entering Sichuan to just under twenty thousand organized into four divisions in the spring of 1933, and forty thousand in four armies in June and July. It was probably then that the soviet boasted the control of forty-two thousand square kilometers and seven million people,* the second largest soviet in Central China.[51] But it faced two serious problems: Many of the new, local recruits were opium addicts;

---

*The seven counties in the Sichuan-Shaanxi soviet had only about two million people. The claim of seven million is obviously a gross exaggeration.

and apart from the few top-ranking leaders, nearly all the cadres from the division level down were illiterate, and so the transmission of orders and directives depended on memory and memory alone. Not surprisingly, an animosity existed between the educated and uneducated cadres, adding to the difficulties of commanding such an army.[52]

In the meantime, the six Sichuan armies, 250,000 strong, now united under the commander-in-chief, General Liu Xiang, mounted another, more protracted encirclement campaign from November 1933 to August 1934. It followed roughly the same pattern as the previous one, with, of course, enough deception and ingenuity to conceal the sameness. The Fourth Front Army was initially pushed back toward the core of the soviet. There followed a period of seesaw battles throughout the lunar new year season and the early spring.[53] As mosquitoes helped spread the summer epidemics and the morale of the Sichuan government troops on such a long campaign dwindled, the Fourth Front Army unleashed a general counterattack that ended in Liu Xiang's resignation from the command in August.[54]

A victory for the Communists though it was, the second campaign with all its ferocity cost both sides dearly. The devastation through spring and summer ushered in food shortages; the slaughter and summer epidemics ended in a labor shortage; the government blockade made it almost impossible for the Communists to exchange the goods they had in overabundance for what they needed—salt, medicine, and cloth.[55]

The defeat of the Sichuan armies altered the nature of the war from what had to that point been principally a provincial effort to annihilate the Communists to a joint effort of both the province and the central government. Chiang Kai-shek's staff officers, money and matériel, and infantry poured into the province via the Yangzi and the mountain paths from Gansu and Shaanxi.[56] The Fourth Front Army was therefore no longer able to enjoy tranquility on its northern front; it had to fight on two fronts. This made it less able to concentrate in a small area and hit out. Winter was approaching. The army, now sixty thousand strong, was ready. It was the strongest Red Army in China and in control of the largest piece of land. The First Front Army had by now abandoned its central soviet in Jiangxi and been badly mauled on the first leg of its Long March. This was the immediate background to the Sichuan-Shaanxi encirclement campaign.

The party center and the First Front Army initially planned to join forces with He Long and Xiao Ke in western Hunan and eastern Guizhou and then to make contact with the Fourth Front Army. As this proved impossible, they wandered to Zunyi in northern Guizhou to take a respite and plan the next step. They wanted to create another soviet somewhere in the vast region stretching from northeastern Guizhou across the Guizhou-Sichuan border to eastern Yunnan and western Sichuan. They urgently needed help from the Fourth Front Army, whose main task was to preserve the Sichuan-Shaanxi Soviet. The tension between giving aid to the comrades in southern Sichuan and defending the soviet was keenly felt in the Zhaohua-Guangyuan campaign in January 1935. The party Center asked the Fourth Front Army to send at least one division to meet it somewhere in Sichuan. But where? No one seemed to know for sure. A division, say, of ten thousand represented about one-sixth of the Fourth Front Army's strength, but it would not be enough if the chosen meeting place was in the heavily defended basin. Even that would jeopardize the existence of the soviet. As it turned out, no troops left northern Sichuan for the south, and the Zhaohua-Guangyuan campaign, which began on January 22 and ended a week later, was a failure for the Communists.[57] On the twenty-second, the party Center telegraphed the Fourth Front Army on its plan to cross the Yangzi at a point between Luzhou and Yibin. Leaving their command posts in the thick of fighting, the top brass of the Fourth Front Army met at Wangcangba to discuss how the two front armies could coordinate their strategic movements. Several crucial questions were raised but none answered: Should the Fourth Front Army dispatch its main force south to meet the oncoming First Front Army? Which route should it take? How strong a force should it send? Could such a force fight its way to the Yangzi? In view of the limited strength the Fourth Front Army had at its disposal, no consensus on any of these questions was found, and so no decision was taken.[58]

Instead, the Fourth Front Army launched a short diversionary campaign in southern Shaanxi. Because of this preoccupation it did not return to Sichuan until the middle of February to rethink how it could coordinate with the First Front Army. By then the party Center had given up the hopeless plan of crossing the Yangzi to turn Sichuan completely red. Zhang Guotao, the party leader of the Sichuan-Shaanxi soviet, began to regard it as a squeezed lemon, in view of the shortages in food, arms, and ammunition. It would be folly to hold onto the area at all cost.[59] To quote from General Xu Xiangqian again:

> A revolutionary base area must support the war efforts, the existence and growth of the Red Army. The army must have human, material, and financial resources at its disposal. It must have food, clothes, new recruits, arms, and ammunition. Without these things, any talk of self-preservation and enemy destruction is just hot air. In the last months of the Sichuan-Shaanxi base area, the condition could be summed up in one word: exhausted.

This was totally different from his first impression of northern Sichuan. He goes on:

> We asked for food, there was none. We asked for tunics, there were none. We asked for new recruits, there were none either. The existence of the army was in the balance, let alone fighting. When the enemy's Sichuan-Shaanxi campaign came, we would lack the necessary human, material, and financial resources to sustain the war. Even if we fought on with grim determination, we could not last long. We could not repeat what had been done in the two previous campaigns. In the final analysis, what our hearts desired was not what we could carry out in reality.[60]

The situation was ominous for the Red Army. Liu Xiang's troops, having taken Wanyuan, were driving toward Tongjiang and Bazhong. The Twenty-ninth Army was pressing on in the southwestern sector of the front. On February 16 the party Center telegraphed the Fourth Front Army its new plan to establish a base area somewhere in the highlands of western Sichuan, either near Yunnan and Guizhou in the south or near Gansu and Shaanxi in the north.[61] In the light of these developments, the Fourth Front Army decided to cross the Jialing and march westward to join forces with the First Front Army. It took eighty thousand soldiers, left behind the soviet it had created and defended for twenty-seven months, and began the battle of the Jialing on March 28, 1935.[62]

The CCP established its first Sichuan party committee in February 1926, nearly five years after Hunan. But by the end of that year, the Lu[zhou]-Shun[qing, now Nanchong] armed uprising took place, led by Liu Bocheng, heralding more than sixty uprisings in the next ten years.[63] Of these, the most noteworthy in the annals of the armed struggles of the CCP in Sichuan was the East Sichuan Guerrilla Column.

Its creator, Wang Weizhou (1887–1970), joined not the CCP but the Korean Communist Party, in Shanghai in 1920. Soon he was sent to Moscow to study for a year. On his return, his mother's illness called him back to Xuanhan, a small city sandwiched between Wanxian and Tongjiang. He and other left-wing scholars in the adjacent counties taught at the primary schools and the Union Secondary School while organizing party cells in a dozen eastern Sichuan counties.[64]

The first guerrilla band led by Wang and Li Jiajun (1903–30), a native of Wanyuan, came into being soon after the end of the alliance between the GMD and CCP. They had the help of the Communist teachers and students at the Fourth Teachers' Training School in Wanxian, another center of left-wing scholars in eastern Sichuan.[65] The guerrillas in the Chengkou-Wanyuan-Wuxi area depended on the traditional social ties of the leaders and their families for cover and for protection. The soldiers came from the fringe elements of rural society and the mutineers of the poorly paid and poorly disciplined army commanded by General Liu Cunhou.[66]

An illustration of the continued usefulness of traditional ties is the exciting anecdote of Wang Weizhou's escape from the jaws of death in the summer of 1931. While on his way back to his guerrilla hideout, he stopped at his brother's home. A number of soldiers came to search the house when Wang himself was out for a walk. A personal friend, an army officer, saw him and quickly hid him in the money shop run by the officer's father. A little later Wang disguised himself as a woman and escaped. Of course, Wang repaid this debt of gratitude after 1949 when he found a job for the officer.[67]

The sphere of the guerrilla column's activities covered the entire area north of the Yangzi and east of the Qu. Although only about three thousand strong, it was influential enough to merit the creation of a party special committee to manage it. By the end of 1929 it was redesignated the First Route of the East Sichuan Guerrillas, which was to become a part of Li Lisan's planned march on Wuhan. Unfortunately, in Fangxian, northwestern Hubei, on its way to Wuhan in the summer of 1930, it was surrounded and destroyed by government troops.[68]

Wang Weizhou regrouped the remnants of the First Route, about six hundred men, to advance eastward, but they were again routed. Later in 1931 he regrouped his men once more, added new recruits, and called it the Third Route of the East Sichuan Guerrillas. By now it was no longer composed of scholars and mutineers, but scholars and peasants.[69]

At the same time other peasant movements rose to respond to Wang's activities. The Second Route of the East Sichuan Guerrillas appeared in the Fuling-Zhongxian area.[70] It joined forces with the Third Route and fought a disastrous battle against a Sichuan government division in August 1933. Another spontaneous peasant rising occurred in a fortress outside the city of Liangshan. When the antitax protesters were cornered in the fortress, the local CCP committee decided to help by organizing the peasants and armed them with knives and spears, to attack the besieging army. The army was overpowered, and in the wake of it a guerrilla band was established.[71] In October 1933 the East Sichuan Guerrillas eventually joined the Fourth Front Army in Xuanhan and were reorganized into the Thirty-third Army.[72]

What I have described so far is the awakened masses and their potential support for the Red Army's efforts in founding a soviet area. Mao Zedong certainly attached much importance to it when he wrote his report on the second congress of the CCP committees of the Hunan-Jiangxi border counties in October 1928 and his subsequent attempt to create a soviet in northwestern Fujian and southern Jiangxi.[73] It was curious that neither He Long nor Zhang Guotao considered it before going to western Hunan or eastern Sichuan. It took He a long time to realize its crucial significance. Zhang was luckier; he simply walked into a situation bubbling with violent defiance, which favored him and his comrades, and they made good use of it.

When the Fourth Front Army entered Sichuan, its highest leaders noticed the welcome and expectation the people expressed, as well as an intense hatred of the evil gentry and local tyrants almost synonymous with a "sharp revolutionary spirit" or "strong vengefulness," in Zhang Guotao's language.[74] Xu Xiangqian was impressed by their eagerness to cooperate with the East Sichuan Guerrillas in the past and with his front army now. Women in particular worked hard in the fields, carried heavy loads, and displayed an activism in revolutionary activities.[75] Of course, the inhabitants had their shortcomings—their faith in gods and spirits, in the former sons of heaven as well as the new one in the person of Comrade Zhang Guotao;[76] and women being cruelly treated by their opium-sodden husbands and in-laws.[77] The non-Communist weekly *Minzhong* (The people) confirms this impression as it cites the fact that several thousand people of Bazhong went to

welcome the Red Army. They were groaning under the crushing burden of taxes; the anti-Reds tax alone amounted to four million yuan for
the county! On the other hand, the Red Army did not press-gang people into doing corvée duties, billet in dwelling houses, or take grain
from the inhabitants. Taking the opportunity of the arrival of the
Fourth Front Army, the people in Nanjiang, Tongjiang, and Bazhong
demonstrated against levying more taxes and pushed their way into big
homes to eat (*chidahu*) to their hearts' content.[78]

This fervor the Fourth Front Army inspired was not mixed with
traditional affinities upon which He Long, relied in western Hunan in
1928. Neither the army nor its leaders were indigenous to Sichuan, so
they had neither relatives nor fellow townsmen to blur their vision.
How did they proceed to strengthen and consolidate this purer political
fervor? Their first step to "mobilize the masses" was to "beat the local
tyrants" (*datuhao*) by sharing out the tyrants' portable property. This
was followed by the redistribution of land. As a means to consolidate
popular support, the efficacy of land redistribution was predicated on
the hypothesis that the majority of the rural population were poor
peasants who owned a disproportionately small share of arable land.
This, of course, implied that a small number of landlords and rich
peasants possessed a shamelessly large share of it. Quoting from Lu
Pingdeng (1936, 183), Lin Chao and his coauthors say that the landowners in the entire soviet area, 9–12 percent of the population, occupied 74–80 percent of the land. Lin also used the Sanchuansi district of
Cangxi as an example. There the landlords (6.8 percent of the households) owned 67 percent of the land; the rich peasants (8 percent)
owned 15 percent; the middle peasants (5.9 percent) owned 8 percent;
and the poor peasants (49.1 percent) owned only 10 percent.[79]

In December 1932, the soviet government announced its land law:
all utilized land—fields, wooded land, and houses—and draft animals
and farming tools belonging to the landlords redistributed to each
adult, taking into consideration his or her ability to work the share of
land. The landlords ended up having no land at all, and rich peasants
only infertile land. All the work of sharing out was done in the presence of the masses after the masses had bitterly and angrily accused
the more prosperous of past wrongdoings. This was supposed to be a
lesson in political education to sharpen the class awareness of the
masses and deepen their commitment to the revolution. A report on the
county of Zhenba described the redistribution in these terms: 16 town-

ships, each having 10 landlords and 100 poor peasants; each landlord owning 111 mu and therefore each poor peasant receiving nearly 2 mu. At other places a person's share was as little as 1 mu. Even that the peasant was said to be very happy to accept.[80]

Zhang Guotao described northeastern Sichuan as "sparsely populated over a wide stretch of land."[81] If this was so, why was its pre-revolution land distribution as unequal as on the plains? Did the oft-cited inequality refer only to the paddy fields on the valley floors and the wooded land, most of which was indeed owned by landlords and rich peasants? On the slopes and plateaus the dry land was in the hands of owner-cultivators, the middle peasants. Personally, I have strong reservations about the perception of extreme inequality of land distribution in northeastern Sichuan before the end of 1932. My own position is stated in chapter 2, and hence the importance I attach to the redistribution of land in mass mobilization is limited. If land redistribution in the highlands was absolutely necessary for both economic and political reasons, each person's share should not have been much lower than four mu. Under peaceful conditions, a smaller share might have been enough, if the poor household could subsidize its livelihood with income from other productive activities such as trade and cash crops or, less importantly, selling one's labor as a part-time porter or builder. On the highland these activities were seldom in high demand. Under war conditions of disrupted transport and economic blockade, cash crops had little chance of getting through to the markets on the lowland. The Communist war imposed an order of economic autarky in which production was more than ever for subsistence.

General Liu Xiang's blockade of the "bandit area," which relied on management by county magistrates, local gentry, and militia groups, aimed at preventing food, salt, war matériel, and paraffin from reaching the Fourth Front Army.[82] Here, as elsewhere, the government blockade of the "bandit areas" was never water-tight. There was money to be made by exporting valuable highland goods, including opium, for lowland cotton, cloth, Western medicine, and salt (especially when Nanbu—a salt producing area—was not in Communist hands). To concentrate the soviet's efforts in running the blockade, twenty-seven state trading firms, called "economic communes" (jingji gongshe), were established. Their capital came from the portable property confiscated by the soviet government, and the smuggling trade was conducted either by straightforward purchase with cash or by an intricate process of barter (exchanging opium for cloth and medicine). We do not know how individuals took part in the economic communes, or how much of the export commodities was paid for by individuals. In any case, the soviet government monopoly of the red-and-white interarea trade deprived the people of an important sideline income. At Maoyuzhen, a market town upgraded to a county, Qijiang, interarea trade slumped. All the dealers in alcoholic drinks, vinegar, tea, salt, *yiner*, and so on went out of business, while a few oil presses, draperies, dyers, and herbists survived by the skin of their teeth.[83]

After the redistribution, the soviet government encouraged the tillers to reclaim new land, to plant food instead of cash crops like opium, and to form cooperatives of draft animals and farming tools in an undivided effort to increase food production. All former taxes were abolished.[84] On entering Sichuan, the Fourth Front Army saw how poverty-stricken and how heavily taxed the people were. Therefore, the soviet government abolished the "nasty" taxes to alleviate the livelihood of the masses.[85] In their place the soviet collected the "public grain" (*gongliang*)—40 percent for maintaining the civil service and transport service, 40 percent for provisioning the army, and 20 percent for elementary social insurance service for the aged, widowed, orphaned, and disabled.[86] At the peak of its prosperity, the soviet had some 2 million people, including 60,000 soldiers and as many civil servants and transport workers. Assuming that each of them ate 1.5 catties of polished grain a day (see chapter 2), the total amount of public grain was in the vicinity of 82 million catties. The seven counties that formed the more stable territory in the soviet had a total cultivated area of 5,985,000 mu, and each mu produced about 250 catties of grain.[87] The total grain output of the soviet was therefore about 1,500 million catties, 5.5 percent of which was paid as public grain. In contrast to the 10 percent tax paid by the people under the old regime, this much lighter burden was welcome news and won their support.

Of course, the Red Army needed supplies other than food. Cloth, salt, opium, draft animals, and cash came from confiscation of rich people's property; arms and ammunition and Western medicine came chiefly from war booty.[88] This made it necessary for the Red Army to foray out of the core area of the soviet to capture what it needed. The inferior quality of Sichuan arms and ammunition, compared with what was used by the central government armies and fell into Communist hands, and the fact that Sichuan soldiers often fled with their weapons caused considerable worry to the Fourth Front Army, which depended on its enemy to supply the weapons to kill him.[89]

Another noteworthy source of revenue for the soviet government was its exclusive power to issue currency. All the monies circulated before the establishment of the soviet were recalled and replaced by the paper, cloth, and metallic currencies of the Workers and Peasants Bank. The assets of the bank consisted chiefly of opium, nearly 10 million soviet yuan of it, but only worth 1,280,000 yuan according to the market price of opium in eastern Sichuan. (see chapter 3). The disparity in prices—3 soviet yuan and 0.40 yuan—indicated the extent of inflation in the soviet. However, against the 10 million soviet yuan of opium, the bank issued 2 million soviet yuan of paper and cloth money and 800,000 soviet yuan of silver and copper coins. The printing and minting machines were left behind by General Liu Cunhou's army when it fled. The fixed rate of exchange between the soviet yuan, nominally in silver, and the wen, nominally in copper, was 1 yuan to 30,000 wen (or 150 two-hundred-wen pieces). So designed, the only good money in the system was the silver coin, which was destined to become the only acceptable medium in the interarea trade, by virtue of which it was soon driven out of circulation inside the soviet. The government hastily stopped its issue and channeled it into the interarea trade monopolized by the economic communes.[90]

In spite of what has been said on opium prohibition, the drug was the pillar of the soviet economy. The bank needed a constant reserve of 200,000 catties against its currency issues, and the economic communes needed the drug for the interarea trade. Many of the local recruits into the Red Army and bureaucracy needed it for their physical comfort and professional efficiency. Ordinary people needed it, too, to satisfy their craving.[91] It is unclear how the soviet authorities came to have so much opium at their disposal. Take the 200,000 catties in the bank, for instance. If it was purchased by the bank, it would cost a staggering amount of money, which the bank was unlikely to have. Probably it was procured free of charge through confiscation and as war spoils.

Soviet government finances seems to have depended upon the public grain that fed its bureaucracy and armed forces, the monopoly on issuing currency for the defrayal of its expenses (without which it would have had to take control of many other key resources), and the opium at its disposal to secure the currency and to barter for cloth, medicine, and so forth from the white area. The soviet was constantly fighting for its survival, and the war was paid for by the public grain and opium. In this way, the people were affected only by the 5.5 percent of the total grain output taken from them as a tax and by the conscripted labor service for transport and for making tunics.[92] Other needs were met by issuing currency, monopolizing the interarea trade, confiscation, and war booty. Of this, opium was the mainstay. Since the land was redistributed, the peasants—part-owners and tenants— were freed from paying rent, 50 percent of the yield of the land, and interest if they were in debt. The population as a whole was obliged to pay a much lighter tax than ever before. Although they had their losses under the soviet regime—for example, they lost much of their considerable sideline income through selling cash crops to the lowlands— these losses were probably blamed on the anti-Communist forces.

Another popular policy adopted by the soviet government was directed at the elimination of the bandits in the soviet area. The origins of Wang Sanchun and Cui Erdan were obscure. Perhaps at some stage they did fly Shaanxi government colors. People like them survived in a zone of ambiguity. In the summer and autumn of 1933 the Fourth Front Army made a determined effort to chase them out of the soviet area. Wang did not try to return to the fringe of the soviet until March 1935 and Cui some seven months later.[93] They continued, however, to roam the countryside of northern Sichuan and southern Shaanxi well into 1937, two years after the Red Army had departed.

Surrounding the soviet, the government-organized and financed guerrillas and "special duty" columns, usually of a bandit origin, carried on in their accustomed ways. Government troops sent to fight the Communists robbed people indiscriminately. As soon as they recovered a piece of territory, the old regime was restored and local bosses and their armed retainers returned.[94] Between the Communist pull and the old regime's push, the soviet found reasons and opportunities to survive for twenty-six months. In the end it attracted some eighty thousand men and women to take part in the Long March and to continue the fight for its cause.

But the devastation of northeastern Sichuan was appalling. From early 1933, when the Twenty-ninth Army launched its first encirclement, to the winter of 1934–35, when the soviet was given up, the Fourth Front Army occupied and reoccupied the seven or eight counties at least four times; the government troops also recovered them four times.[95] Wanyuan provides an example of the situation. In the spring of 1935 when the Fourth Front Army evacuated the city for the last time, it burned the city for seven days and nights. Of the forty-eight market towns in the county, forty-three were in ruins. It was said that only one-third of the inhabitants remained or returned, only two or three hundred head of cattle survived, and only one-tenth of the land was plowed and sowed.[96] The picture of Nanjiang and Jiange was not much better.[97] Both Zhang Guotao and Xu Xiangqian recorded their impressions just before the Long March. To Zhang, it was a "scene of desolation." The land was "ravaged" and "overrun with weeds." To Xu, it was total devastation. The third encirclement fought in the growing season resulted in shortages of food and labor; the blockade caused a shortage of a variety of basic goods for living.[98] The people's support of the Communists was firm, and the Communists' ways to consolidate this support were astute. Both belligerents were determined—one to survive and the other to deny that survival. The Red Army, however, though well-disciplined and well-led, was in the final analysis much weaker than the government armies. It fought on like devils until the war resources were exhausted and it had to flee.

Comparison

It is not the concern of this study to explain why He Long followed a different approach to founding a soviet from Zhang Guotao's and Xu Xingqian's and also from Mao Zedong's. My concern is that since they adopted different ways, their results were also different. He Long had his traditional ties— kinship, commander-subordinate relationship, and local affinity—all of which he depended on and utilized. The original group of followers he gathered around him had more faith in him than in the Marxist-Leninist doctrine, which in all likelihood they did not understand. Since many of his men left for home after the Nanchang uprising and before he joined the Communist Party, they probably did not know in March 1928 that their commander was already a Communist.

They fought to capture cities, not to hold them long enough to introduce socioeconomic reform, land redistribution, and mass mobilization, but for the valuables they could take away and share with the poor. When they needed fresh supplies of arms and ammunition, they took from their enemy. When they needed new recruits, the records show that He Long accepted the cooperation and surrender of defeated warlords' men and of mountain social bandits of the Haiduk type.[99] But to call him and his men "Haiduks" would be doing them an injustice. Although they spent many months on the mountains and in the woods, they did not eschew village and urban life. Throughout the years in western Hunan, He never wavered in his loyal support of the Communist cause. His loyalty always went to the party Center, no matter who happened to head it. He responded to Li Lisan's adventures by trying to attack Shashi and Changsha in the summer of 1930; he followed the directives of the provisional Center led by Qin Bangxian by defending the Hong Lake Base Area; most important of all, he gave his allegiance to Mao Zedong instead of Zhang Guotao in the decisive struggle for power in 1935 and 1936. Chinese party historians who have access to documents written by He himself do not explain whether he supported these party leaders as a matter of discipline or as the result of deliberations. If He's understanding of the issues at stake from 1930 to 1936 was not in any sense penetrating or profound, he probably offered loyalty to his superiors in a manner similar to that he received from his subordinates. As a good soldier, he probably did not deem it necessary to question political decisions. When his behavioral traits are considered, one must hesitate to label him a Haiduk.

If one compares him with other soviet leaders, however, he was decidedly less reliant on socioeconomic reforms for mass mobilization and the consolidation of mass support. Ideology and political consciousness, changes in social institutions, and class relations did not seem to matter much to him. To win, to capture, and to share out spoils were to him the essence of being a good fighter for the oppressed. Therefore, without a stable soviet area, he fought on from one range of mountains to the next, from one river valley to another, always returning to western Hunan with about the same number of men under his flag until he met with Xiao Ke and Ren Bishi. Then there was a change in policy and an increase in the strength of his army in preparation for the Long March.

He's colorful experiences, so outstanding among the founders of soviets in this period, make Zhang Guotao's pale in comparison. Zhang was definitely more orthodox in the creation of his soviet in northeastern Sichuan but more successful in every aspect. In the decisive 1932 campaign against He Long and Duan Dechang in the Hong

Lake area, Chiang Kai-shek deployed four divisions and three brigades. The result was the destruction of the soviet there. In another decisive campaign against He Long and Xiao Ke in 1935, Chiang's commander He Jian led eight divisions of infantry to push the Red Army back to Yongshun and Longshan.[100] In contrast, the second encirclement campaign against the Fourth Front Army saw Chiang's commander Liu Xiang throw into the battle no fewer than 110 regiments of 200,000 troops, only to be defeated by the Red Army.[101] In nine years He Long had not succeeded in creating a solid soviet, while Zhang Guotao's was the second largest, next only to the central soviet. From the winter of 1934 up to December 1936 when Chiang Kai-shek was captured by the mutineers in Xian, the Fourth Front Army stood supreme among the sadly crippled First Front Army, the recently created Second Front Army (commanded by He Long and Xiao Ke since July 1936), and other smaller units. The Fourth Front Army was an essential factor in the calculations of national politics as the second united front between the GMD and the CCP was being formed and an expeditionary force of the army was fighting in the Gansu corridor.

The Central China highlands offered to the Communist movement not just the soviets founded by Zhang Guotao and He Long, the Fourth Front Army, and the Second Front Army commanded by He and Xiao Ke, but also the Fourth Red Army, which was to evolve into the First Front Army and such less mighty units as the Tenth Army Corps under Fang Zhimin. Although many soldiers had died in action in the years of cruel fighting, the three front armies were still able to hold onto the support of impressive numbers of highland fighters and embark on the Long March. The First Front Army consisted then of about 100,000; the Second, about 20,000; and the Fourth, 80,000. It was this group of officers and men, with notable assistance from North China Red Army units such as the Fifteenth Army Corps, that fought and won in the thirteen years after their evacuation from these highlands. It was they who formed the backbone of the Eighth Route Army during the anti-Japanese war and the four field armies of the People's Liberation Army when the civil war resumed from 1946 to 1949.

11
CONCLUSION

IN THE introduction I explained my historical and theoretical concerns in three sequential stages: (1) The commercialization of the highland agriculture failed to lead to social and economic changes away from involution and toward modernity. (2) This failure was partly attributable to population increases, partly attributable to the exploitation of the small peasants by the landed and military elites, and more decidedly attributable to "pumping the economic surplus out of the peasantry" by a "stronger surplus-extracting machinery" organized by the military.[1] (3) The peasants' anger grew out of the loss of this surplus, which was, on the one hand, confirmed by the militant highland tradition and, on the other hand, articulated by the Communists, who came to mobilize them in a revolution against the old regime of the military and gentry.

The body of the study has given the details of these three major concerns. In spite of population increases, the highlanders had enough to eat, and the majority of them were owner-cultivators and part-owners. This is not to deny that there were landless peasants who could be politically aroused to take action by the Communist land redistribution program; chapter 2 and the subsequent discussion, however, make no attempt to exaggerate the role of abject poverty and immiserization in the rebelliousness of the highlanders, as the left-wing social and political analysts of the 1930s argued. In the forty years between 1895 and 1937, the highlanders went through a rapid agricultural commercialization (chapter 3), bringing in additional income to sustain a growing population. This income, enormous in scale, caused neither the mode of production nor the mode of distribution of highland products to be modernized (chapter 4). If my calculations are acceptable, the additional income amounted to no less than 500 million yuan or some 38 yuan per capita in the forty years. At the same time the military expenditures of the region took some 10 percent, not 3 or 4 percent as some economic historians would have one believe, or 2.40 yuan per capita per annum (chapters 5 and 6).

Socially, the majority of the highlanders lived outside cities, towns, and even villages or fortresses. Unprotected by militia or police, uncared for by lineage or government, and uneducated (chapter 7), they had to fend for themselves and rely to a considerable degree on the wisdom of their oral tradition, which was both martial and romantic. Unencumbered by urban refinement, they were still lions, not yet foxes (chapter 8). These highlands happened to be interposed between the northern and southern leagues of militarists. Frequent civil wars brought huge armed concentrations—soldiers, militia, rebels, and bandits— which needed to be fed, clothed, billeted, and equipped by the monies collected from the highlanders (chapter 9).

Indeed, there was plenty of combustible stuff waiting to be ignited by the radicals from the lowlands who had both the vision and the skill to organize the highlanders into a revolutionary force. When the radicals did come to the highlands, the frequency and intensity of civil strife increased, leading to even more devastation (chapter 10).

As history, this study has endeavored to make these points. The highlands went through radicalization and revolution not in a persistent agrarian depression, but in a persistent agrarian prosperity up to the early 1930s. The highlanders' anger was generated and exacerbated not by starvation but by the ruthless appropriation by the state of what they rightfully regarded as their own earnings. The amount extracted from the people was spent by the state neither on productive investment nor on popular welfare, but largely on fighting.

The anger or the conflict between the state and the people should have been moderated by the additional income from the enormously expanded cash crops. But, as I have demonstrated, the income was siphoned away from its producers by a government that represented the interests of both the military and the gentry, whose occlusion prevented them from playing the entrepreneurial role needed for the highland modernization, and even from knowing the wishes and attitudes of the ordinary people.[2]

In the great controversy between moral and political economists, the historian finds it difficult to choose sides due to insufficient factual materials. I simply do not have the detailed knowledge of the individual political decisions of the highlanders to allow me to denote that they were based on either moral indignation or rational weighing of advantages and disadvantages. From the perspective of a Chinese historian, the 1983 symposium in the *Journal of Asian Studies* is unsatisfactory.

The conclusions of this study are that the highlanders were individually defiant and courageous, that they were angry with the rapacity of all the levels of government, and that they were prepared to cooperate with the Communists who came to mobilize them. It is apparent, nonetheless, that what is in question are the social, cultural, and political problems of a people who lived widely dispersed in homesteads and hamlets that had neither motorized vehicles nor telephones to bind them together. More than any other group of people, they lacked solidarity in terms of either social organization or a communal ethos by which to conduct any coherent, long-term political action.[3] Probably more than any other group of people, they needed outside leadership.

To mobilize them by means other than a mere reliance on traditional ties such as patron-client relations, kith and kin, and local affinity, the outsiders had to make good use, initially, of land confiscation and redistribution. Here the position taken by Mao and Chinese Marxist historians seems to be irreconcilable with that of Western scholars such as Wolf, Le Roy Ladurie, and Popkin.[4] Although Mao had consistently sung the praises of the poor peasants' role in the revolution in contrast to Western scholars' stress on the activism of middle peasants (owner-cultivators), he took great care both in theory and in policy in protecting the interests of the middle peasants and against unnecessarily alienating the rich peasants. He appreciated their skills in management and trade. To me, the irreconcilability is more apparent than real. To quote from Petras and Merino, "The peasants who were most militant and aggressive in their behavior against the landlord . . . tended also to have the strongest desire to develop commercial agricultural enterprises."[5]

In the Central Soviet (southern Jiangxi and northwestern Fujian highlands), as in the highlands under study here, the revolutionaries seem to have relied on two waves of enthusiasm—the first from the poor peasants to give aid to the Communist party in the process of conquest, and the second from the middle and rich peasants in the process of land redistribution and policy making. Without the latter, either because of negligence or because of callousness on the part of the revolutionaries, the rural soviet regime could not have been firmly established, let alone enlarged.

APPENDIX A
On Statistics

THIS APPENDIX is not entirely horror stories, although some of the statistical inconsistencies are indeed difficult to understand. For instance, the *Zhonghua minguo tongji tiyao* (Selected statistics of the Chinese Republic) of 1935 reports that the average size of a family farm in Wuxi was only 5.3 mu, but that of Fengdu, 41.7 mu. One wonders why Wuxi peasants did not migrate up the Yangzi to Fengdu. Similarly, the average size of the family farm in Dayong was 3.8 mu, whereas that in nearby Sangzhi was 63.3 mu. Table A.1 is based on two sets of figures.

We are fortunate to have both sets of figures listed in the table, as one confirms the other on a number of useful points. First, in terms of order of importance, western Hubei people depended on maize, wheat, and rice as their staple food. Second, in northwestern Hubei, the cultivation of legumes, either for local consumption or for export, took up a considerable share of the land. Third, wherever a relatively high percentage of land was dedicated to rice cultivation, irrigation was likely to be better. There is in fact no choice between the two sets of data, since those given in set (b) for any one of the counties do not add up to 100.

Governments and private individuals have taken the initiative to compile and publish statistics on various aspects of the affairs of the nation since the opening years of this century. The 1930s saw a prodigious burst of energy in this direction, particularly in the statistical data concerning the economic development of the country. At the central government in Nanjing, the Ministry of Industry, Central Agricultural Experiment Institute, Bureau of Statistics of the Legislative Yuan, and Rural Reconstruction Committee of the Executive Yuan played an indispensable role in it; at the provincial government level, there were at least two offices dealing with the collection and publication of provincial and county statistics—the Department of Reconstruction (Jiansheting) and an Office of Statistics attached to another branch of the government. Then there were semiofficial and private efforts made by banks, newspapers and periodicals, universities and colleges, and so forth. In most cases, however, the methods adopted to discharge their duties were obscure, aside from occasional revelations in the monographs and articles. The author of *Sichuan liangshi yunxiao* (The transport and marketing of Sichuan foodstuffs), for example, mentions the lack of training of the personnel engaged in statistical work, the shortage of reading material on the assigned place for investigation, and the lack of cooperation from people being investigated. Impatience on the part of all concerned and the unstandardized weights and measures were also insurmountable difficulties. In an article in *Ren yu di* (People and their land), the author describes the frustration in collecting statistical data on land lease practices in Sichuan. Questionnaires were issued from Chengdu to all the counties, but very few of them were filled out and returned. More found their way back to Chengdu after telegrams were sent urging the county governments to return them, but the majority contained obvious errors and falsehoods. These had to be sent back for correction. How they were corrected and how they were checked in Chengdu is unknown. The province then had 2 metropolises and 166 counties. Exactly one-half of them eventually sent in more or less usable answers.

It is perfectly true that inconsistency and unreliability are common in the statistics concerning the highland. This does not in any sense mean that socioeconomic research based on Chinese data is hopeless. There are gems to be discovered, such as the cost of growing opium and the detailed information on the taxes in Fuling, Wang Chengjing's article on southeastern Sichuan, Zhang Xiaomei's monograph on Sichuan, the *Zhongguo shiyezhi*'s report on Hunan, and others. The researcher can hope for the luxury of having the same thing done twice or three times by different investigators, allowing one to collate and compare in order to achieve consistency and coherence of the whole picture. To illustrate this point, let me use a decree issued by Chiang Kai-shek in 1935. It reads in part:

> Since the reorganization of the aforesaid [Sichuan] provincial government [in 1935], the various military regions have voluntarily renditioned their administrative powers [to it]. Thereafter all the civilian and military expenses of the whole province, all the nasty taxes and exemptions from them handled by the provincial treasury have systematically been readjusted. However, unless the chaotic public finance of the counties is thoroughly reformed, it is impossible to alleviate the suffering of the people, to wipe clean the accumulated shabby practice, and to ease the needs of the government.[1]

How is this passage, which is about one of the most difficult financial problems, the finances of the garrison regions, to be interpreted? We are lucky indeed to have two reports on the finances of the garrison region of the Twenty-first Army: one by Zhang Xiaomei, and another by Lu Pingdeng.[2]

The two reports differ in coverage: Zhang has omitted revenues from salt, opium, taxes in advance, the "nasty" taxes, and bonds, while Lu, writing at least two years before Zhang, has included them. While Zhang gives the amount of 10,861,694 yuan as the region's revenue in 1933, Lu offers the amount of 47,800,000 yuan, which was to rise to 72,316,600 yuan in the following year. Even as late as 1936, the region still had its own budget to prove that Chiang's optimism about financial unity in Sichuan was premature. If one compares this set of figures on revenue with the estimates of the defense expenses of the province through the great war between Liu Xiang of the Twenty-first Army and Liu Wenhui of the Twenty-fourth Army in 1932–33 and the war against the Red Army in the two following years, it is apparent that even Lu's figures for 1934 and 1936 were very modest understatements.

The heart of the matter is not precise knowledge, which may not be attainable, but a reliable pattern or trend to weave into a coherent story. That I believe is often attainable. For that one needs a great deal of patience, extensive reading, careful collation, and a robust common sense consolidated by theoretical and historical reading.

Table A.1

Land Devoted to Major Food Crops in the 1930s, West Hubei (percent)

County		Rice	Wheat	Barley	Maize	Sorghum
Badong	A	9.4	28.0	6.8	31.6	15.0
	B	13.89	41.67	10.0	20.27	22.72
Baokang	A	5.0	20.0	8.0	61.3	2.3
	B	6.67	27.78	11.11	16.39	3.11
Enshi	A	18.6	11.7	7.0	32.7	9.3
	B	17.39	10.87	6.52	37.33	8.69
Fangxian	A	13.0	39.0	6.5	18.3	12.3
	B	19.23	57.69	8.62	46.67	18.0
Hefeng	A	22.0	26.0	9.0	25.0	—
	B	17.85	21.43	7.14	40.83	—
Jianshi	A	22.0	14.4	5.3	33.0	3.7
	B	13.51	8.78	3.24	30.43	2.23
Laifeng	A	42.6	18.6	13.0	15.0	2.0
	B	28.57	12.5	8.73	38.18	1.36
Lichuan	A	16.0	14.0	7.0	26.0	—
	B	23.33	20.0	10.0	35.83	—
Wufeng	A	4.3	17.0	14.0	28.0	6.0
	B	6.19	28.75	20.62	20.59	8.15
Xianfeng	A	21.6	17.0	11.0	37.0	—
	B	20.62	16.66	10.31	10.0	—
Xuanen	A	13.0	16.0	15.0	31.0	13.5
	B	15.3	20.45	18.18	20.0	12.28
Yunxi	A	6.0	48.0	7.0	28.8	1.0
	B	6.76	54.05	8.11	46.67	1.08
Yunxian	A	14.7	27.8	8.3	30.5	3.0
	B	18.93	35.71	10.11	47.62	3.93
Zhushan	A	14.7	9.0	4.6	45.8	5.0
	B	29.41	11.76	5.88	39.29	6.47
Zhuxi	A	15.9	10.0	5.0	4.2	27.7
	B	17.89	11.11	5.56	58.82	3.11
Zigui	A	18.5	27.8	9.25	13.0	3.0
	B	28.57	42.86	14.29	75.0	4.57

County		Sweet potatoes	Soy beans	Peas	Broad beans	Sesame
Badong	A	4.0	3.8	0.5	0.4	—
	B	6.11	5.56	0.72	0.56	0.22
Baokang	A	0.3	—	—	—	2.6
	B	0.44	—	—	—	3.55
Enshi	A	18.7	0.7	1.2	0.1	—
	B	17.39	0.65	1.08	0.11	—
Fangxian	A	0.3	5.2	10.0	0.8	0.3
	B	0.46	7.3	1.5	10.95	4.62
Jianshi	A	10.2	7.5	3.1	0.5	—
	B	6.22	4.59	1.88	2.84	0.1
Laifeng	A	0.8	3.2	2.7	2.0	—

	B	0.54	2.14	1.79	1.23	—
Lichuan	A	2.3	34.4	—	—	—
	B	3.33	49.33	—	—	—
Wufeng	A	0.8	28.5	0.6	0.4	—
	B	1.25	41.25	0.84	6.27	—
Xianfeng	A	0.5	5.5	6.0	0.9	—
	B	0.5	5.33	5.79	0.87	—
Xuanen	A	6.6	2.0	2.0	13.0	
	B	8.19	2.27	2.28	1.64	—
Yunxi	A	3.6	1.9	3.6	—	—
	B	4.06	1.89	4.06	—	—
Yunxian	A	1.1	13.9	0.4	0.3	—
	B	1.43	17.86	0.47	0.36	—
Zhushan	A	—	11.4	0.6	0.4	—
	B	—	14.71	0.77	5.88	
Zhuxi	A	5.0	16.9	2.0	1.0	—
	B	5.56	19.0	2.22	1.17	—
Zigui	A	1.0	9.25	10.5	—	7.8
	B	1.57	14.29	16.14	—	12.0

Sources: Set A is derived from the table in *Hubei nianjian* (1936, 164-65); set B is from *Hubeisheng zhi tudi liyong yu liangshi wenti* (1977, 24198-99).

APPENDIX B
The Folk Tradition

FOLK SONGS and tales are performing arts for entertainment and at the same time depositaries of a tradition. They are always subject to external cultural and other influences and to internal alterations and revisions, but they are never meant to be performed for monetary gain. However crude, rough, and extreme in their depiction of human emotions, they are sincere expressions of the singers and tellers.

As art forms and as research documentation, their value attracted the attention of scholars of literature and folklorists, perhaps under Japanese influence, during the May Fourth movement. Two centers of ethnography, one in the north at National Beijing University and another in the south at Sun Yat-sen University, emerged to collect, edit, and publish China's folk songs and folk tales.

Zhou Zuoren was an enthusiastic participant in this venture, but not all the other folklorists were as liberal and cosmopolitan as he was.[1] Zhou's basic principles in collecting songs and tales, riddles and sayings were absolute faithfulness and utter indiscrimination. He himself did not go to the villages to do fieldwork; those who did rejected his faithfulness and lack of a sense of censorship. The disagreement occurred in selecting what was to be collected and what was to be published. The majority could not convince themselves to separate the act of publication from its moral responsibility to the reader. To corrupt the reader intentionally or unintentionally can never be morally justified or forgiven. Therefore, in Beijing or Guangzhou, it was decided to exclude what was considered "obscene" (*huiyin*) and "thievish" (*huidao*).[2] The self-imposed censorship was particularly sensitive to obscenity. According to tradition, the clear differentiation of virtuous odes from vicious songs dates back to Confucius, and the tradition remained even among modern-minded folklorists in spite of the iconoclasm of the May Fourth movement. In two studies, "Filthy Songs" and "Aspects of Folk Songs," folks songs and songs performed at certain types of tea-houses and brothels are treated as the same.[3] Both were for popular entertainment during the chaotic warlord years.

When Chiang Kai-shek promoted his ideals of New Life, the government decreed that arts and literature, including songs, must take seriously their function as vehicles of popularizing traditional virtues. Therefore, "obscene songs" were to be prohibited.[4] The government did not differentiate between folk songs and tea-house songs. For instance, the Zhuang people of the Left and Right River region in Guangxi were forbidden to sing and dance their traditional festival songs and dances in the name of protecting people from moral corruption.[5]

The Communist party took its task as a defender of correct thought and behavior even more seriously than its predecessors. Since 1950, the key word has been "healthy," to both the bodies and souls of the people. The party's policy toward folk traditions has been antifeudal, anticapitalist, and antiobscene.[6] In the years of revolution, the party song writers composed many folk songs to accentuate class struggle and, for a period, the national struggle against Japan. These songs usually took a prominent position in the anthologies of folk songs published after 1950, underlining people's class and national hatred. And hatred, more than any other feeling, is to be found in most of the anthologies. The party's opposition to the principles of faithfulness and censorship is an intense and angry one. As mainstream arts and literature must follow Mao Zedong's dictum of politics taking precedence, folk songs and tales must do the same.

An example taken from the *Sichuan daxue xuebao* says: "Old folk songs belong to the past. What they sing does not correspond to what we need today. . . . However, we cannot deny that they are still shaping many people's thoughts. . . . Of course we cannot demand people of the past to write to meet our needs, but the influence of what they wrote on the present day must be carefully weighed."[7] The author of this essay deems it entirely correct to edit a line in a folk song written by a school leaver who went back to her native village to farm. The original line reads *"Shengxue buqi zuo zhuangjia"* (I farm because I can't afford to go to college). The edited line reads, *"Shengxue buru zuo zhuangjia"* (I farm, because it's better than going to college). The final version is *"Yaozai nongcun lai anjia"* (I want to settle down in my village).

The same method of editing a text is applied to a traditional folk song on an eighteen-year-old wife who married a three-year-old husband. There are three stanzas in it, the second and third of which deal with the conflicts between mother-in-law and daughter-in-law and the young woman's sexual craving. Both have been deleted by the editor because they are feudalistic and obscene.

In other words, we are dealing with a distorted, impoverished folk tradition. How much of it has been lost and how much still remains among the people who sing and tell stories is anybody's guess. Even in the 1920s when Beijing and Guangdong folklorists were trying to rescue what they could, few of them ventured as far as the remote mountains. Perhaps their financial resources allowed them to do their fieldwork only at places adjacent to their native villages and they did their work of love during summer vacation when they went home. Yet we know that the unimpoverished tradition, uncensored and unrefined by urban influence, exists in precisely the remote places. I am nonetheless extremely lucky to have found the few songs and tales for my analysis above, especially in chapter 8. But more and better organized collections are required for future research before the traditions are lost to us forever.

NOTES

Weights, Measures, and Monies

1. Chen Hansheng and Wang Yinsheng (1929, 1); *Caizheng jikan* (1:6).
2. Zhang Xiaomei (1938, W2–10).
3. *Chuanyan tekan*, no. 12: 9–12; no. 179: 35; and no. 180: 10; *Xinshubao* 1, 6 (1934).
4. *Zhonghang yuekan*, no. 10 (1930): 60–61; Li Changlong (1940, 17, 38); Li Shifeng (1934, 39–40).
5. Woodhead (1938, 216–17).
6. Ibid., 203.
7. Lu Pingdeng (1936, 40–41).
8. Zhang Youyi (1957, 3:30); *Shunong jikan*, no. 3: 3–4.

Chapter 1

1. *Hubei ziran dili* (1980, 35–37, 39).
2. Zheng Lijian (1947, 47–48); Gao and Dou (1981, 61–62, 70).
3. Zheng Lijian (1947, 159–60); *Hubei ziran dili* (1980, 35–43).
4. *Hubei ziran dili* (1980), 43, 49.
5. Ibid., 103–4.
6. Wang Chengjing (1944, 7); Liu Haipeng (1952, 31).
7. Gao and Dou (1981, 61–62, 70).
8. *Hubeisheng nianjian* (1936, 16–17, table 2).
9. *Zhongguo jingji nianjian* (1934, 3: c.22).
10. Skinner (1977, 213).
11. Ibid., pp. 258–59.
12. *Sichuan yuebao*, 8/5 (vol./no.), 39–40.
13. Wang Chengjing (1940, 65, 67).
14. *Sichuan yuebao*, 3/1, 138–43.
15. Wang Chengjing (1940, 67–69).
16. Ibid., 72; *Sichuan yuebao*, 3/1, 147–50, 153–56.
17. *Sichuan yuebao*, 3/1, 153–56.
18. Shen Congwen (1982, 203); Wang Chengjing (1940, 69–70).
19. *Hubeisheng yizhan*, 1:5.
20. Ibid., 1:2; also relevant county gazetteers.
21. *Sichuansheng nongqing baogao*, 3/5, 9–11; Feng Hefa (1933, 1:820).
22. *Sichuan jingji jikan*, 2/2, 266–67.
23. Ibid., 383–84.

24. *Sichuan yuebao*, 3/1, 135–37, 150–52.
25. Shen Congwen (1982, 9:202).
26. *Hubeisheng nianjian*, 633–34, 644; *Wuhan ribao*, January 19, 1935, February 12, 1936; *Zhongguo jingji*, 3/8, 2; *Sichuan yuebao*, 9/3, 43–49, 9/6, 162; Zhang Xiaomei (1938, G8–9, 11–12); Fang Xianting (1938, 2:640); *Sichuan wenxian*, V25, 10–13; *Hunan jinbainian* (1958, 2:640); *Jingji yanjiu*, 1/1, 6.
27. *Sichuan gonglu yuekan*, 11:12–13; Fang Xianting (1938, 2:1911–12).
28. *Sichuan gonglu yuekan*, 13:13–27.
29. Lu Pingdeng (1936, 60); *Sichuan gonglu yuekan*, 11:8; *Luxing zazhi*, 3/1, 30.
30. Zhang Xiaomei (1938, G14); *Sichuan gonglu yuekan*, 9:10.
31. Xue Shaoming (1937, 162, 196).
32. *Sichuan yuebao*, 10/5, 232–351 *Sichuansheng nongqing baogao*, 3/5, 9–11; *Shehui jingji yuebao*, 5/11–12, 660–67; Zhou Yishi (1957, 147); Feng Hefa (1933, 1:820).
33. Zhang Xiaomei (1938, G10, 12–13); *Xinyuji huikan*, 50:24; *Sichuansheng nongqing baogao*, 3/5, 9–10.
34. Wang Guang (1966, 406); Shen Congwen (1948, 11).
35. Chen Yanjiong (1936, 16–17).
36. Shen Congwen (1982, 9:153).
37. Wang Guang (1966, 406); Shen Congwen (1948, 11).
38. *Zhongguo shiyezhi* (1935, 3:203–6J); Shen Congwen (1948, 15).
39. Myers (1970, 13–24).
40. Huang (1985, pt. 1, chap. 1; pt. 3, chaps. 15–16).
41. Myers (1970, 31).
42. Skinner (1964–65, pt. 2, 199–200; Baker (1882, 9); von Richtofen (1903, 181).
43. Hsiao (1967, 275–306); Fei (1962, 106); Myers (1970, 126).
44. Blum (1960, 3).
45. Bambo (1977, 181).
46. Skinner (1971); E. R. Wolf (1957).
47. Shanin (1975, 246); Southworth and Johnston (1967, 77).
48. Watson (1982, 595, 606–7).
49. Wang Xizhi, (1891, F6/v3, 280); Zhang Xiaomei (1938, M42–44); my Dayong and Sangzhi diary, May 15 and 19, 1989.
50. *Yunxi xianzhi*, ch. 3); *Wanyuan xianzhi*, ch. 2.
51. *Wanxian zhi*, chs. 2, 9.
52. *Sichuan yuebao*, nos. 3, 4.
53. Ibid., 9/2.
54. Lu Pingdeng (1936, 71); *Sichuan yuebao*, 2/7, 22.
55. Hilton (1974, 217).
56. Geertz (1971, 48–9); Le Roy Ladurie (1979a, 6–7).
57. Braudel (1979, 2:298).
58. Solomon (1948, 525–34).
59. Le Roy Ladurie (1979a, 5).
60. Redfield (1956, 49).
61. Li Changlong (1940, 146).
62. *Sichuan yuebao*, 6/1, 87.
63. Aston and Philpin (1985, 13–14).
64. *Cambridge Modern History* (1968, 2:26ff, 37ff).

65. Shanin (1975, 79).
66. Rogers (1969, 14).
67. Aston et al. (1985, 15–18, 31).
68. Ibid., 27, 11.
69. Huang (1985, chaps. 6, 8, 10).
70. Zhang Youyi (1957, 2:84–88).
71. Ibid., 48–49; my Guling diary.
72. Zhang Youyi (1957, 2:76).
73. Ibid., 3:705; Zhang Xiaomei (1938, A24–26); *Nongmin congkan*, 2:152–53; *Xinshubao*, March 18, 1935; *Xinxin xinwen*, March 12, 1935.
74. Huang (1985, 262–74).
75. *Nongqing baogao*, 4/7, 175.
76. *Zhongguo zudian* (1942, 6–8).
77. *Donfang zazhi* 32/4, 116.
78. Feng Hefa (1933, 2:112).
79. *Xinshubao*, April 6, 1937.
80. Zheng Wanggu (1934, 99–103); *Sichuan jingji yuekan*, 6/5, 11–12.
81. *Decennial Report* (1892–1931, 484).
82. *Sichuan xuchan* (1941, 1:4); *Sichuansheng zhi shanhuo* (1935, 2:97).
83. Zhang Xiaomei (1938, V12–27); *Sichuan yuebao*, 9/10, 11.
84. *Sichuan yuebao, 9/10, 11.*
85. My Dayong diary, May 15, 1989.
86. Tawney (1964, 17, 52–53).
87. Scott (1976, 167).
88. Ibid., 57, 167, 182.
89. Davis (1970, 351–52).
90. Polachek (1983, 807–25).
91. *Hunan jinbainian* (1958, 1:112); *Xinshubao*, January 17 and November 18, 1935; *Sichuan yuebao*, 6/2, 179; my Shaowu and Gulin diaries, August 31 and September 19, 1983, and my Dayong diary, May 16, 1989.
92. Keyes (1983, 865).
93. Huang (1985, 5–7).
94. Popkin (1979, 16–19, 23–24, 27).
95. Ibid., 31.
96. Schultz (1964, 48–52); Southworth and Johnston (1967, 37–40).
97. Popkin (1979, 32–62).
98. Ibid., 253.
99. Ibid., 259–60, also 245–51.
100. Scott (1976, 240).
101. Redfield (1956, 68–69); Le Roy Ladurie (1979a, 79–80).
102. Le Roy Ladurie (1979a, 95–96); Scott (1976, 305).
103. Geertz (1973, 12, 17–18, 44–48).
104. Redfield (1947, 293–308).
105. Holy and Struchlik (1981, 29).
106. Kaufman (1985, 8).
107. Geertz (1973, 401).
108. Piers and Singer (1971, 23–24, 31–32).
109. Scott (1985, 17, n. 52); Le Roy Ladurie (1979b, 174, 185, 199–200).
110. Blum (1978, 47–48, 114–15); Hobsbawm (1973a, 12–13).

111. Huizer (1973, 18).
112. Le Roy Ladurie (1974, 151, 159–60); Lopreato (1967, 71); Lewis (1964, 494).
113. Rogers (1969, 26–38); Hobsbawm (1973, 6).
114. Le Roy Ladurie (1979, 13–14); Lewis (1951, chap. 12; 1964, 495).
115. Rogers (1969, 30–31).
116. Scott (1985, 282–84); Huizer (1973, 13).
117. Foster (1965, 296).
118. Ibid., 301–5.
119. Kennedy (1966, 1218); Piker (1966, 1207).
120. Lewis (1964, 493–94); Lopreato (1967, 66, 115).
121. Lewis (1964, xliii, 53); Lopreato (1967, 73); Shanin (1975, 23).
122. Lewis (1964, 424); Lopreato (1967, 120–21); Redfield (1956, 126–27);
Le Roy Ladurie (1974, 302).
123. Thomsen (1969, 25).
124. Kaufman (1985, 14–15, 24–25, 103–4); Piers and Singer (1971, 39).
125. Boggs (1978, 38–41).
126. Scott (1985, 317–19).
127. Geertz (1973, 90–91, 125–27).
128. E. Wolf (1974, 38–39).
129. Ibid., 146–59, 174–75).
130. Lewis (1969, 185); E. Wolf (1966, 99).
131. E. Wolf (1964, 238–42).
132. Diamond (1988).
133. *Dongfang zazhi*, 23/6, 57.
134. Shen Congwen (1982, 9:119, 160).
135. Skocpol (1979, 7–11, 14–18).
136. Russett (1964, 442–54); Huntington (1968, 57); Moore (1967, 473).
137. E. Wolf (1969, 277–78, 294); Petras and Merino (1972, 17); Shanin
(1975, 250); Popkin (1979, 71).
138. Huntington (1968, 56); Paige (1977, 58–59).
139. Schram (1963, 183–84); Takeuchi (1971, 7:125).
140. Mao (1964, 1:32–33).
141. Jackson (1966, 35–36).
142. E. Wolf (1975, 268; 1969, 290); Shanin (1975, 268).
143. Feeny (1983, 782).
144. Takeuchi (1971, 2:47–48).
145. Mao (1982, 272).
146. Takeuchi (1971, 2:219–25).
147. Zhongyang (1982, 1:191–92, 339).
148. Arendt (1963, 54–59).
149. Skocpol (1976, 206; 1979, 286–87).
150. Hobsbawm (1973a, 19).

Chapter 2

1. Xu Zhenying (1950, 6–7).
2. Needham (1984, 9, 25, 98).
3. *Sichuansheng nongqing baogao*, 1/5, 159–72.
4. Buck (1937, 192); Needham (1984, 123–25).

5. This includes *Sichuansheng jingji jikan, Sichuan yuebao, Hunan nianjian, Dagongbao, Zhonghang yuekan,* and the works by Lu Pingdeng, Wang Chengjing, Zhang Xiaomei, and Zheng Wanggu.

6. *Jingji yanjiu,* 1/7, 28/ *Sichuansheng nongqing baogao,* 1/5, 152, 1/5, 505–6.

7. Zheng Zhaojing (1939, 79).

8. Bannermen's land, garrison land, minority officials' land, county government land, temple land, clan association land, school land, protected forest land, etc. (Buck [1937, 192–93]; Li Wenzhi [1957, 1:178–83, 201, 205, 210, 214]).

9. Zhang Xiaomei (1938, 11); Lu Pingdeng (1936, 131–32).

10. Li Wenzhi (1957, 1:178–79).

11. Zhujichu (1942, 11).

12. *Jingji nianjian,* 7:G77; *Jingji yanjiu,* 3/3 303–4.

13. *Jingji nianjian,* 7:G79–80.

14. Zhang Youyi (1957, 2:84).

15. *Nongmin congkan,* 2:145–46.

16. Meng Guangyu (1943, 33–40).

17. *Zhongguo shiyezhi* (1935, 3:22–41 [*yi*]).

18. Ibid.

19. Meng Guangyu (1943, 33–40).

20. Zhujichu (1942, 88–89); Chen Zhengmo (1936, 61).

21. Zhang Youyi (1957, 2:105–6).

22. Lu Pingdeng (1936, 200).

23. Zhang Xiaomei (1938, m5).

24. Lu Pingdeng (1936, 200).

25. Zhang Youyi (1957, 3:256–62).

26. Lu Pingdeng (1936, 97–98).

27. Cheng Lichang (1938, n.p.); Zhang Xiaomei (1938, A14–7, B14–7); *Zhongguo shiyezhi* (1935, 3:8–10 [*yi*]).

Chapter 3

1. *Gongshang banyuekan,* 7/3, 106.

2. Zhang Xiaomei (1938, H5).

3. Wang Chengjing (1944, 20); Zhang Xiaomei (1938, N32).

4. Chen Yanjiong (1935, 29); *Sichuan yuebao,* 9/5, 143; 10/6,127.

5. Wang Chengjing (1944, 20).

6. *Zhonghua nongxuehuibao,* no. 135, 65–68.

7. Ibid., 70; Zhang Xiaomei (1938, N53).

8. *Sichuansheng jingji jikan,* 4/2–3–4, 122.

9. *Zhonghua nongxuehuibao,* no. 135, 70.

10. *Sichuansheng jianshe gongbao,* no. 4, 222; *Sichuan jingji jikan,* 2/2, 234.

11. *Chuanyan tekan,* no. 182, 5, 9.

12. Wang Chengjing (1944, 43); *Chuanyan tekan,* no. 159, 2–3; no. 174, 15–24; *Xinshubao,* October 30, 1935.

13. *Jingji nianjian,* 10:J156–57.

14. *Zhongguo shiyezhi,* 3:63–66, 107 (*si*); *Nongshang gongbao,* 7/2, 36.

15. *Nongshang tongjibiao,* 3:519–29; *Jingji nianjian,* 10:157–58; Zhang Xiaomei (1938, R61–63).

16. Chen Bingfan (1954, 1:76–77, 148; 2:259).

17. *Nongshang tongjibiao*, 3:573–79; 6:549–50; 5:577.

18. *Sichuansheng zhi yaocai* (1934, 162–66); *Sichuan kaocha baogaoshu* (1935, 59, 61); Zhang Xiaomei (1938, T92–93).

19. *Sichuan kaocha baogaoshu* (1935, 81); Zhang Xiaomei (1938, N51–53).

20. Cai Wuji and Mei Shudong (1951, 1–2); *Zhuzong* (1940, 13–14).

21. *Zhuzong* (1940, 6–11).

22. *Tongji yuebao*, no. 3, 15–20.

23. *Sichuan yuebao*, 5/4, 135–37.

24. *Dagongbao*, July 23, 24 and 25, 1922.

25. *Dagongbao*, July 6, 1922; *Jingji yanjiu*, 1/7, 36.

26. Li Changlong (1940, 24–26).

27. Ibid., 148; Lu Pingdeng (1936, 296).

28. Li Changlong (1940, 6–8); Li Shifeng (1934, 37–38); Zou Xupu (1944, 14).

29. Li Changlong (1940, 4–6); *Sichuan yuebao*, 8/3, 3–4.

30. *Jingji yanjiu*, 1/1, 17.

31. Li Changlong (1940, 15–7, 47–51); Zhang Xiaomei (1938, 68–70).

32. He Kai and Liu Hu, eds. (1934, 27–28).

33. Ibid., 30; *Sichuan yuebao*, 8/3, 16–17.

34. *Tongyou* (1941, 51–52).

35. *Sichuan yuebao*, 8/3, 16–17; Kanda Masao (1936, 556).

36. Zhang Xiaomei (1938, R73–77).

37. *Sichuan yuebao*, 7/2, 22–26.

38. *Haiguan* (1940, 1a:202); *Sichuan jingji jikan*, 1/2, 124; 1/3, 426–45. Two recent contributions, both well-researched, to the study of tong oil are W. T. Rowe, "Tung Oil in Central China: The Rise and Fall of a Regional Export Staple" (1989), and Hou Kunhong, "Kangzhan shiqide zhongguo tongyu shiye" (1989). Although their scopes and focuses are different from mine, they should be consulted for comparison.

39. *Zhongguo jingji*, 1/1, 13.

40. *Li Wenzhi* (1957, 1:458).

41. F. O. 371, July 7, 1911, 1072, no. 16037.

42. *Shibao*, January 11 and September 17, 1919.

43. *Decennial Reports* (1892–1931, 484); Lu Pingdeng (1936, 330–31); Spence (1975, 154).

44. Hall (1976, 121–22).

45. *Eastern Miscellany*, 32/14, July 16, 1935, 105–6.

46. *Shenbao yuekan*, June 15, 1935, 51.

47. *Sichuan jinyan yuekan*, 3/4, 3; *Xinshubao*, April 6, 1937.

48. *Hunan nianjian* (1933, 272–77).

49. Liu Haipeng (1952, 27–28); Gao Guanmin and Dou Xiuying (1981, 129, 132); and my Dayong and Sangzhi diaries, May 16 and 19, 1989.

50. *Hubeisheng zhengfu gongbao*, no. 309, 41–44.

51. *Shibao*, December 27, 1923; March 18, 1924; *Dongfang zazhi*, 23/20, 33.

Chapter 4

1. *Zhongguo shiyezhi*, 3:203–6 (*ding*); Wang Chengjing (1944, 46).

2. Liu Ts'ui-jung (1980, 15, 18–20).

3. Liu Ts'ui-jung (1980, 13–16, 17–18); *Luxing zazhi*, 7/6, 16.

4. Liu Ts'ui-jung (1980, 27); *Luxing zazhi*, 7/6, 16; *Xibei yanjiu*, no. 7, 9.
5. Liu Ts'ui-jung (1980, 18–20); *Hanjiang liuyu maoyi jice* (1905, pt. 1); Chen Yan (1937, 59).
6. *Xin youji huikan*, 8:V50, 26–28.
7. Wang Chengjing (1944, 44–48); Wang Guang (1966, 384–87).
8. Wang Chengjing (1944, 44–48).
9. Shen Congwen (1948, 10–11, 16, 36; 1982, 9:153, 189–91).
10. *Hunansheng zhi, Dilizhi*, 2:756; Wang Guang (1966, 395–96); *Jingji yanjiu*, 2/12, 28–29.
11. Zheng Zhaojing (1939, 167–68).
12. *Luxing zazhi*, 3/1, 29; 5/9, 25.
13. Zhang Xiaomei (1938, H20).
14. Ibid., H5–6, 20; *Sichuan wenxian* (V45:17–18).
15. Zhang Xiaomei (1938, H5–6).
16. Zheng Zhaojing (1939, 168).
17. Fang Xianting (1938, 2:1170).
18. Shen Congwen (1982, 9:202).
19. *Sichuansheng nongqing baogao*, 3/5, 9–11; *Hubeisheng yizhan*, 1:14–21; *Hunan sizhi*, V.
20. *Sichuansheng nongqing baogao*, 3/5, 9–11.
21. Wang Chengjing (1944, 50); *Sichuan jingji jikan*, 2/1, 383–84.
22. *Hunan miaofang tunzheng*, 1883, ch. 1, 37, 81–84; *Hubeisheng yizhan*, 2:33–34; *Hubei tongzhi*, ch. 50, 52; *Dagongbao*, March 2, 1919; my diary in Fenghuang, September 10, 1983.
23. Zhang Xiaomei (1938, G8–9).
24. Ibid., G14.
25. Xue Shaoming (1937, 162, 196).
26. *Xinshubao*, February 22, 24, 1935, March 6, 1936; *Sichuan yuebao*, 6/2, 162–63; 8/2, 228.
27. Zhang Xiaomei (1938, C138).
28. Wang Chengjing (1944, 60–62).
29. Shen Congwen (1948, chap. 2).
30. Ibid., 38–39; Ling Chunsheng and Rui Yifu (1947, 72).
31. *Zhongguo shiyezhi*, 3:161–62 (*bing*).
32. Shen Congwen (1948, 5); *Cili xianzhi*, chap. 16.
33. Du Shougu (1986, 1: chaps. 2, 5, 12).
34. Wang Chengjing (1944, 63–65).
35. Ibid., 46.
36. Ibid., 63, 71–72; *Sichuan yuebao*, 3/1, 135–43.
37. Shen Congwen (1982, 9:203); Wang Chengjing (1944, 69–70).
38. Wang Chengjing (1944, 67–69).
39. *Decennial Reports* (1912–21, 1:245).
40. *Xinshubao*, October 29, 1934.
41. *Sichuan yuebao*, 3/1, 131–35.
42. *Tongji yuekan*, 1/4, 19.
43. Zhang Xiaomei (1938, B9); *Wanxian diaocha*, 1.
44. *Sichuan jingji jikan*, 1/2, 124.
45. *Sichuan yuebao*, 8/3, 1–13.
46. *Shiye zhoubao*, no. 3, 2–5.

47. *Chuanyan tekan*, no. 17, 1; *Sichuan yuebao*, 9/4, 105.

48. *Xinshubao*, April 7, 1934.

49. *Sichuan yuebao*, 1/5, 25–8; 8/5, 103.

50. *Jingji zazhi*, 1/3, 44.

51. *Sichuan yuebao*, 6/4, 13–8; *Xinshubao*, October 4, 5, 18, 1934; *Yinhang zhoubao*, 19/36, 3–4, 13–14.

Chapter 5

1. *Hubei wenxian*, 1:13; *Dongfang zazhi*, 31/14, 98; *Tianfu andu*, 5, Hunan, 1–2; *Tianfu wenti*, 1936, 2:202.

2. Kapp (1973, 35–37); Pu Xiaorong (1986, 502–5).

3. Fan Chongshi (1962, 5–6).

4. Zhang Xiaomei (1938, C152–53); *Shibao*, January 8 and June 8, 1928; January 14, 1929; Feizhi (1933, 299–301); *Sichuan yuebao*, 6/1.

5. J. Ch'en (1979, chap. 3).

6. *Huazi ribao*, September 14, 1920.

7. *Shibao*, May 5, 1931.

8. *Dagongbao*, September 10, 1934.

9. Kapp (1973, 46, 57); Sheridan (1966, 105, 113); *Huazi ribao*, October 20, 1920; *Shibao*, June 23, 1932.

10. *The China Yearbook* (1926, 436).

11. *Nongcun fuxing weiyuanhui huibao* (1934, 140); *Wuhan ribao*, July 16, 1933; May 24, 1936.

12. Lu Pingdeng (1936, 461–62); Zhu Xie (1935, 348).

13. *Hunan nianjian* (1933, 287); *Wuhan ribao*, April 23, 1934.

14. Chen Hansheng, *Donfang zazhi*, October 10, 1928, 230.

15. McDonald (1978, 231).

16. Li Baihong (1962, 82–83); Liu Shiren (1935, 94–95).

17. *Republican China*, 10, 2:44.

18. *Xinshubao*, September 29, 1935; table 5.6 above.

19. Lu Pingdeng (1936, 490–91).

20. Zhu Xie (1935, 347–53).

21. *Shichuan yuebao*, 9/2, 38; *Zhongguo nongcun*, 1/2, 83.

22. *Shenbao yuekan*, June 15, 1935, 52.

23. Lu Pingdeng (1936, 17–18).

24. Zhang Xiaomei (1938, C26, 83–84, 143–46).

25. *Chuanyan tekan*, no. 10:17, no. 12:11, no. 119:11; *Yanwu gongbao*, no. 29:171.

26. *Yanwu gongbao*, no. 29:167–68.

27. *Chuannan gequ yanchang*, 323; *Chuanyan tekan*, no. 178:8.

28. *Yanwu gongbao*, no. 1:82–84.

29. *Chuanyan tekan*, no. 138:3–5.

30. *Hubei wenxian* 1:14; *Wuhan ribao*, May 20, 1932.

31. *Wuhan ribao*, July 9, 1933.

32. *Zhongguo jingji*, 1/6, 2–4; *Sichuansheng zhi yaocai* (1934, 171); *Nongcun fuxing weiyuanhui huibao* (1934, 221–23).

33. *Tongyou* (1940, 68–70).

34. *Zhuzong* (1940, 33–39).

35. Zhang Xiaomei (1938, 146–53).
36. *Shangwu guanbao*, no. 23:30; *Zhongguo shiyezhi*, Hunan, 3:71–73 *ding*.
37. *Zhongguo shiyezhi*, Hunan, 3:171–72 *bing*.
38. *Dagongbao*, September 2, 1917; December 22, 1918; September 23, 1920; *Xinshubao*, November 19, 1933; August 25, 1933; *Dongfang zazhi*, 31/14, 214.
39. Myers (1970, 65).
40. *Sichuan jingji jikan*, 1/2, 174–79; *Dagongbao*, October 26, 1921; March 15, 1924; March 26, 1925; March 28, 1925; April 8, 1925; April 22, 1925.
41. *Sichuan shanhouhuiyilu*, 1:23.
42. *Judu yuekan*, no. 78, quoted in *Shenbao yuekan*, June 15, 1935, 49; *Nongxue yuekan*, 2/4 31; see below.
43. *Shibao*, December 27, 1923; March 18, 1924; *Dongfang zazhi*, 23/20, 33.
44. Shen Congwen (1948, 68); my Fenghuang diary, September 19, 1983.
45. Zhou Yujin (1961, 23–26).
46. *Wuhan ribao*, January 18, 1934; *Yinhang zhoubao*, 18/1, 29.
47. *Dagongbao*, September 25, 1920.
48. For example, *Dagongbao*, 3, 4/9, October 21, 1924; January 1, 1925; April 4, 1925.
49. *Sichuan wenxian*, V95, 10–11; Lu Pingdeng (1936, 18–19); Zhang Xiaomei (1938, C154).
50. *Sichuan wenxian*, V95, 11–12; *Yinhang zhoubao*, 19/28, 2–3; 19/40, 8; 20/12, 2; 20/12, 5–6; *Xinshubao*, November 29, 1933; March 2, 1934; November 5, 1934.
51. *Hubei wenxian*, 8:42–43; *Yinhang zhoubao*, 10/20, 5.
52. *Hubei nianjian* (1937, 418–25).
53. *Xinminbao*, April 10, 1937; May 4, 1937; *Gongshang banyuekan*, 6/13, 59; Feng Hefa (1933, 1:269).
54. Zhang Xiaomei (1938, F2–4).
55. Lu Pingdeng (1936, 40–41).
56. Ibid., 42; Wei Jianyou (1955, 206).
57. *Dongfang zazhi*, October 10, 1928, 15–17; *Shibao*, July 31, 1924; *Xinshubao*, February 2, 1935; *Yinhang zhoubao*, 18/7, 10–11; *Sichuan yuebao*, 5/6, 48; 7/3, 85–86; 7/4, 70.
58. *Dongfang zazhi*, 24/16, 35–36.
59. *Yinhang zhoubao*, 20/16, 6; 20/18, 10–12; *Sichuan yuebao*, 5/3, 46; 7/3, 90; 8/3, 79.

Chapter 6

1. *Jingji nianjian* (1934, D193–94).
2. *Huibao* (1934, 184).
3. Pu Xiaorong (1986, 491); Feizhi (1933, 103–8).
4. *Shenbao yuekan* (May 1932, 6); see also Kapp (1973, 37); Feizhi (1933, 293–98); Li Baihong (1962, 75–78).
5. *Shibao*, December 31, 1932.
6. *Shenbao yuekan*, 4/12, 47.
7. Ding Wenjiang (1926, 1:203–4, 208–11).
8. *Chengfu gongbao*, November 12, 1916; Tao Juyin (1948, 31).
9. *Xiandai shiliao* (1934, 1:19–20).

10. *Huazi ribao*, January 1, 1923; *Hunan jinbainian dashi jishu* (1958, 2:484).
11. *Dagongbao*, September 19, 1917; *Xin Hunanbao* (1951, 29–30).
12. *Dagongbao*, February 10, 1919; February 5, 1922; June 30, 1922; McCord (1988, 178–79).
13. Takeuchi (1972, 1:232–33).
14. Lary (1985, 42–43); J. Ch'en (1979, 79–80).
15. *Wuhan ribao*, September 12, 1933).
16. Feng Hefa (1934:1:827).
17. *Shibao*, August 8, 1924; July 19, 1925; July 1, 1926, August 2, 1926.
18. *Sichuan yuebao*, 10/1, 262; 3/4, 144; 1/5, 112–13; 9/6, 218; *Xin Sichuan zazhi*, 1:45–46.
19. *Xinshubao*, February 3, 1934; December 23, 1934; February 21, 1935; *Dagongbao*, February 14, 1920; *Wuhan ribao*, September 12, 1933.
20. J. Ch'en (1985, 46).
21. Su Yunfeng (1981, 350, 367).
22. Zhang Pengyuan (1983, 307).
23. Su Yunfeng (1981, 394).

Chapter 7

1. Zhang Xiaomei (1938, A3, 16); *Sichuan wenxian*, V83, 19–20.
2. *Sichuan jingji jikan*, 2/2, 315.
3. Wang Chengjing (1944).
4. Zhang Xiaomei (1938, B9, 15).
5. *Sichuan jingji jikan*, 2/2, 315.
6. *Sichuan wenxian*, V83, 20.
7. *Nanchuan xianzhi* (1926, ch. 2, 81–83).
8. Wang Chengjing (1944, 71); *Sichuan tongji yuekan*, 1/4, 19.
9. *Xinshubao*, February 12, 1935.
10. *Nanchuan xianzhi* (1926, ch. 9, 210–11).
11. Ibid., 212–13.
12. Ibid., chs. 4, 94; ch. 7, 12.
13. Ibid., ch. 7, 13.
14. *Jingji yanjiu*, 1/7, 31–32.
15. Chen Yanjiong (1936, 2–3); Wang Chengjing (1944, 65–67).
16. Wang Chengjing (1944, 63).
17. *Dongfang zhazhi*, 32/14, 116.
18. *Xinzhonghua*, 2/23, 86; *Sichuan yuebao*, 6/1, 105–7.
19. Lu Pingdeng (1936, 69).
20. *Sichuan yuebao*, 8/4, 210.
21. *Zhongguo shiyezhi* (1935, 3:11, 34 [*jia*], 47 [*yi*]); McDonald (1978, 62).
22. *Hunan nianjian* (1933, 9–10).
23. Shen Congwen (1982, 9:139–40).
24. *Dagongbao*, July 16, 1922.
25. Tan Xinzhi (1976, 138).
26. See, e.g., *Xin youji huikan*, 5/30, 21–27.
27. *Fenhuang tingzhi*, ch. 1, 20–27; ch. 8, 3; *Yongsui tingzhi*, ch. 8, sec. 8.
28. Ling and Rui (1947, 35).
29. Wu Xinfu (1983, 33).

30. *Yongsui tingzhi*, ch. 19; *Hunan miaofang tunzhengkao* (1883, ch. 5); Shen Congwen (1982, 9:127–28).
31. Wu Xinfu (1983, 36); Sheng Xiangzi (1943, 5).
32. *Hunan jinbainian dashijishu* (1958, 2:681–82).
33. Hsiao (1967, 144–52, 153).
34. Zhang Xiaomei (1938, Y30).
35. *Hubeisheng nianjian* (1936, 778–79); *Hunan nianjian* (1933, 906–8); *Jingji yanjiu*, 1/6, 84–85.
36. Kuhn (1970, 39–43).
37. *Xiushan xianzhi*, ch. 4, 7.
38. *Dongfang zazhi*, 24/16, 38, 44.
39. *Sichuan yuebao*, 3:80.
40. Ibid., 3:10–11; 4:13, 22–23, V22.
41. Ibid., 4:18; 8:49; 19:76.
42. *Guangyi gongbao* (1906, 4:10).
43. *Sichuan jiaoyu*, 7:1.
44. *Sichuan xuebao*, 19:21.
45. *Sichuan jiaoyu*, 29–30.
46. *Sichuan nongxuehui huikan*, 1:136–39.
47. *Sichuan jiaoyu*, 19:25–27.
48. *Sichuan xuebao*, 2:1–3; 8:1–9; 9:8–11, 14; 10:16–18.
49. Hu Hua (1980–86, 1:75–124; 7:1; 20:157–58; 22:88–93, 197–240; 24:147–50); Wen Xianmei (1984, 26, 74–75, 132); *Sichuan dangshi renwuzhuan* (1984, 2:195, 240).
50. *Sichuan yuebao*, 5/2. 169–71; 8/5, 261–68.
51. *Sichuan yuebao*, 9/6, 204–5; *Sichuan gonglu yuekan*, 13:28.
52. *Sichuan yuebao*, 7/4, 199.
53. *Xinshubao*, September 14, 1936.
54. *Sichuan gonglu yuekan*, 13:28; *Sichuan yuebao*, 6/2, 171.
55. *Sichuan yuebao*, 9/6, 204–5.

Chapter 8

1. Stacey (1983, chap. 2, esp. pp. 33–34); Laslett (1971, 3).
2. Braudel (1979, 1:486).
3. Handlin et al. (1963, 33).
4. *Wuhan ribao*, August 22, 1933.
5. Xu Xiangqian (1985, 2:258, 267); *Bashan fenghuo* (1981, 177).
6. Xu Xiangqian (1985, 2:270).
7. Several Hunan and Sichuan counties had wolves, jackals, wild boars, and even tigers. See the gazetteers of Cili and Sangzhi; Shen Congwen (1948, 38); Shou Zhenhuang (1964, 23–24); *Xinxin xinwen*, September 26, 1935.
8. Shen Congwen (1944, 63–64, 85; 1982, 119, 140).
9. Shen Congwen (1982, 119).
10. *Huiyi He Long* (1979, 79, 113); Zhang Ermu (1979, 24–26, 29); Boorman and Howard (1967, 2:69).
11. *Huiyi He Long* (1979, 79).
12. Ibid.
13. Wu and Chen (1942, 85); *Huiyi He Long* (1979, 113).

14. Shen Congwen (1948, 76–84); my Fenghuang diary, September 11, 1983.

15. *Xiangcun jianshe jikan*, 1/1, 3–31.

16. Lary (1985, 20–23).

17. *Lishi yanjiu* (August 1978, 31).

18. My Guilin diary, September 19, 1983.

19. *Sichuan yuebao*, 6/2, 173–75.

20. Kuang Jingqiu (1981, 103); *Huiyi He Long* (1979, 201); *Xinshubao*, January 6, June 19, and August 16, 1934.

21. Zheng Gusheng (1933, 25–26).

22. *Xiao Fanghuzhai*, fasc. 6, 3:2156.

23. *Minsu congsu*, no. 30.

24. Tan Xinzhi (1976, 135).

25. Cheng Ying (1962, 60–61).

26. Ibid., 325–26.

27. Zhu Yuzun (1933, 21).

28. *Minjian wenyi jikan*, 3; September 1, 1951, 121.

29. *Hunan miaofang tunzhengkao* (1883, ch. 5); Wu Xinfu (1983, no. 3, 32–36).

30. *Fenghuang tingzhi*, ch. 1, 20–27); *Yongsui tingzhi*, ch. 8, sec. 8; Wu Xinfu (1983, no. 3, 32).

31. *Hunan tongzhi*, ch. 85; Wu Xinfu (1983, no. 3, 36).

32. *Hunan miaofang tunzhengkao*, ch. 5.

33. Sheng Xiangzi (1943, 4).

34. Ibid., 7–8; *Hunan jinbainian dashi jishu* (1958, 2:681–82).

35. Sheng Xiangzi (1943, 8).

36. Ibid., 5; Wu Xinfu (1983, no. 3, 37); my Fenghuang diary, September 11, 1983.

37. J. Ch'en (1979, 161).

38. *Geyao ziliao*, 2a, 21.

39. *Minjian*, no. 12, 156.

40. J. Chen (1979, 161).

41. *Geyao ziliao*, 2b, 16.

42. Wu Zelin (1942, 302).

43. *Guizhou Miaoyi geyao*, 56.

44. Wu Zelin (1942, 113–48).

45. Zhu Ziqing (1957, 132).

46. Yishuo, *Nongcun qingge*, 23.

47. Shen Congwen (1957, 13–14).

48. *Geyao zhoukan*, 2/11, 3.

49. Ibid.

50. *Minjian wenxue* (1961, no. 7, 59.

51. Li Yuenan (1954, 169).

52. *Geyao ziliao*, 2a, 76.

53. Mei Zi (1930, 23).

54. J. Ch'en (1979, 161–62). The "fifth curfew" is dawn.

55. Tan Xinzhi (1976, 135).

56. Zhu Ziqing (1957, 27).

57. Chen Zhiliang (1950, 36).

58. Ling and Rui (1947, 93–99); *Fenghuang tingzhi*, ch. 2, 53–57.

59. Wu Zelin (1942, 91–92); Chen Zhiliang (1950, 36).

60. Ling and Rui (1947, 93–99); my Gulin diary, September 17, 1983.

61. Wu Zelin (1942, 9–10, 30); Liu Jie (1925, 9); Chen Zhiliang (1950, 34); Tan Xinzhi (1976, 138–39); Sheng Xiangzi (1945, 25–26); my Gulin diary, September 17, 1983.

62. Wu Zelin (1942, 72).

63. *Fenghuang tingzhi*, ch. 2, 57; Wu Zelin (1942, 273); Chen Zhiliang (1950, 34).

64. *Fenghuang tingzhi*, ch. 2, 57.

65. Shen Congwen (1957, 21).

66. *Shenbao yuekan*, July 15, 1935; *Zhongguo shaoshu minzhu* (1981, 447).

67. Wu Zelin (1942, 224–25); Ma Shaoqiao (1956, 7–9); Chen Zhiliang (1950, 82); Liu Jie (1925, 3); my Fenghuang and Gulin diary, September 10 and September 17, 1983.

68. My Fenghuang diary, September 10, 1983.

69. Lewis (1964, 494–95); Lopreato (1967, 1210–21); Le Roy Ladurie (1979, 154).

70. Le Roy Ladurie (1982, 49–53).

Chapter 9

1. J. Ch'en (1979, chap. 3).

2. Lary (1985, 73–74).

3. *Shibao*, January 13 and February 15, 1928.

4. Mao Sicheng (1936, 8g:116); *Guowen zhoubao*, 3/19, 30.

5. *Dagongbao*, January 18, 1920.

6. Ma and Xiao (1983, chap. 9).

7. *Shangwu ribao*, October 25, 1929.

8. Zhang Xiaomei (1938, C152–53); also the tables at the end of this chapter.

9. *Shibao*, August 15 and September 13, 1920.

10. Fan Chongshi (1962, 18–19).

11. Ding Wenjiang (1926, 1:207); *Shibao*, January 11 and February 13, 1925.

12. *Shibao*, February 10 and 12, 1927.

13. Pu Xiaorong (1986, 502–6).

14. *Huazi ribao*, June 11, 1928; Li Baihong (1962, 75–78).

15. *Dagongbao*, September 10, 1917; Laijiang Zhuowu (1962, 72).

16. *Dagongbao*, September 10, 1929.

17. Freedman (1965, 645); *Wuhan ribao*, April 18, 1933.

18. *Shibao*, November 7, 1925; *Dongfang zazhi*, 24/16, 38–39; Feng Hefa (1933–35, 1:1128).

19. *Wuhan ribao*, September 12, 1933; *Sichuan wenxian*, V133, 3–10; *Dagongbao*, September 19, 1917.

20. *Wuhan ribao*, June 7–8, 1933; Takeuchi (1972, 1:232–33); Feng Hefa (1933–35, 1:827).

21. Reprinted in *Sichuan yuebao*, 6/1.

22. Billingsley (1988, esp. chap. 7); Lu Pingdeng (1936, 561–67); *Xinshubao*, June 16, 1935; *Sichuan wenxian*, V82, 22.

23. Shen Yunlong (1963, 132).

24. Zhou Gucheng (1931, 225–26).

25. *Shibao*, April 14, 1919.
26. *Sichuan tongji yuekan*, 1/1 and 1/3; *Xiangcun jianshe jikan*, 1/1.
27. *Sichuan wenxian*, V41–42, 42; *Tongyi pinglun*, 58/10–12; Li Wenzhi (1957, 1:943); *Dagongbao*, December 24, 1918.
28. *Xinshubao*, January 17, 1935; *Sichuan wenxian*, V/41–42, 42.
29. *Xinshubao*, February 21, 1935, May 3, 1936; *Dagongbao*, February 14, 1920; *Sichuan gonglu yuekan*, 13:31–32.
30. Ma Boyuan (1925).

Chapter 10

1. Chen Tiejian (1986, 307).
2. Zhang Ermu (1979, 114, 128).
3. Kuang Jingqui (1981, 101).
4. Zhang Guoxing (1988, 43–44).
5. *Xinghuo liaoyuan*, I/B, 604.
6. *Shibao*, July 1, 1929; *Lishi yanjiu*, no. 8, (1978):32–33.
7. *Xinghuo liaoyuan*, I/B, 613–16.
8. *Jiaofei zhanshi*, 4:725–32.
9. *Xinghuo liaoyuan*, 2:254; *Jiaofei zhanshi*, 4:729–32.
10. *Lishi yanjiu*, no. 8, (1978):35.
11. *Shibao* (May and June 1931).
12. *Shibao*, August 18, 1932.
13. Kuang Jingqiu (1981, 105); *Shibao*, September 10 and 27, 1932.
14. *Shibao*, October 18, 1932; Zhang Ermu (1979, 211); Mu Xin (1981, 34–35).
15. *Lishi yanjiu*, no. 8, (1978):39.
16. *Xiangechuanqian* (1985, 5–7, 8–11).
17. Ibid., 23; *Xinghuo liaoyuan*, I/B, 617; *Lishi yanjiu*, no. 8, (1978):41–42.
18. *Zhongguo gongnong hongjun* (1987, 601); Xu Xiangqian (1985, 2:386); *Xiangechuanqian* (1985, 23).
19. Sheng Liyu (1959, 17–18); *Xiangechuanqian* (1985, 16–17).
20. *Xinghuo liaoyuan*, 2:262; Zhang Ermu (1979, 251–59); *Xiangechuanqian* (1985, 66–67); Xiao Ke (1980, 679); *Jiaofei zhanshi*, 5:852–54; and contemporary newspaper reports.
21. Based on *Shibao*, *Xinshubao*, and *Xinxin xinwen* of this period; also *Xinghuo liaoyuan*, 2:262, 320–24, 343; *Jiaofei zhanshi*, 5:852–55.
22. For instance, in *Huiyi He Long* (1979, 5, 6, 21, 37).
23. Xu Xiangqian (1984, 1:99–101, 111–13).
24. *Shibao*, March 1, 1925; *Dagongbao*, April 22, 1925.
25. Zhang Ermu (1979, 25, 97); *Geming wenwu*, no. 4 (1977):16.
26. *Xinxin xinwen*, October 16, 1931.
27. *Geming wenwu*, no. 4 (1977):16.
28. *Xin Hunanbao* (1951, 60–62); *Xinghuo liaoyuan*, I/B, 606–8.
29. *Xinghuo liaoyuan*, I/B, 623–27; *Lishi yanjiu*, no. 8 (1978):29.
30. *Huiyi He Long* (1979, 79, 94–95).
31. Zhang Ermu (1979, 139).
32. *Xinghuo liaoyuan*, I/B, 608; *Lishi yanjiu*, no. 8 (1978):29–30; Zhang Ermu (1979, 156); *Huiyi He Long* (1979, 164).

33. Liao and Tian (1987, 89–90, 141–42).
34. Mao Zedong (1964, 1:13).
35. Xiao Ke (1982, 56); *Huiyi He Long* (1979, 165); *Xiangechuanqian* (1985, 82).
36. *Xinghuo liaoyuan*, I/B, 608.
37. *Huiyi He Long* (1979, 198–207, 265).
38. Kuang Jingqiu (1981, 104).
39. *Xinghuo liaoyuan*, I/B, 662–63.
40. *Lishi yanjiu*, no. 2 (1982):56–58.
41. Ibid.
42. *Xiangechuanqian* (1985, 9, 11, 33).
43. Ibid., 72–73.
44. Ibid., 51–62.
45. Liao Guoliang (1987, 123, 126–27, 135); *Xiangechuanqian* (1985, 18–19, 28–30, 57–58, 72–73, 87–91).
46. Xu Xiangqian (1985, 2:252).
47. Zhang Guotao (1972, 2:312–15, 334–35); Xu Xiangqian (1984, 1:229–30); Lin Chao et al. (1982, 22–24, 36–37).
48. Xu Xiangqian (1985, 2:255–56); *Sichuan yuebao*, 2/2, 107–8.
49. Xu Xiangqian (1985, 2:276–77); *Shenbao yuekan*, 2/4, 141.
50. Xu Xiangqian (1985, 2:288–90); *Chuanyan tekan*, no. 171, 7–8; *Sichuan wenxian*, V8, 12.
51. Lin Chao et al. (1982, 73).
52. Xu Xiangqian (1985, 2:274–75, 298–99).
53. *Xinshubao*, December to May, especially February 2, 1934; *Shibao*, the same period; Lin Chao et al. (1982, 218); Xu Xiangqian (1985, 2:342–70).
54. *Shibao*, August 29, 1934; Lin Chao et al. (1982, 272).
55. Xu Xiangqian (1985, 2:380–81).
56. *Xinshubao*, October 10, 18, 1934; Xu Xiangqian (1985, 2:381).
57. *Xinshubao*, January 23, 1935; Xu Xiangqian (1985, 2:388).
58. Xu Xiangqian (1985, 2:393–94); Lin Chao et al. (1982, 311–12).
59. Zhang Guotao (1972, 2:360–61).
60. Xu Xiangqian (1985, 2:407).
61. Lin Chao et al. (1982, 320).
62. Xu Xiangqian (1985, 400).
63. *Lushun qiyi* (1986, 4).
64. *Bashan fenghuo* (1981, 145–46); Bing Kun (1984, 57–100); *Geming huiyilu* (1980, 100–2).
65. Lin Chao et al. (1982, 175).
66. Bing Kun (1984, 100–3); *Bashan fenghuo*, 149; *Zhonggong dangshi ziliao*, no. 1 (1982:88–90).
67. *Geming huiyilu* (1960, 1:104–5).
68. Lin Chao et al. (1982, 175–91); *Bashan fenghuo* (1981); Bing Kun (1984, 104–8).
69. *Bashan fenghuo* (1981, 150–52); Lin Chao et al. (1982, 12–13).
70. Lin Chao et al. (1982, 608–09); Li Baihong (1962, 73).
71. Lin Chao et al. (1982, 183–86).
72. Ibid., 192.
73. Takeuchi (1971, 2:18).

74. Zhang Guotao (1972, 2:348–50).
75. Xu Xiangqian (1985, 2:258, 267–68).
76. Zhang Guotao (1972, 2:346–47).
77. Xu Xiangqian (1985, 2:267–68).
78. Lin Chao et al. (1982, 38).
79. Ibid., 84.
80. Ibid., 86–87, 95, 101.
81. Zhang Guotao (1972, 2:348).
82. *Xinshubao*, November 15, 1933.
83. Lin Chao et al. (1982, 151–53, 448).
84. Ibid., 396–405.
85. Zhang Guotao (1972, 2:317–19).
86. Lin Chao et al. (1982, 467–68).
87. Zhang Xiaomei (1938, A15–16).
88. Lin Chao et al. (1982, 465–67).
89. Zhang Guotao (1972, 2:336–37, 361).
90. Lin Chao et al. (1982, 485).
91. Xu Xiangqian (1985, 2:302); Zhang Guotao (1972, 2:326); Lin Chao et al. (1982, 408).
92. Lin Chao et al. (1982, 78); Zhang Guotao (1972, 2:325); *Xinshubao*, February 11, 1934.
93. *Xinxin xinwen*, April 19, 1935; Lin Chao et al. (1982, 78, 100); *Xinshubao*, March 6 and October 3, 1935.
94. *Xinshubao*, November 18, 1933; June 23, 1934.
95. Xu Xiangqian (1985, 2:255–56, 277–81, 283–86, 320, 341–70, Chap. 11); Zhang Guotao (1972, 2:343–58).
96. *Xinshubao*, January 5, February 21, and March 18, 1935; *Xinxin xinwen*, April 19, 1935.
97. *Xinshubao*, September 22, 1934; *Sichuan gonlu yuekan*, 6:115.
98. Zhang Guotao (1972, 2:359–60); Xu Xiangqian (1985, 2:380–81).
99. Hobsbawm (1969, 66–70; 1973, 155).
100. *Jiaofei zhanshi* (1966, 4:717); (1967, 5:854); *Lishi yanjiu*, no. 8, (1978):38.
101. Lin Chao et al. (1982, 218–19).

Chapter 11

1. Moore (1967, 473); R. Brenner in Aston and Philpin (1985, 238).
2. Paige (1977, 18–23); Skocpol (1979, 180); Wolf (1969, 286).
3. Paige (1977, 6); Moore (1967, 475).
4. E. Wolf (1975, 268, 270); Le Roy Ladurie (1979, 96); Popkin (1979, 263–64).
5. Petras and Merino (1972, 33).

Appendix A

1. Zhang Xiaomei (1938, C20).
2. Ibid., C143–46; Lu Pingdeng (1936, 17–21).

Appendix B

1. Zhong Jingwen (1928, 53).
2. Ibid., 51; *Minsu zhoukan*, 5:64.
3. Cited by Zhu Ziqing (1957, 162–63).
4. *Wuhan ribao*, May 9, 1934.
5. *Dongfang zazhi*, 32/14, 111.
6. *Minjian wenxue*, Beijing, no. 4 (1964):23.
7. *Sichuan daxue xuebao*, no. 1 (1958):43–46.

BIBLIOGRAPHY

Amano Motonosuke. 1937. *Shina nogyo keizai ron* (On the Chinese farm economy). Tokyo: Kaizosha.

———. 1952, 1953. *Chugoku nogyo no shomondai* (Problems of Chinese agriculture). 2 vols. Tokyo.

Arendt, H. 1963. *On Revolution*. London.

Arrigo, L. G. 1986. "Landownership Concentration in China—The Buck Survey Revisited." *Modern China* 12/3.

Aston, T. H., and C. H. E. Philpin. 1985. *The Brenner Debate: Agrarian Class Structure and Economic Development in Pre-industrial Europe*. Cambridge.

Averill, S. C. 1983. "The Shed People and the Opening of the Yangzi Highlands." *Modern China* 9/1.

Bai Wen. 1937. *Shanjing* (A discourse on mountains). Shanghai.

Baker, E. C. 1882. *Travels and Researches in Western China*. London.

Bambo, A. T. 1977. "Close Corporate and Open Peasant Communities: Reopening a Hastily Shut Case," *Comparative Studies in Society and History* 19/2.

Banfield, E. 1958. *The Moral Basis of a Backward Society*. Illinois.

Bashan fenghuo (Beacon fires on the Daba mountains). 1981. Chengdu.

Bennett, J. 1966. "Further Remarks on Foster's 'Image of Limited Good,'" *American Anthropologist* 68: 206–10

Billingsley, P. 1988. *Bandits in Republican China*. Stanford.

Bing Kun. 1984. *Wang Weizhou zhuan* (A biography of Wang Weizhou). Beijing.

Blum, J. 1961. *Lord and Peasant in Russia: From the Ninth to the Nineteenth Century*. Princeton.

———. 1978. *The End of the Old Order in Rural Europe*. Princeton.

———, ed. 1982. *Our Forgotten Past—Seven Centuries of Life on the Land*. London.

Boggs, Carl. 1978. *Gramsci's Marxism*. London.

Boorman, H. L., and R. C. Howard, eds. 1967. *Biographical Dictionary of Republican China*. New York.

Bowen, J. R. 1986. "War of the Words: Agrarian Change in Southeast Asia," *Peasant Studies*, 14/1

Braudel, F. 1979. *The Structure of Everyday Life* (vol. 1) and *The Wheels of Commerce, Civilization and Capitalism, 15th–18th Century* (vol. 2). New York.

Brenner, R. 1976. "Agrarian Class Structure and Economic Development in Pre-industrial Europe," *Past and Present* 70.

———. 1982. "The Agrarian Roots of European Capitalism," *Past and Present*, 97.

Buck, J. L. 1930. *Chinese Farm Economy: A Study of 2,866 Farms in Seventeen Localities and Seven Provinces in China*. Chicago.

———. 1937. *Land Utilization in China: A Study of 16,786 Farms in 168 Localities and 38,256 Farm Families in Twenty-two Provinces in China, 1929–1933*. Shanghai.

Cai Wuji and Mei Shudong. 1951. *Zhongguo di zhuzong* (Chinese bristles). Shanghai.

Chaianov, A. V. 1931. "The Socio-economic Nature of Peasant Farm Economy," in *A Systematic Source Book in Rural Sociology*, ed. P. A. Sorokin et al. Minnesota.

Chang Guotao (Kuo-t'ao). 1971. *The Rise of the Chinese Communist Party, 1921–28, 1928–38*. Lawrence, Kansas.

Chatfield, C. 1949. *Food Composition Tables, FAO Nutritional Studies*, no. 3. Washington, DC.

Chen Bingfan. 1954. *Zhongguo kuangchan ziyuan* (China's mineral resources). Taibei.

Chen Hansheng. 1928. "Zhongguo nongmin fudan di fushui" (The tax burden of Chinese peasants," in *Nongmin* (Peasants), ed. Wang Zhongmin, 129–79, or *Eastern Miscellany* 10/10.

———. 1932a. "Bengkuizhong di Guanzhong di xiaonong jingji" (Bankrupting small peasants' economy in the Guangzhong region), *Shenbao yuekan* (*Shenbao* monthly) 1/6.

———. 1932b. "Pochanzhong di Hanzhong di pinnong" (Bankrupting poor peasants in the Hanzhong region), *Eastern Miscellany* 30/1.

Chen Hansheng and Wang Yinsheng. 1929. *Mu di chayi* (Different mus). Institute of Social Sciences, Academia Sinica. Shanghai.

Ch'en, Jerome. 1979. *The Military-Gentry Coalition: China under the Warlords*. Toronto.

———. 1985. "Local Government Finance in Republican China," *Republican China* 10/2.

Chen Shijian. 1950. *Zhongguo di heliu* (Chinese rivers). Beijing.

Chen Tiejian. 1987. "Lun xilujun" (On the West Route Army), *Lishi yanjiu* 1987/2.

Chen Yan. 1937. *Shaangan diaochaji* (A survey of Shaanxi and Gansu). N.p.

Chen Yanjiong. 1935. *Wanxian jingji diaocha* (A survey of Wanxian economy). Japanese ed. Tokyo.

———. 1936. *Fuling jingji diaocha* (A survey of the Fuling economy). Japanese ed. Tokyo.

Chen Zhengmo. 1936. *Zhongguo gesheng di dizu* (Rent in the provinces of China). Shanghai.

———. 1971. *Zhongguo nongjing ziliao sanzhong* (Three sets of Chinese agricultural materials). Taibei.

Chen Zhiliang. 1950. *Xinan fengqingji* (Customs and culture in the southwest). Shanghai.

Cheng Lichang. 1938. *Hubei zhi nongye jinrong yu diquan yidong zhi guanxi* (Hubei agricultural finance and the changes in the ownership of land), Land Administration Research Institute monograph no. 86, 1977.

Cheng Ying. 1962. *Zhongguo jindai fandi fanfengjian lishi geyao xuan* (Selected anti-imperialist and anti-feudal folksongs in modern Chinese history). Beijing.

China Postal Atlas. 1933. Nanjing.

Chuanbei shuisheng (The sound of water in north Sichuan). 1944–45. Mimeographed, irregular. Zitong.

Chuannan gequ yanchang (South Sichuan salterns). N.d. N.p.

Chuanshaan geming genjudi lishi wenxian xuanbian (Selected documents on the Sichuan-Shaanxi revolutionary base area). 1979. Chengdu.

Chuanyan tekan (Sichuan salt, supplements). 1928–35. Issued every five days, 1928–30, thereafter fortnightly until 1935. Chongqing.

Cili xianzhi (Cili county gazetteers). 1894 and 1923.

Cumings, B. 1981. "Interest and Ideology in the Study of Agrarian Politics," *Politics and Society* 10/4.

Dagongbao. 1917–. Changsha (photocopy, heavily censored in 1918 probably by Governor Zhang Jingyao's administration).

Davis, J. 1970. "Morals and Backwardness," *Comparative Studies in Society and History* 12.

Decennial Reports, 5th issue. 1892–1931. Issued by the Chinese Maritime Customs. Shanghai.

Deng Fuan. 1935. *Hunan kuangchan gaikuang* (The general situation of the Hunan mining industry). Japanese ed. Shanghai.

Diamond, N. 1988. "The Miao and Poison: Interactions on China's Southwestern Frontier," *Ethnology* 1/1988.

Ding Wenjiang. 1926. *Minguo junshi jinji* (Recent developments in Republican military affairs). Shanghai.

Dongfang zazhi (Eastern miscellany). 1904–. Shanghai.

Du Shougu and Zhang Huejun. 1986. *Jindai Sichuan changzhen jingjizhi* (Market town economy of modern Sichuan), vol. 1. Chengdu.

Eastern Miscellany. 1927. "Gedi nongmin zhuangkuang diaocha" (A survey of the peasants' conditions at various places), August, 24/16.

Eberhard. W. 1982. *China's Minorities: Yesterday and Today*. Berkeley.

Elvin, M., and G. W. Skinner, eds. 1974. *The Chinese City Between Two Worlds*. Stanford.

Enshi xianzhi (Enshui county gazetteer). 1937.

Exi shichaji (A fact-finding trip to west Hubei). 1934. Hankou

Fan Chongshi. 1962. "1920–22 nian di Sichuan junfa hunzhan" (The confused fighting among Sichuan warlords in 1920–22). *Jindaishi ziliao* (Modern history materials). 1962/4.

Fang Xianting, ed. 1938. *Zhongguo jingji yanjiu* (A study of the Chinese economy). Shanghai.

Fangxian zhi (Fangxian County gazetteer). 1866.

Feeny, D. 1983. "The Moral or Rational Peasant? Competing Hypotheses of Collective Action" *Journal of Asian Studies* 42/4.

Fei, Hsiao-tung. [1938] 1962. *Peasant Life in China, a Field Study of Country Life in the Yangtse Valley*. London.

Feizhi neizhan datongmeng zonghui (The anti–civil war Alliance). 1933. *Sichuan neizhan xiangji* (A detailed account of the Sichuan civil wars). Shanghai.

Feng Hefa. [1931] 1934. *Nongcun shehuixue dagang* (An outline of agrarian sociology). Shanghai.

———. 1933–35. *Zhongguo nongcun jingji ziliao* (Materials on the Chinese rural economy). Shanghai.

Feng Wu and Zhang Lude. 1952. *Zhongguo di zhiwuyou* (Chinese vegetable oils). Shanghai.

Fengdu xianzhi (Fengdu county gazetteer). 1894. Rev. ed., preface date 1927.

Fenghuang tingzhi (Fenghuangting gazetteer). 1824.

Fengjie xianzhi (Fengjie county gazetteer). 1893.

Foster, G. M. 1965. "Peasant Society and the Image of Limited Good," *American Anthrolopogist* 67.

———. 1966. "Foster's Reply to Kaplan, Saler, and Bennett," *American Anthropologist* 68.

Freedman, M. ed. 1970. *Family and Kinship in Chinese Society.* Stanford.

Fried, M. H. 1952. "Chinese Society: Class as Subculture," *Transactions of the New York Academy of Sciences,* ser. II, 5/14.

———. 1953. *Fabric of Chinese Society: A Study of the Social Life of a Chinese County Seat.* New York.

Fuzhou zhi (Fuling prefectural gazetteer). 1870. Rev. ed., 1928

Gao Guanmin and Dou Xiuying. 1981. *Hunan ziran dili* (Hunan natural geography), Changsha.

Geertz, C. 1971. *Agricultural Involution: The Processes of Ecological Change in Indonesia.* Berkeley.

———. 1973. *The Interpretation of Culture.* New York.

———. 1983. *Local Knowledge—Further Essays in Interpretive Anthropology.* New York.

Geming huiyilu (The revolution recalled). 1960, 1980. Beijing.

Geming wenwu (Revolutionary artifacts). 1976–. Bimonthly. Beijing.

Geyao (Folksongs). 1922–35. Weekly.

Gongshang banyuekan. 1934. Semimonthly.

Graham, D. C. 1954. *Songs and Stories of the Ch'uan Miao.* Washington, DC.

Gu Bao. 1982. "Xiangexi suqu tudi geming zhengce di jige tedian" (Some characteristics of the land revolutionary policies of the West Hubei-Hunan Soviet), *Dangshiyanjiu* (Studies in the history of the CCP) 1982/2.

Gu Gengyu. 1980. "Wo jingying zhuzong ershiyunian di huigu" (Recollections on my dealing in bristles for a quarter of a century), *Wenshi ziliao xuanji* (Selected materials on literature and history), no. 5. Beijing.

Guangyuan xianzhi (Guangyuan County gazetteer). Rev. ed. 1940.

Guangyi congbao (General knowledge). 1906. Chongqing.

Guiyang zhouzhi (Guiyang prefectural gazetteer). 1868.

Guizhou zhi (Zigui prefectural gazetteer). 1901.

Gunde, R. "Land Tax and Social Change in Sichuan, 1925–1935," *Modern China* 2/1.

Guo Tingyi, ed. 1984. *Zhonghua minguo shishi rizhi 1931–1937* (A daily chronology of the Republic of China, 1931–37), vol. 3. Taibei.

Guomingemingjun zhanshi (The battle history of the National Revolutionary Army). N.d. 17 vols. N.p.

Guowen zhoubao (National affairs). 1935–36. Weekly. Shanghai.

Haiguan zhongwai mouyi tongji niankan (The yearbook of China's foreign trade statistics). 1940. Compiled by Chinese Maritime Customs. Shanghai.

Hall, J. C. S. 1976. *The Yunnan Provincial Faction, 1927–1937.* Canberra.

Handlin, O., and J. Burchard, eds. 1963. *The Historian and the City.* Cambridge, MA.

Hanjiang liuyu mouyi jice (Manual on the trade of the Han valley). 1905. Hankou(?).

Hatano Kenichi, ed. 1924–25. *Gendai Shina no kiroku* (A record of modern China). Tokyo.

He Kai and Liu Hu, eds. 1934. *Tongyou yu tongshu* (Tong oil and tong trees). Japanese ed. Shanghai.

He Long. 1928. "He Long baogao Shimen baodong, " (He Long's report on the Shimen uprising), *Zhonggong dangshi cankao ziliao* (Reference materials on CCP history), vol. 3, 1979.

Hilton, R. 1974. "Medieval Peasants: Any Lessons?" *Journal of Peasant Studies* 1/2.

Hobsbawm, E. J. 1959. *Primitive Rebels—studies in archaic forms of social movement in the nineteenth and twentieth centuries* New York.

———. 1969. *Bandits*. London.

———. 1973a. "Peasants and Politics," *Journal of Peasant Studies* 2/1.

———. 1973b. "Social Banditry," in *Rural Protest: Peasant Movements and Social Change*, ed. H. A. Landsberger. New York.

Hobsbawm, E. J., and G. Rude. 1968. *Captain Swing*. New York.

Hofheinz, R. 1969. "The Ecology of Chinese Communist Success: Rural Influence Patterns, 1923–25," in *Chinese Politics in Action*, ed. A. Doak Barnett. Seattle.

Holy, L., and M. Struchlik, eds. 1981. *The Structure of Folk Models*. New York.

Hsiao, Kung-ch'uan. 1967. *Rural China—Imperial Control in the Nineteenth Century*. Seattle.

Hu Hua et al., eds. 1980–86. *Zhonggong dangshi renwu zhuan* (Biographies in the CCP history). Xian.

Hu Puan, ed. 1968. *Zhonghua quanguo fengsuzhi* (Chinese customs). Taibei.

Hu Zhaoliang. 1956. *Hunansheng jingji dili* (Hunan economic geography). Changsha.

Huang, P. C. C. 1985. *The Peasant Economy and Social Change in North China*. Stanford.

Huang Shaohuai. 1958. *Woguo shaoshu minzu di zongjiao he fengsu* (Religions and customs of the minorities of our country), vol. 1. Beijing.

Huang Zecang. 1935. *Zhongguo tianzai wenti* (The problem of natural disasters in China). Shanghai.

Huang Zhuyi. 1927. "Chuanbei nongmin xiankuang zhi yiban" (The general conditions of north Sichuan peasants," *Dongfang zazhi* (Eastern miscellany). August. 24/16.

Huazi ribao (The Chinese mail). 1895–. Hong Kong.

Hubei caizheng jilue (A brief account of the public finance of Hubei). 1917. Wuhan.

Hubei fengwu zhi (Customs and special products of Hubei). 1986. Wuhan.

Hubei quansheng diding kao (The land and poll taxes of Hubei). N.d. Manuscript, n.p., in the Diet Library, Tokyo.

Hubei quansheng zhouxian gekuan qianliang xizhang (The details of the taxes of Hubei prefectures and counties). N.d. Manuscript, n.p., in the Toyobunko, Tokyo.

Hubei tongzhi (Hubei provincial gazetteer). 1921. Wuchang.

Hubei wenxian (Historical materials on Hubei). 1966–. Taibei.

Hubeisheng nianjian (Hubei yearbook). 1937. Hankou(?).

Hubeisheng yizhan sizhi tucheng lishu xianxing shike qingce (Manual of courier stations, distances, and time allowed to reach them in the province of Hubei). N.d. 2 vols. N.p.

Hubeisheng zhengfu gongbao (Hubei government gazettes). 1928–. Weekly. Wuchang.

Hubeisheng zhi tudi liyong yu liangshi wenti (Land utilization and food problems in Hubei), in *Dizheng yanjiushuo congkan*. Land Administration Research Institute monographs, no. 47. Taibei.

Huiyi He Long (Remember He Long). 1979. Shanghai.

Huiyi He Long xuji (A sequel to *Remember He Long*). 1984. Shanghai.

Huizer, G. 1973. *Peasant Rebellion in Latin America*. Middlesex.

Hunan caizheng shuomingshu (An explanation of Hunan government finance). 1911. 6 volumes. Changsha.

Hunan jiangyu yichuan zongzuan (Complete manual on the area and courier service of Hunan). 1888. Changsha(?).

Hunan jinbainian dashi jishu (Important events of the last hundred years in Hunan). 1958. Changsha.

Hunan lujun junyong ditu (Hunan army ordnance maps). 1915–27. Changsha(?).

Hunan miaofang tunzhengkao (Defense against the Miao and the administration of the garrison fields). 1883. Changsha.

Hunan nianjian (Hunan yearbook). 1934. Shanghai.

Hunan sizhi shuilu tuchengce (Manual of Hunan roads and waterways). N.d. 5 vols. N.p., in the Toyobunko, Tokyo.

Hunan tongzhi (Hunan provincial gazetteer). 1885. Changsha.

Hunansheng zhi (The province of Hunan). 1981–82. Vol. 2, Geography. Changsha.

Huntington, S. 1968. *Political Order in Changing Societies*. New Haven.

Jackson, G. D. 1966. *Comintern and Peasant in East Europe, 1919–1930*. New York.

Jia Dehuai. 1941. *Minguo caizheng jianshi* (A brief history of the finance of the Republican government). Changsha.

Jia Shiyi. 1932–34. *Minguo xu caizhengshi* (Sequels to the history of finance of the Republican government). Shanghai.

Jiang Zhizheng. 1981. "Zhou Yiqun yu Xiangexi suqu" (Zhou Yiqun and the west Hubei-Hunan soviet), *Huazhong shiyuan xuebao* 1981/1.

Jiangexian xuzhi (Revised county gazetteer of Jiange). 1927.

Jiaofei zhanshi (History of military action against the communist rebellion). 1967. Taibei.

Jingji banyuekan (Semimonthly economic journal). 1923–. Originally called *Zhongwai jingji zhoukan* (China-foreign economy weekly). Beiping.

Jingji tongji (Economic statistics monthly). 1926– Ed. by *Shanghai Banking Weekly*. Shanghai.

Jingji yanjiu (Economic study). 1939–. Monthly. Shanghai.

Jingji zazhi (Economic magazine). 1936–. Monthly. Ed. by Sichuan Economic Society. Chongqing.

Jingzhen chengan huibian (A compilation of precedents on tax matters). 1908–09. 8 issues. Chengdu(?).

Jinyan yuekan (Opium prohibition). 1937–. Monthly. Chengdu.

Kanda Masao. 1936. *Shisensho soran* (A general survey of Sichuan). Tokyo.
Kaplan, D., and B. Saler. 1966. "Foster's 'Image of Limited Good': An Example of Anthropological Explanation," *American Anthropologist* 68.
Kapp, R. 1973. *Szechwan and the Chinese Republic*. New Haven.
Kaufman, G. 1985. *Shame, the Power of Caring*. Cambridge, MA.
Kennedy, J. G. 1966. "Peasant Society and the Image of Limited Good: A Critique," *American Anthropologist* 68.
Keyes, C. F. 1983. "Economic Action and Buddhist Morality in a Thai Village," *Journal of Asian Studies* 42/4.
Kinkley, J. C. 1987. *The Odyssey of Shen Ts'ung-wen*. Stanford.
Kuang Jingqiu. 1981. "Xiangexi geming genjudi chuangjian shimo" (The creation of the West Hubei-Hunan Revolutionary Base Area), *Changde shizhuan jiaoxue yu yanjiu* 1981/4.
Kuhn, P. A. 1970. *Rebellion and Its Enemies in Late Imperial China*. Cambridge, MA.
Kuizhou fuzhi (Kuifu [Fengjie] prefectural gazetteer). 1891.
Laifeng xianzhi (Laifeng county gazetteer). 1866.
Laijiang Zhouwu (pseud.). 1962. *Zhiwan zhanzheng shimoji* (An account of the Zhili-Anhui War). Beijing.
Langzhong xianzhi (Langzhong county gazetteer). 1916.
Lary, D. 1985, *Warlord Soldiers*. Cambridge.
Laslett, P. 1971. *The World We Have Lost*. London.
Le Roy Ladurie, E. 1974. *The Peasants of Lanquedoc*, Illinois.
———. 1979a. *Montaillou, the Promised Land of Error*. New York.
———. 1979b. *The Territory of the Historian*. Sussex .
———. 1982. *Love, Death, and Money in the Pays D'oc*. New York.
League of Nations. 1926. *Report of the First Opium Conference*. Geneva.
Lewis, O. 1951. *Life in a Mexican Village: Tepoztean Restudied*. Illinois.
———. 1964. *Pedro Martinez—a Mexican Peasant and His Family*. New York.
Li Baihong. 1962. "Ershinianlai zhi chuanfa zhanzheng" (Sichuan warlords' civil wars in the past 20 years), *Jindaishi ziliao* (Modern history materials), no. 4.
Li Changlong. 1940. *Tongyou* (Tong oil). Shanghai.
Li Feigan (Bajin, signed Yu Yi). 1934. *Jiangjun* (The general). Shanghai.
Li Jiannong (signed Bansu). 1929. *Zhongshan chushihou Zhongguo liushinian dashiji* (Important events in the sixty years after the birth of [Sun] Yatsen). Shanghai.
Li Shifeng. 1934. *Hunansheng zhi tongyou yu tongyouye* (Tong oil and tong oil trade in Hunan). Japanese ed. Shanghai.
Li Wenzhi. 1957. *Zhongguo jindai nongyeshi ziliao* (Historical materials of modern Chinese agriculture). Vol. 1. Beijing.
Li Xin et al. 1981–87. *Zhonghua minguo shi* (A history of the Republic of China). Beijing.
Li Yuenan. 1954. *Minjian xiqu geyao sanlun* (Discussions on operas and folksongs). Shanghai.
Li Yuhua, ed. 1952. *Zhongguo di senlin he tezhong linchan* (Chinese forests and special forest products). Shanghai.
Li Zhenghong. 1938. *Sichuan nongye jinrong yu diquan yidong zhi guanxi* (The relationship between Sichuan agricultural finance and changes in land ownership), in Xiao Zheng, ed., Land Administration Research Institute monograph no. 89, 1977. Taibei.

Li Zhiping. 1934. *Hunan tianfu zhi yanjiu* (A study of Hunan land taxes), in Xiao Zheng, ed., Land Administration Research Institute monograph no. 11, 1977. Taibei.

Liang Qin. 1981. "Guanyu Xiangexi suqu di sange wenti" (Three questions concerning the west Hubei-Hunan soviet), *Jianghan luntan* 1981/4.

Liao Guoliang and Tian Yuanle, eds. 1987. *Zhongguo gongnong hongjun shijie renwu lu* (Events and personalities of the Chinese Workers and Peasants Red Army). Shanghai.

Lichuan xianzhi (Lichuan county gazetteer). 1894.

Lin Chao, Wen Xianmei, and Liu Bingqiang. 1982. *Chuanshaan geming genjudi lishi changbian* (Detailed history of the Sichuan-Shaanxi revolutionary base area). Chengdu.

Lin Lan. 1930. *Minjian chuanshuo* (Folktales). Shanghai.

Ling Chunsheng and Rui Yifu. 1947. *Xiangxi miaozu diaocha baogao* (Survey report on the Miao of west Hunan), History and Language Institute, Academia Sinica, monograph no. 18. Shanghai.

Lishi yanjiu (Historical studies). 1978–. Bimonthly. Beijing.

Little, D., and J. W. Esherick. 1989. "Testing and Testers," *Journal of Asian Studies* 48/1.

Liu Bochuan et al. 1936. *Tianfu wenti yanjiu* (A study on the problems of the land tax). Shanghai.

Liu Cuirong. See Ts'ui-jung Liu.

Liu Dajun. 1929. *Woguo diannong jingji zhuangkuang* (The economic conditions of the tenant farmers in our country). Shanghai.

Liu Haipeng, ed. 1952. *Zhongguo di turang* (The soil of China). Shanghai.

Liu Hanyuan. 1938. *Xiangxi tuntian zhi yanjiu* (A study on the garrison fields in west Hunan), in Xiao Zheng ed., *Zhongguo dizheng yanjiusuo congkan*, no. 67. 1977. Taibei.

Liu Jie. 1925. *Miao huang xiaoji* (Notes on the wilderness of the Miao country). Shanghai.

Liu Shiren. 1935. *Tianfu wenti yanjiu* (A study of the problems of the land tax). Shanghai.

Liu Ts'ui-jung. 1980. *Trade on the Han River and Its Impact on Economic Development, 1800–1911*, Economics Institute, Academia Sinica, monograph no. 16. Taibei.

Liu Zhaoji. 1946. *Xinan caifenglu* (Gathering songs in the southwest). Shanghai.

Lixian zhi (Lixian county gazetteer). 1939.

Longshan xianzhi (Longshan county gazetteer). 1878.

Lopreato. J. 1967. *Peasants No More*. San Francisco.

Lou Zikuang et al., eds. 1928. *Zhongshan daxue minsu congshu* (Sun Yatsen University monographs on ethnography). 30 issues. Guangzhou. Reissued 1969, Taibei.

Lu Pingdeng. 1936. *Sichuan nongcun jingji* (Sichuan rural economy). Shanghai.

Lu Siman. 1952. *Zhongguo di maopi* (Chinese furs and hides). Shanghai.

Lushun qiyi (The Luzhou-Shunqing [Nanchong] uprising). 1986. Chengdu.

Luxing zazhi (The China traveler), 1929–. Monthly. Shanghai.

Luo Yunyan. 1929. *Zhongguo yapian wenti* (The opium problem in the Far East, 1933). Shanghai.

McCord, E. A. 1988. "Militia and Local Militarization in Late Qing and Early

Republican China," *Modern China* 14/2.

McDonald, A. W. 1978. *The Urban Origins of Rural Revolution, Elites and the Masses in Hunan Province, China, 1911–1927.* Berkeley.

Ma Boyuan. 1925. *Hanxulu* (The record of sorrow). N.p.

Ma Ji. 1952. *Zhongguo di senlin* (Chinese forests). Shanghai.

Ma Shaoqiao. 1956. *Qingdai miaomin qiyi* (Miao uprisings in the Qing dynasty). Wuhan.

Ma Xuanwei and Xiao Bo. 1983. *Sichuan junfa Yang Sen* (Yang Sen, the Sichuan warlord). Chengdu.

Mao Sicheng. 1936. *Minguo shiwunianqian zhi Jiang Jieshi xiansheng* (Mr. Chiang Kai-shek before 1926). Shanghai.

Mao Zedong. 1964. *Xuanji* (Selected works). Beijing.

———. 1982. *Nongcun diaocha wenji* (Collected writings on rural survey). Beijing.

Mei Zi, ed. 1930. *Sichuan qingge* (Love songs from Sichuan). Shanghai.

Meng Guangyu. 1943. "Sichuan zudian xiguan" (Land lease practice in Sichuan), *Ren yu di* (Man and land) 3/2–3.

Minjian (Among the people). 1931–. Monthly. Ed. by Tao Moukang. Shaoxing.

Minjian wenxue (Folk literature). 1958–. Monthly. Beijing.

Minjian wenyi jikan (Folk literature). 1951. No. 3. Beijing(?).

Minsu congshu (Ethnographical monographs). Peking University, Beijing.

Minsu xuezhi (Ethnography journal). 1942–43. Beiping.

Minsu zhoukan (Ethnography weekly). 1927–33. Sun Yat-sen University, Guangzhou.

Moore, B. 1967. *Social Origins of Dictatorship and Democracy.* Boston.

Mu Xin. 1981. "Renmin di zhongcheng zhanshi Guan Xiangying" (Guan Xiangying, a loyal fighter for the people), *Jinyang xuekan* 1981/4.

Myers, R. H. 1970. *The Chinese Peasant Economy: Agricultural Development in Hopei and Shantung, 1890–1949.* Harvard.

Nanchuan xianzhi (Revised Nanchuan County gazetteer). 1926. Chengdu.

Nanjiang xianzhi (Nanjiang county gazetteer). 1922. Chengdu.

Needham, J. 1984. *Science and Civilisation in China*, vol. 6, book 2. Cambridge.

Nongbao (Farming). 1936–. Issued every ten days. Central Agricultural Experiment Institute. Nanjing.

Nongqing baogao (Report on agricultural conditions). 1933–38. Central Agricultural Experiment Institute. Nanjing.

Nongcun (Villages). 1933–36. Quarterly. Shanghai.

Nongcun fuxing weiyuanhui huibao (Bulletin of the Agricultural Reconstruction Commission). 1934. Nanjing.

Nongcun jingji (Rural economy). 1934(?). Ed. by Wang Yunwu and Li Shengwu. Shanghai.

Nongmin congkan (Peasants). 1927–. Shanghai.

Nongshang gongbao (Journal of the Ministry of Agriculture and Commerce). 1915–. Beijing.

Nongshang tongjibiao (Agricultural and trade statistics). 1914–24. Ministry of Agriculture and Commerce. Beijing.

Nongxue yuekan (Agriculture monthly). 1935–. Agricultural College, National University of Beiping. Beiping.

Nongye jianshe (Agricultural reconstruction). 1937–. Monthly. Changsha.

Nongye zhoubao (Agriculture weekly). 1931. Nanjing.

Nongyou (Friends of peasants). 1934–. Monthly. Hankou.

Paige, J. 1977. *Agrarian Revolution.* New York.

Peng Yuxin. 1945. *Xian difang caizheng* (County government finance). Chongqing.

Perkins, D. 1969. *Agricultural Development in China 1368–1968.* Chicago.

Perry, E. J. 1980. *Rebels and Revolutionaries in North China, 1845–1945.* Stanford.

Petras, J., and H. Z. Merino. 1972. *Peasants in Revolt, a Chilean Case Study, 1965–1971.* Austin.

Piers, G., and M. Singer. 1971. *Shame and Guilt.* New York.

Piker, S. 1966. "'The Image of Limited Good': Comments on an Exercise in Description and Interpretation," *American Anthropologist* 68.

Polachek, J. M. 1983. "The Moral Economy of the Kiangsi Soviet, 1928–1934," *Journal of Asian Studies* 42/4.

Popkin, S. L. 1979. *The Rational Peasant—the Political Economy of Rural Society in Vietnam,* Berkeley.

Pu Xiaorong, ed. 1986. *Sichuan zhengqu yuange yu zhidi jinshi* (The evolution of Sichuan administrative districts and their modern names). Chengdu.

Qianjiang xianzhi (Qianjiang County gazetteer). 1894.

Redfield, R. 1956. *Peasant Society and Culture.* Chicago.

Ren Bishi. 1979. Changsha.

Rogers, E. M. 1969. *Modernization among Peasants: The Impact of Communication.* New York.

Rozman, G. 1982. *Population and Marketing Settlements in Ch'ing China.* Cambridge.

Rui Yifu. See Ling Chunsheng.

Russett, B. M. 1964. "Inequality and Instability: The Relation of Land Tenure to Politics," *World Politics* 16 (April).

Samuel, R., ed. 1981. *People's History and Socialist Theory.* London.

Sands, B., and R. H. Myers. 1986. "The Spatial Approach to Chinese History: A Test," *Journal of Asian Studies* 45/4.

Sangzhi xianzhi (Sangzhi County gazetteer). 1873.

Schram, S. R. 1963. *The Political Thought of Mao Tse-tung.* New York.

Schultz, T. W. 1964. *Transforming Traditional Agriculture.* New Haven.

Scott, J. C. 1976. *The Moral Economy of the Peasant.* New Haven.

———. 1985. *Weapons of the Weak—Everyday Forms of Peasant Resistance.* New Haven.

Sha Ding (Yang Tongfang). 1953. *Duanpian xiaoshuoji* (Short stories). Beijing.

———. 1960. *Ji He Long* (Notes on He Long). Beijing.

Shangwu guanbao (Commerce, the government bulletin). 1907–11. Beijing.

Shangwu ribao (Business daily news). 1925–. Chongqing.

Shanin, T., ed. 1975. *Peasants and Peasant Societies.* Middlesex.

Shehui jingji yuebao (Social economy monthly). 1934–. Social Economic Studies Institute. Shanghai.

Shen Congwen. 1934. *Biancheng* (A border town). Shanghai.

———. 1943. *Xiangxing sanji* (Notes on a trip to Hunan). Shanghai.

———. 1948. *Xiangxi* (West Hunan). Shanghai.

———. 1957. *Shen Congwen xiaoshuo xuanji* (Selected short stories). Beijing.

————. 1960. *Congwen zizhuan* (Autobiography). Hong Kong.

————. 1982. *Shen Congwen wenji* (Collected essays of Shen Congwen). Hong Kong.

Shen Yunlong. 1963. *Li Yuanhong pingzhuan* (A critical biography of Li Yuanhong. Taibei.

Shen Zonghan. 1952. *Zhongguo nongye ziyuan* (China's agricultural resources). Taibei.

Shenbao yuekan (Shenbao monthly). 1932–35. Shanghai.

Sheng Yuli. 1959. *Zhongguo jiefangjun sanshinian shihua* (An informal history of the thirty years of the Chinese People's Liberation Army). Tianjin.

Sheng Xiangzi. 1934. "Hunan zhi miao yao" (The Miao and Yao of Hunan), *Xin Yaxiya* 8/4.

————. 1935. "Hunan miao yao wenti kaoshu" (An analysis of the Miao and Yao problems in Hunan," *Xin Yaxiya* 10/5.

————. 1945. *Xiangxi miaoqu zhi zhengzhi jiqi xianzhuang* (The administration in the western Hunan Miao regions and its present situation). Chongqing.

Sheridan, J. E., 1966. *Chinese Warlord: The Career of Feng Yu-hsiang*. Stanford.

Shi Daoyuan. 1945. *Sichuansheng zhi zhuzong* (The bristles of Sichuan). Chongqing.

Shibao (Eastern times). 1918–48. Daily. Shanghai.

Shimen xianzhi (Shimen County gazetteer). 1889.

Shinan fuzhi (Shinan prefectural gazetteer). 1837. Rev. ed. 1885.

Shiye zhoubao (Business weekly). 1934–. Chongqing.

Shou Zhenhuang, ed. 1964. *Zhongguo jingji dongwuzhi* (Marketable animals of China). Beijing.

Shufeng (Sichuan culture). 1914–. Monthly? Chengdu.

Shufeng (Sichuan culture). 1936–. Chengdu.

Shuiwu huikan (Tax affairs). 1929?. Issued irregularly. Chongqing.

Sichuan caizheng huibian (Sichuan public finance). 1914. Monthly. Bureau of Finance. Chengdu.

Sichuan caizheng jikan (Sichuan public finance). Quarterly. Chengdu.

Sichuan dangshi renwu zhuan (Biographies in Sichuan CCP history). 1984. Vol. 2. Chengdu.

Sichuan gonglu yuekan (Sichuan motorways monthly). 1936–. Sichuan Bureau of Motorways. Chengdu.

Sichuan jiaoyu (Sichuan education). No. 19.

Sichuan jingji jikan (Sichuan economy quarterly). 1943–. Chongqing.

Sichuan jingji yanjiu zhuankan (Sichuan economic studies) 1944. Issued irregularly. Chengdu.

Sichuan jingji yuekan (Sichuan economy monthly). 1936–. Chengdu.

Sichuan kaocha baogaoshu (Sichuan, an investigation report). 1935. National Economic Commission, Japanese ed. Shanghai.

Sichuan nongcun bengkui shilu (A true record of the bankruptcy of Sichuan rural economy). 1935. West China Modern Archives. Chengdu?.

Sichuan nongxuehui huikan (Bulletin of the Sichuan Agricultural Society). 1925–. Monthly? Beijing.

Sichuan nongye (Sichuan agriculture). 1934–. Monthly. Chongqing.

Sichuan shanhou huiyilu (The report of the Sichuan Rehabilitation Conference). 1926. Chengdu.

Sichuan shengli nongxueyuan yuankan (Bulletin of the Sichuan Agricultural College bimonthly). 1934–. Chengdu.

Sichuan shuiwu huikan (Sichuan taxation). 1914–. Monthly. Chengdu.

Sichuan tongji yuekan (Sichuan statistics monthly). 1939–. Chengdu.

Sichuan tongzhi (Sichuan provincial gazetteer). 1816.

Sichuan wenxian (Historical documents on Sichuan). 1964–. Ed. by Zhou Kaiqing. Taibei.

Sichuan xuchan (Sichuan animal products). 1941. Ed. by Pan Hongsheng. Chengdu.

Sichuan xuebao (Sichuan studies). 1905–. Issued irregularly. Chengdu.

Sichuan yuebao (Sichuan monthly). 1932–37. Chongqing.

Sichuansheng jianshe gongbao (Sichuan reconstruction, issued twice a year). 1939-. Chengdu.

Sichuansheng jinyan yuekan (Sichuan opium prohibition monthly). 1937–. Chengdu.

Sichuansheng nongqing baogao (Reports on Sichuan agriculture). 1938–. Issued irregularly. Chengdu.

Sichuansheng shengyihui huikan (Bulletin of the Sichuan Provincial Council). 1926–. Chengdu.

Sichuansheng zhengfu gongbao (Sichuan government gazette). 1931–. Fortnightly. Chengdu.

Sichuansheng zhi shanhuo (Sichuan mountain goods). 1935. Chongqing.

Sichuansheng zhi yaocai (Sichuan herbal medicine). 1934. Chongqing.

Skinner, G. W. 1971. "Chinese Peasants and the Closed Community: An Open and Shut Case," *Comparative Studies in Society and History* 13/3.

Skinner, G. W. 1964–65. "Marketing and Social Structure in Rural China," *Journal of Asian Studies* 24/1, 24/2.

———. 1977. *Cities in Late Imperial China.* Stanford.

Skocpol, T. 1979. *States and Social Revolutions—A Comparative Analysis of France, Russia, and China.* Cambridge.

Solomon, M. R. 1948. "The Market in Underdeveloped Economies," *Quarterly Journal of Economics* 62/3.

Song Zhe, ed. 1961. *Hunan minjian gushi* (Hunan folktales). Hong Kong.

Southworth, H. M., Johnston, B. F. 1967. *Agricultural Development and Economic Growth.* Ithaca.

Spence, J. 1975. "Opium Smoking in Ch'ing China." In *Conflict and Control in Late Imperial China,* ed. F. Wakeman and C. Grant. Berkeley.

Spencer, J. E. 1940. "The Szechwan Village Fair," *Economic Geography* 16/1.

Stacey, J. 1983. *Patriarchy and Socialist Revolution in China.* Berkeley.

Su Yunfeng. 1981. *Zhongguo xiandaihua di quyu yanjiu Hubeisheng. 1860–1916* (Regional study of China's modernization: Hubei, 1860–1916). Taibei.

Sun Jingzhi. 1958. *Huazhong diqu jingji dili* (An economic geography of central China). Beijing.

Takeuchi, M., ed. 1971. *Mao Zedong ji* (Collected works of Mao Zedong). Tokyo.

Tan Xinzhi. 1976. *Zhongguo shaoshu minzu xinmao* (A new outlook for China's minority nationalities). Hong Kong.

Tang Wenya, Ye Xueqi, and Yang Baoliang. 1980. *Hubei ziran dili* (A natural geography of Hubei). Wuhan.

Tao Juyin. 1957–9. *Beiyang junfa tongzhi shiqi shihua* (An informal history of the period dominated by the northern warlords). Beijing.

Tawney, R. H. 1964. *Religion and the Rise of Capitalism*. Middlesex.

Thomsen, M. 1969. *Living Poor—A Peace Corps Chronicle*. New York.

Thompson, E. P. "The Moral Economy of the English Crowd in the Eighteenth Century," *Past and Present* 50.

Tianfu andu huibian (Documents on land taxes). 1912–15. Beijing.

Tianfu wenti yanjiu (A study of the problems of land taxes). 1936. In *Hanxue congshu*. Shanghai.

Tongji tiyao (Statistical summary). 1935. Comp. by Statistical Bureau. Nanjing.

Tongji yuebao (Statistics monthly bulletin). Ed. by the Legislative Yuan. Nanjing.

Tongji yuekan (Statistical monthly). Ed. by the Statistics Bureau. Nanjing.

Tongyou (Tong oil). 1941. Ed. by the Bureau of International Trade. Nanjing.

von Richtofen, F. 1903. *Letters 1870–1872*. Shanghai.

Wang Zheng. 1977. "Jinian He Long" (Commemorating He Long), *Renmin ribao* July 28.

Wang Chengjing. 1940 or 1944. *Sichuan dongnan shandiqu zhi jingji dili yu jingji jianshe* (An economic geography and the economic reconstruction of the southeast mountain region of Sichuan). Chongqing.

———. 1947. *Chuanxibei buxingji* (Northwest Sichuan on foot). Chongqing.

Wang Guang. 1966. *Zhongguo shuiyunzhi* (On China's waterways). Taibei.

Wang Xiaowen and Chen Chuangang. 1937. *Zhongguo tudi wenti* (The land problems of China). Shanghai.

Wang Xiqi, ed. 1891. *Xiao fanghuzhai yudi congchao* (Writings on geography and travels edited in the Little Square Bottle Studio). Shanghai.

Wang, Yeh-chien. 1973. *An Estimate of the Land-tax Collection in China, 1753–1908*. Harvard.

Wanxian zhi (Wanxian County gazetteer). 1926.

Wanyuan xianzhi (Wanyuan County gazetteer). 1932. Rev. ed.

Wasserstrom, R. 1978. In *Journal of Peasant Studies* 7/2 .

Watson, J. L. 1982. "Chinese Kinship Reconsidered: Anthropological Perspectives on Historical Research," *The China Quarterly* 92.

Wei Jianyou. 1955. *Zhongguo jindai huobishi* (A history of modern Chinese currency). Shanghai.

Wei Yingtao, Li Youming, et al. 1985. *Sichuan jindaishi* (A modern history of Sichuan). Chengdu.

Wen Gongzhi. 1930. *Zuijin sanshinian zhongguo junshishi* (A military history of China in the last thirty years). Shanghai.

Wen Xianmei. 1984. *Chuanshaan geming genjudi yingliezhuan* (Martyrs of the Sichuan-Shaanxi revolutionary base area). Vol. 1. Chengdu.

Wolf, A. P. 1974. *Religion and Ritual in Chinese Society*. Stanford.

Wolf, E. R. 1957. "Closed Corporate Peasant Communities in Mesoamerica and Central Java," *Southwestern Journal of Anthropology* 13/1.

———. 1964. *Sons of the Shaking Earth—The People of Mexico and Guatemala—Their Land, History, and Culture*. Chicago.

———. 1966. *Peasants*. New Jersey.

———. 1969. *Peasant Wars of the Twentieth Century*. New York.

Woodhead, H. G. W., ed., *China Yearbook*. 1926, 1938. Shanghai..

Wu Xinfu. 1983. "Shilun qingdai 'tunzheng' dui xiangxi miaozu shehui fazhan di yinxiang" (A discussion on the "garrison administration" and its impact on the social development of the Miao people in western Hunan), *Minzu yanjiu* 1983/3.

Wu Zelin and Chen Guojun. 1942. *Guizhou miaoyi shehui yanjiu* (A study of the Miao society in Guizhou). Guiyang.

Wuhan ribao (Wuhan daily). 1931–37. Wuhan.

Wushan xianzhi (Wushan County gazetteer). 1893.

Xiandai shiliao (Materials of modern history). 1934. Shanghai.

Xianfeng xianzhi (Xianfeng county gazetteer). 1865.

Xiang Qing. 1983. *Gongchan guoji he zhongguo geming guanxidi lishi gaishu* (A brief history of the relations between the Comintern and the CCP). Guangzhou.

Xiangcun jianshe jikan (Rural reconstruction quarterly). 1935-. Chengdu.

Xiangechuanqian geminggenjudi shigao (A draft history on the Hunan-Hubei-Sichuan-Guizhou Revolutionary Base Area). 1985. Changsha.

Xiao Bo. See Ma Xuanwei.

Xiao Ke. 1980. "Hong er-liu juntuan huishi qianhou" (Before and after the union of the Second and Sixth Red Army Corps), *Jindaishi yanjiu* 1980/1.

Xie Benshu et al., eds. 1984. *Huguoyundong shi* (A history of the Republic Protection movement). Guiyang.

Xin youji huikan (A new collection of travelogues). 1921. Shanghai.

Xinghuo liaoyuan (A single spark can start a prairie fire). 1960. Beijing.

Xinminbao (New citizens daily). 1926-. Hankou.

Xinshubao (New Sichuan daily). 1921-. Chongqing.

Xinxin xinwen (New, new, news). 1930-. Daily. Chengdu.

Xinzheng yuekan (New administration monthly). 1936-. Chengdu.

Xinzhonghua (New China). 1933-. Monthly. Shanghai.

Xiushan xianzhi (Xiushan county gazetteer). 1891.

Xu Xiangqian. 1984–85. *Lishi di huigu* (Looking back to history). Beijing.

Xu Zhengxue. 1934. *Zhongguo nongcun bengkui yuanyin di yanjiu* (An analysis of the causes of the bankruptcy of Chinese rural economy). Nanjing.

Xu Zhenying. 1950. *Zhongguo di xumu* (Chinese animal husbandry). Shanghai.

Xue Shaoming. 1937. *Qiandianchuan luxingji* (Travels in Guizhou, Yunnan, and Sichuan). Shanghai.

Xuxiu Badong xianzhi (Revised county gazetteer of Badong). 1866.

Xuxiu Pingli xianzhi (Revised county gazetteer of Pingli). 1897.

Yanwu gongbao (The bulletin of salt administration). 1929-. Monthly. Nanjing.

Yanye (Tobacco). 1941. Ed. by the Bureau of International Trade. Shanghai.

Yengoyan, A. A. 1966–67. "Ecological Analysis and Traditional Agriculture," *Comparative Studies of Society and History* 9.

Yinhang zhoubao (Banking weekly). 1935-. Shanghai.

Yishuo (Minguo Yishou), ed. 1931. *Nongcun qingge* (Rural love songs). Shanghai.

Yongsui tingzhi (Gazetteer of Yongsuiting). 1909.

Yuan Renyuan. 1951. "Xiangexi geming douzheng huiyi" (Recall the revolutionary struggles in west Hubei-Hunan), *Xin Hunan bao*, June 22.

Yuewangan sisheng zhi zudian zhidu (The land lease systems in Henan, Hubei, Anhui, and Jiangxi). 1936. Nanjing.

Yunxi xianzhi (Yunxi County gazetteer). 1938.

Yunxian zhi (Yunxian County gazetteer). 1866.
Yunyang xianzhi (Yunyang County gazetteer). 1935. Rev. ed.
Zeng Zhaoxuan. 1979. *Zhongguo di dixing* (China's topography). Guangzhou.
Zeng Zhonggang. 1942. *Hunan zhi mucai* (The timber of Hunan). Changsha.
Zhang Ermu. 1979. *He Long zai Xiangexi* (He Long in western Hubei-Hunan). Changsha.
Zhang Guoxing. 1988. "Pingyuan youjizhan zhanlue fangzheng di zhiding jiqi yiyi" (The formulation and significance of the strategic guidance to plains guerrilla warfare), *Zhonggong dangshi yanjiu* 1988/3.
Zhang Pengyuan, ed. 1983. *Zhongguo xiandaihua di quyu yanjiu—Hunansheng 1860–1916* (Regional studies of China's modernization—Hunan, 1860–1916). Taibei.
Zhang Xiaomei. 1938. *Sichuan jingji cankao ziliao* (Reference materials of Sichuan economy). Shanghai.
Zhang Youyi. 1957. *Zhongguo jindai nongyeshi ziliao* (Historical materials of modern Chinese agriculture). Vols. 2 and 3. Beijing.
Zhao Lingjing. 1977. *Sichuan liangshi wenti zhi yanjiu* (A study of the food problem of Sichuan), Land Administration Research Institute monographs, no. 49. Taibei.
Zhaohua xianzhi (Zhaohua County gazetteer). 1845.
Zhengfu gongbao (Government gazette), 1912–28. Beijing.
Zheng Gusheng. 1933. *Zhongguo minjian chuanshuoji* (Chinese folktales). Shanghai.
Zheng Lijian. 1947. *Sichuan xindizhi* (A new geography of Sichuan). Shanghai.
Zheng Wanggu. 1934. "A Survey of Agriculture in Fuling," *Sichuan shanhou duban gongshu tudian gaijin weiyuanhui yuekan* 1/4.
Zheng Zhaojing. 1939. *Zhongguo zhi shuili* (China's water resources). Changsha.
Zhong Jingwen. 1928a. *Geyao lunji* (On folk songs). Shanghai.
———. 1928b. *Minjian wenyi luncong* (Essays on folk literature). Shanghai.
Zhonggong dangshi shijian renwu lu (Events and personalities in CCP history). 1983. Shanghai.
Zhongyang geming genjudi shiliao xuanbian (Selected historical materials on the Central Revolutionary Base Area). 1982. 3 vols. Nanchang.
Zhongguo geyao ziliao (Materials of Chinese folk songs). 1959. Ed. by Society of Chinese Folk Literature. Beijing.
Zhongguo gongchandang lingdao hunan renmin yingyong duozheng di sanshinian (The thirty years of the heroic struggle of the Hunan people led by the CCP). 1951. Changhsha.
Zhongguo gongnong hongjun shijian renwu lu (Events and personalities of the Chinese Workers and Peasants Red Army). 1987. Shanghai.
Zhongguo jingji (Chinese economy). Ed. by Chinese Economy Research Society. Monthly. Nanjing.
Zhongguo jingji nianbao (Chinese economic yearbook). 1934, 1935. Shanghai.
Zhongguo jingji nianjian (The Chinese economic yearbook). 1934. Shanghai.
Zhongguo jingji nianjian xubian (A sequel to the *Chinese Economic Yearbook*) 1935. Shanghai.
Zhongguo jingji pinglun (Comments on Chinese economy), August 31, 1936.
Zhongguo nongcun (Chinese agriculture). 1934-. Shanghai.
Zhongguo shaoshu minzu (China's minorities). 1981. Beijing.

Zhongguo shiyezhi (Chinese economy). 1935. Vol. 3: Hunan. Ed. by Bureau of International Trade. Shanghai.

Zhongguo tongyou difang wuchanzhi (Products along the postal routes of China). 1936. Ed. by General Post Office. Shanghai.

Zhongguo zudian zhidu zhi tongji fenxi (A statistical analysis of China's land lease system). 1942. Chongqing.

Zhonghang yuekan (Bank of China monthly). 1930–38. Shanghai.

Zhonghua nongxuehuibao (The bulletin of the Chinese Agricultural Society). 1929-. Shanghai.

Zhongzhou zhilizhou zhi (The gazetteer of the directly controlled Zhongzhou Prefecture [Zhongxian]). 1873.

Zhou Gucheng. 1931. *Zhongguo shehui zhi bianhua* (Changes in Chinese society). Shanghai.

Zhou Kaiqing. 1967. *Jindai zhongguo jingji congbian* (Collected writings on modern Chinese economy). Taibei.

Zhou Wen. 1937. *Yanmiaoji* (The poppy season). Shanghai.

———. 1940. *Zhou Wen duanpian xiaoshuoji* (Zhou Wen's short stories). Shanghai.

Zhou Yishi. 1957. *Zhongguo gonglushi* (A history of China's motorways). Taibei.

Zhou Yujin. 1961. *Zhongguo gongzhai zhidu zhi gaige* (Reform of the public loan system of China). Taibei.

Zhu Xie. 1935. *Tianfu fujiashui diaocha* (A survey of land surtaxes). Shanghai.

Zhu Xie. 1934. *Zhongguo caizheng wenti* (Problems of Chinese public finance). Shanghai.

Zhu Yuzun. 1933a. *Minjian geyao quanji* (Collected folk songs). Shanghai.

———. 1933b. *Minjian shenghuaji* (Collected fairy tales). Shanghai.

Zhu Ziqing. 1957. *Zhongguo geyao* (Chinese folk songs). Beijing.

Zhujichu. 1942. *Zhongguo zudian zhidu zhi tongji fenxi* (A statistical analysis of China's land lease system). Chongqing.

Zhushan xianzhi (Zhushan county gazetteer). 1865.

Zhuxi xianzhi (Zhuxi county gazetteer). 1867.

Zhuzong (Bristles). 1940. Ed. by Bureau of International Trade. Shanghai.

Zou Xupu. 1944. *Zhongguo youtong yu tongyou* (China's tong-oil trees and tong oil). Shanghai.

Index

Jerome Ch'en received his B.A. from Southwest Associated Universities (the wartime association of Beijing, Qinghua, and Nankai Universities) in 1943 and his Ph.D. from the University of London. He has taught at universities around the world and since 1987 has been Professor Emeritus at York University, where he was Distinguished Research Professor of History. He was made a Fellow of the Royal Society of Canada in 1980.

Professor Ch'en's major publications include *Yuan Shih-k'ai* (1961; Japanese translation, 1979) and *Mao and the Chinese Revolution* (1965; Spanish edition, 1966; Italian edition, 1966; French edition, 1968; Japanese edition, 1969).

For Product Safety Concerns and Information please contact our EU
representative GPSR@taylorandfrancis.com
Taylor & Francis Verlag GmbH, Kaufingerstraße 24, 80331 München, Germany